Linux System Administration Handbook

Mark F. Komarinski
Cary Collett

Prentice Hall PTR
Upper Saddle River
New Jersey 07458
http://www.phptr.com

ISBN 0-13-680596-5

90000

9 780136 805960

Library of Congress Cataloging in Publication Data

Komarinski, Mark (Mark F.)
      Linux System Administration Handbook / Mark F. Komarinski, Cary Collett.
          p.   cm
      Includes index.
      ISBN 0-13-680596-5 (alk. paper)
      1. Linux. 2. Operating systems (Computers) I. Collett, Cary. II. Title.
QA76.76.063K6483   1998
005.4'4769—dc21   97-52143
                                      CIP

Editorial/Production Supervision: *Joanne Anzalone*
Acquisitions Editor: *Mark L. Taub*
Cover Design Director: *Jerry Votta*
Cover Art: *Daniel Corley, dcorley@umr.edu, http://www.umr.edu/~dcorley*
Manufacturing Manager: *Alexis R. Heydt*
Marketing Manager: *Dan Rush*
Editorial Assistant: *Tara Ruggiero*

© 1998 Prentice Hall PTR
Prentice-Hall, Inc.
A Simon & Schuster Company
Upper Saddle River, New Jersey 07458

Prentice Hall books are widely used by corporations and government agencies for training, marketing, and resale. The publisher offers discounts on this book when ordered in bulk quantities.
For more information, contact
Corporate Sales Department,
Prentice Hall PTR
One Lake Street
Upper Saddle River, NJ 07458
Phone: 800-382-3419; FAX: 201-236-7141
E-mail (Internet): corpsales@prenhall.com

Printed in the United States of America
10 9 8 7 6 5 4

ISBN 0-13-680596-5

Prentice-Hall International (UK) Limited, *London*
Prentice-Hall of Australia Pty. Limited, *Sydney*
Prentice-Hall Canada Inc., *Toronto*
Prentice-Hall Hispanoamericana, S.A., *Mexico*
Prentice-Hall of India Private Limited, *New Delhi*
Prentice-Hall of Japan, Inc., *Tokyo*
Simon & Schuster Asia Pte. Ltd., *Singapore*
Editora Prentice-Hall do Brasil, Ltda., *Rio de Janeiro*

To Brenda—
You'll always be first in my book!
—Mark

To Linux users everywhere,
especially my loving wife!
—Cary

Table of Contents

Chapter 12   *Applications for Linux,* *153*

Chapter 17   *Securing Linux,*   *247*

Chapter 18   *Kernel Administration,*   *259*

Appendix D,   359

Thanks and Acknowledgments

Mark would like to thank:

There are a lot of people who helped out on this book and gave some good suggestions based on my first book *Linux Companion—The Essential Guide for Users and System Administrators* also published by Prentice Hall PTR. First and foremost is my wife Brenda, who helped keep me writing during the past few months. My parents, Peter and Mary Kay, along with my brothers, Derrick, Scott, and Allen, and sister, Kathleen, for all their motivation and help while writing, get thanks as well. Next my co-author Cary, who accepted the challenge of writing the best Linux book around. The cover art for this book and my first book were done by Daniel Corley, master of the POVray rayshading program.

Cary would like to thank:

My wife! Not just for not killing me while I was writing this, but also for supporting me and lending massive amounts of help in proofreading and editing. Next I want to thank Mark for asking me to help with this book; it's been quite an experience. I don't want to repeat it soon, but maybe in a year or so. . . . Also, I'd like to thank one of my close Net friends, Paul Saab. Paul and I have been experimenting with bleeding edge and/or strange freeware for years now. Without him I would likely never have begun many of the pursuits which helped me gain the knowledge I've spewed forth here. Lastly I'd like to thank John Shipman and Jason Van Patten for being both fonts of technical knowledge and the sources of much mirth, which from time to time during this busy summer I was sorely in need of.

Together both of us would like to thank:

Rachel Collett. Rachel helped out far, far above any sense of duty derived from friendship or marriage. Without her help in editing and proofing, our publisher would likely have admonished us for the state of our book. Many thanks to A. Rich and Nelson Chadderdon from Oceanwave Consulting (http://www.oceanwave.com) for their chapters on NetNews and connecting to the Internet. Their help is greatly appreciated. Also, thanks to Daniel Corley (dcorley@umr.edu) for his great expertise with POVray and making our cover image.

Most anything relating to Microsoft or Windows 95, NT, or 3.1 are either trademarks or registered trademarks of the Microsoft Corporation. Post-Script is a registered trademark of Adobe. Solaris is a trademark of Sun Microsystems, Inc. Linux is a registered trademark of Linus Torvalds, but the software itself is free. The wayga.net domain is owned by Mark F. Komarin-ski, and he won't give it to you. He owns it. The ratatosk.org domain is owned by Cary Collett, and Cary won't give it to you either. All other trademarks are owned by their respective companies.

Introduction   1

Get into Linux. The easy way.

Linux is probably one of the fastest growing operating systems around. It has about 5 million worldwide users, and that number is growing each day. For something that started as an idea by a college student in Finland in 1991, that is pretty darn good.

Linux is now used everywhere there is a need for a good, robust operating system. Companies run their businesses on Linux, but many may not know it. It is used for E-mail servers; WWW servers; to provide file and printer access for Microsoft and Apple machines; and even other UNIX machines.

This is a guide to give you (the reader) as much knowledge as we (the authors) have attained in our years of Linux administration. The kinds of projects that administrators have to go through are varied, but they all have a common base—managing users, E-mail, the network, hardware, and making sure that you don't mess up anything too badly while trying to make an improvement.

1.1   Oh No! Not Another Linux Book

This is not just a Linux book. This is the Linux book. Anyone can write some theoretical book about the way networks should run, but how many of these authors are actually the administrators of networks? How many are stuck in the trenches, reading the cryptic man pages to "printcap" while users are complaining about their printouts? We've been there, we are there, we will be there. We enjoy it.

The proof of this exists throughout the book. While everyone else goes on about IDE drives, we personally and professionally recognize the power of the small computer systems interface (SCSI) bus and use it in our systems. It's more expensive and, at times, a pain to work with, but the benefits are enormous.

Anyone can tell you how a program like samba is set up, but what happens in the real world where things aren't quite the same as they are in the manual pages?

1.2   Linux Theory

The UNIX theory is: "Do it your way." But Linux is more than a chain of hamburgers. Linux allows you to not only choose what you want on your hamburger, but also what's in it, how the cow is grown, what spices you add to the mixture, and how long you cook it. Linux gives you all the same abilities that commercial UNIX packages (such as Solaris or AIX) give, plus so much more.

1.3   Is It Really Free?

Yes and no. The Gnu's not UNIX (GNU) Public Licence (which is how Linux is licensed) says that you can charge for a binary distribution, but the source code must be either included or available for the cost of duplication. In the days of the Internet and CD-ROMs, the cost for duplicating is low indeed.

Note that this really covers only the Linux kernel, and the GNU utilities included with most distributions. This does not prevent a company like Walnut Creek, WorkGroup Solutions, or RedHat from assembling all these programs, adding a few special ones (installation and administration scripts, for example), producing a CD-ROM, and charging you $30 for it. The Linux kernel and source code are there. The source code to all the other GNU utilities is either also available or pointers to the source code exist. Thus, these companies have met their end of the GNU licence. Many of these also sponsor Linux-related events or offer free CD-ROMs to software contributors.

Companies such as RedHat have a more expensive product, but they add things that may not be covered by the GNU Public License (GPL). For example, RedHat sells a copy of their distribution for three different architectures for about $30. Or you can get a copy specifically for any of the three (Alpha, Sparc, and Intel) for about $50 and get copies of commercial software, such as MetroX, along with customer support—which the $30 version doesn't offer. Companies like Caldera take this step further and have a full Linux system for Intel, complete with custom software to talk to NetWare networks, for about $100.

1.4 Why Linux?

So why would you (or your company) want to use Linux in a personal or business setting? The answer goes past the shortsighted "anti-Microsoft" response. Microsoft makes a fair product for a new user. But so does Apple. Linux gives you things that Windows 95 can only dream about:

- Source code for the entire kernel.
- Full configurability of the operating system.
- Ability to turn features of the system on and off without rebooting.
- Full 32-bit operating system. This is 64-bit for the Alpha series processors, and by the time you read this, the Sun UltraSparc will probably also be supported and 64-bit.
- Access to the 25 years of software that makes up the UNIX world. This includes compilers, Web servers, editors, games, and Internet tools.

As an inexpensive Web server, Linux will beat NT hands down for performance on equivalent hardware. As a network server, a Linux machine hidden in the corner of an office can handle a small workgroup or a large office with months between reboots (usually to either upgrade the kernel or add new hardware). With the emergence of Java[1] as a truly portable language, applications such as Corel's Office For Java will bring commercial applications to

---

[1]Linux was one of the first operating systems to handle Java applications in the kernel.

Linux just as fast as applications for NT or Windows 95. Many commercial applications (Netscape, Word Perfect, Applix, Motif, Flagship) are already available for Linux, with more being added.

1.5   Is Linux SYSV or BSD?

The simple answer to this is "Yes." Linux takes the best of System Five (SYSV) (like startup files) and the best of Berkley System Distribution (BSD) (ps aux, getty) and combines them. As a downside, some features of each are missing (like streams) and you should make yourself aware of what features of each are in Linux.

1.6   Support

Contrary to popular belief, commercial support for Linux is available. While there is seldom a need for it, companies such as RedHat have telephone and E-mail support for their Linux distribution. Caldera is distributing a "MS Windows killer" in their OpenLinux product. Support contracts and shrink-wrapped packages are available. With the number of users that have Linux on their machines, devices from the latest S3-based video cards to the Mattel PowerGlove have drivers available, and everything in between. The support is often somewhat better than from other operating systems, as the author of a particular driver is sometimes available via E-mail and is often willing to help if your driver is not behaving properly. Some hardware drivers have released patches within 24 hours to users.

1.7   What You Need

So what do you need in order to run Linux? It varies greatly depending on what you want to do with it. If you're going to use Linux to dial up the Internet, a low-end 486 with 8 Mb of memory will suffice just fine. If you want to have a dial-in pool to give access to traveling engineers or salespeople, a 100-Mhz 486 is great. If you want a killer development system or something to write a book with, a Pentium or K6 will do just fine.

What's that? A spare SparcStation 1 with nothing better to do? Turn it into a Linux samba server. Let the people running Windows 3.1, 95, or NT access Network File System (NFS) partitions without having all that messy NFS software installed on the PCs. While it's doing that, it could also handle POP E-mail for the same group of people.

You just bought that great new Alpha machine and NT is having trouble with it? Slap Linux on there and be up and running before you remember what NT stands for.

Here's the bare minimum suggestions for running Linux:

- 386 or better (or Sparc or Alpha or Macintosh)
- 8 Mb of memory
- 300 Mb of hard drive space—Intregrated Drive Electronics (IDE) or SCSI
- Industry Standard Architecture (ISA), Video Electronics Standards Association (VESA), or Personal Computer Interconnect (PCI) bus (Linux doesn't work on Micro Channel Architecture (MCA) quite yet)
- Ethernet card or graphics card, monitor, and keyboard

Once you have these items assembled, you can use the instructions with the Linux distribution to install Linux on your system. See the appendix on installing the included CD-ROM on your system.

Linux Boot and Shutdown

2

What happens when you boot? What happens when you shut down the machine?

Booting Linux is not like starting DOS, but the concepts are somewhat similar.

The first process that Linux kicks off once the kernel has entered memory and the root (/) partition is mounted is init. The init process is always process 1. Killing this process will do the same thing as running halt or shut down. Once init starts, there are a few ways it can go based on your installation. We prefer the way RedHat does it (the SVR4 method), so we'll work on that setup. The advantage to the RedHat method is that it's the same as other commercial Operating Systems (OS) such as Solaris 2.x

2.1 LILO

Configuring the Linux Loader

The LILO program allows you to select a boot partition for your system. If you have multiple operating systems (DOS, Windows 95, Linux, etc.) all on different partitions and want to choose which one you want to boot, LILO will let you do this.

In addition, LILO allows you to send boot parameters to the kernel before it starts up, much as the Sun architecture allow you to send boot parameters to Solaris. For example, you can specify root drive, what devices you have installed, and pass instructions to the *init* command.

The Boot Prompt

When you start your machine up after installing Linux, you probably have the **LILO:** prompt awaiting your command. At this point, you can choose to boot whatever operating systems were configured previously (Linux or DOS, for example). If you're starting something like DOS or Windows 95, there isn't much you need to worry about, and you can just type in "DOS" or "Win95" or however you configured LILO when it was installed. If you forget, you can hit the TAB key to see a list of what operating systems LILO knows about and will boot.

If you're starting Linux, there's a bunch of configuration parameters you can use at the end of the name you use to start Linux. For our example, let's say that we configured that name just as "linux."

`root=partition`   This signals Linux to use a different root partition than is configured in the kernel. When you build Linux on one system, it assigns a default of what the current root partition is. For example, if you build a Linux kernel on an SCSI-based machine where the root partition was on the first drive, first partition, Linux will assign the boot device to be /dev/sda1. If you were to put this kernel on a floppy drive and use it to boot an IDE-based system, it would not boot correctly, since there is no SCSI system to boot off of. Adding in the `root=/dev/hda1`, for example, would tell the kernel to boot off of the first IDE drive, first partition. So, the same kernel can be used for multiple systems.[1]

`ro`   This signals Linux to mount the root filesystem in read-only mode. No changes can be made to the filesystem when in read-only mode. The advantage to this is the startup scripts can perform a filesystem check (fsck) to verify the integrity of the filesystem. If the fsck succeeds, the root partition is mounted read-write and normal bootup continues. If there is a problem with fsck, the partition remains in read-only mode

---

[1] Assuming, of course, that all the drivers that each system needs are installed.

and the administrator will have to either do a manual fsck or reload from tape if the problem is severe. Read-only mode is used by default, so it would be rare when you need this flag.

rw   This signals Linux to mount the root filesystem in read-write mode, as opposed to read-only mode (see above). This is dangerous, since a filesystem check of the root filesystem cannot be performed.

mem=   Some BIOSes won't recognize above 64 MB of RAM in your system. Since Linux needs the BIOS to tell it how much memory is installed, systems with more than 64 MB of RAM will be incorrectly reported. The mem= option tells Linux to ignore the BIOS and know how much memory is there. You can either use a hex address (mem=0x1000000 which is 16 MB), or use a number followed by *k* or *M* (16384k or 16M).

NOTE: If you lie here and tell Linux you have 128 MB when you really have only 64 MB, it will crash at some point. Also, due to paging and some BIOS settings, you may not have the full amount of memory accessible to your system. Check your BIOS or motherboard documentation for how much memory is used.

debug   Kernel hackers may want to use this when booting experimental kernels. Kernel messages are sent to the screen instead of being sent to disk or to the syslog facility.

init=   Specifies what program to boot as the init program. Normally, the kernel looks for /sbin/init, then /etc/init, then gives up and runs /bin/sh. This way, if the init program is corrupted, you can still get into the system.

panic=   When (if?) your kernel panics, it normally waits for the administrator to come by and physically press the power or reset switch. Setting this option will allow the kernel to try and reboot x seconds after a panic. For example, a setting of panic=60 will have the kernel try and reboot 60 seconds after a panic.

vga=   LILO has the ability to change VGA video modes from the standard 80x24 to other modes, such as 80x50 or 132x44. A setting of vga=ask will provide a list of video modes and allow you to choose when it boots.

SCSI, CD-ROM, Ethernet, and other controllers—There are a number of options to tell the kernel that you have a controller on a non-standard IRQ or IO address, or Linux for some reason is not probing the right IRQ or IO address for your device. The most common is Linux's not recognizing some

IDE CD-ROM drives. This can be fixed by explicitly adding `hdb=cdrom` to the LILO boot config. This tells Linux that the second IDE device is really a CD-ROM drive. The rest of the options can be found in the LILO documentation or the BootPrompt HOWTO.

Configuring LILO

Once you have Linux started the way you want, there is a way to have LILO add your favorite options each time you boot. The `/etc/lilo.conf` file contains information that LILO uses each time it starts. This is where the operating systems you want to boot are configured. Here's a sample `lilo.conf` file.

```
# Tell LILO to install itself as the primary boot loader on /dev/hda
boot = /dev/hda
# The boot image to install; you probably shouldn't change this
install = /boot/boot.b

# The stanza for booting Linux
image = /vmlinuz        # The kernel is in /vmlinuz
   label = linux        # Give it the name "linux"
   root = /dev/hda2     # Use /dev/hda2 (first drive, second parti-
   tion)
                        # as the root filesystem
   vga = ask            # Prompt for VGA mode
   append = "hdc=cdrom" # Tell Linux that the third IDE drive is
                        # really a CD-ROM

#The stanza for booting MS-DOS
other = /dev/hdb1       # This is the MS-DOS partition
   label = msdos        # Give it the name "msdos"
   table = /dev/hdb     # The partition table for the second drive
```

In the above setting, the first section (the `boot` and `install` lines) configure LILO itself. The boot line tells LILO where to install. Since it's the first drive, LILO gets configured as the primary boot loader. If you have another boot loader such as the OS/2 boot loader or System Commander, you can configure LILO to use the Linux root partition to be a secondary boot loader. In this case, set the `boot` line to be the root partition of Linux. In the above case, that would be /dev/hda2. You could also take out references to other operating systems, since the primary boot loader would handle booting to other operating systems.

The section for Linux handles many of the configuration options mentioned in the previous section. The label, root partition, VGA setting, and CD-ROM are all configured. Once you chose a VGA mode that suits your needs (you'll enter a number for which video mode you choose), you can replace the *ask* parameter with the number you choose. One important line here is the *image* section. This line tells LILO which file to boot. Some Linux installations configure the kernel to be in the root partition (/) and some put the kernel in the /boot directory. You should be sure which setting you want to use when configuring LILO. A feature of the *image* line is you can boot multiple versions of the kernel all using the same Linux installation. For example, if you're developing new kernels and want to have a "safe" kernel around that you know boots correctly, you can create a "safe" entry in LILO. Its configuration would look something like this:

```
# Create a safe entry for Linux.  I know this kernel works.
image = /boot/vmlinuz.safe   # Boot this file.  Make sure it exists!
   label = safe              # The label for this is "safe"
   root = /dev/hda2          # Specify the root partition just in case
   vga = ask                 # Not really needed, but helpful
   append = "hdc=cdrom"      # Make sure Linux knows about the CD-ROM
```

In the event that a kernel you build doesn't work correctly and you are unable to boot it, you can just enter "`safe`" in the LILO prompt and boot the older kernel. Note that this will not help if there is some problem not related to the kernel, like hardware failure or serious partition corruption.

Once your `/etc/lilo.conf` file is configured to your liking, you can run the `/sbin/lilo` command as root to install the configuration file. The next time you boot the machine, you should see the LILO boot prompt. If at some future time you need to remove LILO from your system, you can do this from DOS (and presumably Windows 95 as well) with the `fdisk /mbr` command. This tells fdisk to reinstall the Master Boot Record (MBR) to the first partition of the first drive.

The *rdev* Command

The `rdev` command allows you to change parameters without using LILO. For example, you can use the `dd` command to put a Linux kernel on a diskette, then move it to another machine to boot. To change the root partition, you can just use the following command:

```
rdev kernel root
```

Where `kernel` is the kernel file and *root* is the new root partition you want to use, if the kernel is on a floppy diskette (you used dd to put it there or *make floppy* when compiling the kernel), the command would look like this:

```
rdev /dev/fd0 /dev/hda1
```

This would configure the kernel file on /dev/fd0 (the floppy diskette) to change its root partition to use /dev/hda1 instead of the default. For a list of other features that rdev has, use the rdev -h command for a list of features.

2.2 Kernel Boot

While the kernel is starting up, you'll get a series of messages flying across the console. Most of these messages you can catch, due to the delay while the next driver initializes. If you miss something, the dmesg command will list all the kernel messages since and during boot time.

Here's about what the boot looks like on an AMD K6 with SCSI:

```
Console: 16 point font, 400 scans
Console: colour VGA+ 80x25, 1 virtual console (max 63)
pcibios_init : BIOS32 Service Directory structure at 0x000f92f0
pcibios_init : BIOS32 Service Directory entry at 0xf0480
pcibios_init : PCI BIOS revision 2.10 entry at 0xf04b0
Probing PCI hardware.
Calibrating delay loop.. ok - 333.41 BogoMIPS
Memory: 30732k/32768k available (592k kernel code, 384k reserved, 696k
    data)
Swansea University Computer Society NET3.035 for Linux 2.0
NET3: Unix domain sockets 0.13 for Linux NET3.035.
Swansea University Computer Society TCP/IP for NET3.034
IP Protocols: ICMP, UDP, TCP
VFS: Diskquotas version dquot_5.6.0 initialized
Checking 386/387 coupling... Ok, fpu using exception 16 error report-
    ing.
Checking 'hlt' instruction... Ok.
Linux version 2.0.27 (root@wayga) (gcc version 2.7.2.1) #4 Sun May 18
    02:31:25 EDT 199
7
Serial driver version 4.13 with no serial options enabled
tty00 at 0x03f8 (irq = 4) is a 16550A
tty01 at 0x02f8 (irq = 3) is a 16550A
PS/2 auxiliary pointing device detected -- driver installed.
Ramdisk driver initialized : 16 ramdisks of 4096K size
md driver 0.35 MAX_MD_DEV=4, MAX_REAL=8
scsi-ncr53c7,8xx : at PCI bus 0, device 11,  function 0
scsi-ncr53c7,8xx : warning : revision of 18 is greater than 2.
scsi-ncr53c7,8xx : NCR53c810 at memory 0xe6000000, io 0xe000, irq 11
scsi0 : burst length 16
scsi0 : NCR code relocated to 0x80600 (virt 0x00080600)
scsi0 : test 1 started
```

```
scsi0 : NCR53c{7,8}xx (rel 17)
scsi : 1 host.
Started kswapd v 1.4.2.2
scsi0 : target 0 accepting period 100ns offset 8 10.00MHz FAST SCSI-II
scsi0 : setting target 0 to period 100ns offset 8 10.00MHz FAST SCSI-II
  Vendor: SEAGATE   Model: ST31055N      Rev: 0532
  Type:   Direct-Access                  ANSI SCSI revision: 02
Detected scsi disk sda at scsi0, channel 0, id 0, lun 0
scsi0 : target 1 accepting period 100ns offset 8 10.00MHz FAST SCSI-II
scsi0 : setting target 1 to period 100ns offset 8 10.00MHz FAST SCSI-II
  Vendor: TOSHIBA   Model: CD-ROM XM-5701TA  Rev: 0167
  Type:   CD-ROM                         ANSI SCSI revision: 02
Detected scsi CD-ROM sr0 at scsi0, channel 0, id 1, lun 0
scsi0 : target 2 accepting period 100ns offset 8 10.00MHz FAST SCSI-II
scsi0 : setting target 2 to period 100ns offset 8 10.00MHz FAST SCSI-II
  Vendor: SEAGATE   Model: ST51080N      Rev: 0913
  Type:   Direct-Access                  ANSI SCSI revision: 02
Detected scsi disk sdb at scsi0, channel 0, id 2, lun 0
scsi : detected 1 SCSI cdrom 2 SCSI disks total.
SCSI device sda: hdwr sector= 512 bytes. Sectors= 2069860 [1010 MB]
  [1.0 GB]
SCSI device sdb: hdwr sector= 512 bytes. Sectors= 2109840 [1030 MB]
  [1.0 GB]
Partition check:
 sda: sda1 sda2 sda3
 sdb: sdb1 sdb2 sdb3 sdb4
RAMDISK: Compressed image found at block 0
VFS: Mounted root (ext2 filesystem).
scsi-ncr53c7,8xx : at PCI bus 0, device 11,  function 0
scsi-ncr53c7,8xx : warning : revision of 18 is greater than 2.
scsi-ncr53c7,8xx : IO region 0xe000 to 0xe07f is in use
VFS: Mounted root (ext2 filesystem) readonly.
Trying to unmount old root ... okay
Adding Swap: 55992k swap-space
```

There are other messages that will probably come by here as programs start up. For example, output of things like fsck will not be in a dmesg output. But messages that will be added to the dmesg is changes of CD-ROMs or floppies (VFS disk change detected on device xx:xx) or if modules get loaded (for PPP or the parallel port, for example).

These messages are also stored in the `/var/log/messages` file which is the default location where syslog stores its messages.

2.3   init

The `/etc/inittab` file is read by init which tells it what init level to start out on, and what processes to start. This would include programs like getty (which is what gives you the login prompt on the console). Other scripts are run based on what runlevel you've entered.

An entry in the `/etc/inittab` file has four fields:

```
l0:0:wait:/etc/rc.d/rc 0
```

The fields are delimited by colons. The first field is one unique to the file and is just an arbitrary two-letter (or -digit) sequence. The second field tells init what runlevel to reference this field on. In this case, it's runlevel 0. The third field is an option to init on what to do while the script is running. Since you don't want to cause problems by having multiple runlevel change scripts running at once, init will wait until the script has finished before running any other scripts. Other options include "respawn" which will restart the process if it dies or stops (for getty), and "once" meaning that the process should be run only once and never again. The fourth field lists the script or process to run. I'll get into how these scripts work below.

2.4   What's a Runlevel?

The runlevel of the machine determines what functionality the system should be providing. Just as Windows 95 provides a "safe mode," UNIX has a single-user safe mode, plus other configurations available:

Runlevel	Functionality
0	Halt
1	Single-user mode
2	Multiuser, no NFS
3	Multiuser, with NFS
4	Unused
5	X11 console (xdm)[a]
6	Reboot

a. In Solaris 2.x, runlevel 5 will power down the system. It won't do that in Linux

Two of these runlevels are really for stopping or rebooting the machine. Runlevel 1 allows only root to log in, and only the root partition is mounted. This is primarily for emergency situations where one of the other partitions is corrupted. The default runlevel for RedHat 4.1 is 3, which is a typical multiuser system, and starts the network file system daemons as well. If you're not using NFS, you can use runlevel 2 if you like.

The first script that gets run by init, no matter what runlevel you're using, is the `/etc/rc.d/rc.sysinit` script. This script activates swap partitions, checks the filesystem consistency on any partitions it's about to mount, and a few other functions we won't worry about yet. In short, the rc.sysinit script runs all the programs that would be required no matter what runlevel you'd be using.

Once the rc.sysinit script completes successfully, init goes on and calls the `/etc/rc.d/rc script` with an option being the number of the runlevel to enter (0-6). Here's where things get interesting.

Under the `/etc/rc.d` directory are six directories called rc.[0-6].d to look at. Each directory has a number of scripts that start with either a K or an S, a two-digit number, and a program name. The S is for start scripts, and they are run when init enters that runlevel. This is for starting up programs that are specific to that runlevel. The K is for kill scripts, and they do the reverse of the S scripts, killing any programs that are not in that runlevel. The numbers give an order to the apparent chaos, as scripts with a lower number are executed first, allowing the networking software to initialize the Ethernet card before the NFS daemons try to start. In all this, the name is just a descriptive one to the user. Kill scripts are run before start scripts.

All these scripts are links to the `/etc/rc.d/init.d` directory, which contains the master of all the scripts. This allows one master script to not only control starting and killing processes but also allows you to find all the scripts in one location.

You can change your init level on the fly using the telinit command.[2] The telinit command takes only one argument—the runlevel you want to go to. This has to be run as root, since you don't want just anyone dropping your system into single-user mode or making it reboot. telinit will handle running all the scripts to kill or start new processes.

---

[2]telinit is really just a link to init, so you could use init <number> instead.

2.5   When Something Goes Wrong

There are only a few places during the boot sequence that will cause the kernel to not finish loading (or load at all). These include the following.

- Can't mount the root partition. The kernel may be trying to load a partition other than the one that is really root. Your kernel may not have the right drivers for the hard drive loaded. This can happen with SCSI drives, where each controller has its own driver. You'll have to boot an older or emergency kernel and fix this.

- Can't auto-fsck a partition. In this case, the system will give you a warning and drop you into single-user mode. At this point, only the root partition is mounted, and you should use fsck to try and fix whatever damage was done. If you can't fix the partition, you'll have to restore it from a tape or reinstall Linux.

- Kernel was told to start up in runlevel 1. Check the `/etc/inittab` to see what the default runlevel is. It should be 2 or 3. You can go to runlevel 2 or 3 using the telinit or init commands.

- Other errors loading drivers. This usually signifies a hardware error, such as a card not being found. In general, if a non-essential card isn't working (Ethernet, sound card, serial port card, etc) the kernel will still boot. If the card is severely damaged,[3] it can cause the entire motherboard to start to fail. Remove all non-essential cards and try rebooting again.

- Bad startup scripts. If a script in `/etc/rc.d` is not written correctly, it can cause the system to go into a loop and appear locked up before it gets to the point where you can log in. Note the point where the machine appears to lock up, and boot into single-user mode (if possible) or boot an emergency floppy. Once you get access to the system, find the script that is causing trouble and look for any problems. You may want to keep backup startups scripts handy just in case.

To make a quick summary, here's the things you should have ready after installing Linux:

---

[3]Static is one of the quickest ways to ruin a card. Be sure you're grounded before working on the inside of a machine.

- Emergency boot floppy. Many Linux installations require a boot floppy anyway, so you probably already have this.

- Root floppy with fsck, mkext2fs, fdisk, copies of startup scripts, tar or program to restore backups. This will allow you to re-create partitions, format them, and restore the last backup to the hard drive if necessary.

- Known good kernel on the root partition—the one used to install the system if you have it available. It may not have all the drivers, but you will be able to boot.

- Screwdrivers and a grounding strap. Just in case you suspect a hardware problem.

2.6   System Shutdown

Shutting Linux down is somewhat easier than starting it, since all you need to do is kill off all the available processes and tell the kernel to either stop or reboot the system.

There are a few ways to shut the system down, depending on how and when you want it to happen. The fastest way is the following:

```
sync;sync;sync;/sbin/halt
```

The three sync commands tell the system to sync up the internal hard drive cache and the hard drive itself. Anything that has to get written to the hard drive gets done at this time. Why three sync commands? There are varying reasons, but the simplest one is that by the time the last sync is done, the buffers have had time to clear. Another idea is that the three sync commands make sure that all the buffers are cleared, as the hard drive cache may have changed or may not have been completely flushed.

There are a few other methods of telling the machine to halt, including using `kill -9 1` and `telinit 0`. In typical UNIX fashion, more than one command will work.

If you choose to reboot the system, you can replace halt with `reboot` or `telinit 6`.

All of the above commands are for shutting down the system right now. If you choose to have a planned shutdown and want to give users time to finish their work and log out in an orderly fashion, you'll want to use the shutdown command.

Shutdown Command

When shutdown is run, the following options are available:

- `-r`   Reboot after shutdown.
- `-h`   Halt after shutdown.
- `-c`   Cancel an already running shutdown.
- `time`   When to shut down, either +minutes or hh:mm for an absolute time. You can also use "now" which is really +0.
- `message`   Warning message to send to all users.

Once shutdown is started, only root will be able to log in until the machine is rebooted, or the shutdown is canceled.

Shutdown is really a nice front end to the init process, since once shutdown has determined that it's time to shut down, it sends a signal to init to change to runlevel 6 or 0.

CTRL-ALT-DELETE

Yes, the famed "three-finger salute"—CTRL-ALT-DELETE—will shut down Linux as well, in a pinch. The init process is watching for this and will shut the machine down if it receives that signal. The default setting is to run the reboot command immediately.

If you're in a common lab area and don't want just anyone to be able to reboot the machine on a whim, you can take the line out of the `/etc/init-tab` and you're all set. Unfortunately, this doesn't prevent malicious people from hitting the power switch or pressing the reset button.

2.7   Keeping a PC Safe from Reboots

During a reboot, a Linux box has very low security. If you're trying to keep a PC safe, the standard architecture makes it very hard to do. First, the PC can boot an OS (DOS) that can fit on a floppy, plus contain enough programs on it to completely ruin a hard drive, a virus can infect the Master Boot Record (MBR) of a hard drive, which is what Linux needs to boot, or a user can bring their own Linux boot floppy to get root access, mount the hard drive, and start editing the `/etc/passwd` file.

Plus, the fun with users hitting the power switch or reset button is always a factor. Running any kind of program remotely on a publicly accessible system is not a good idea, as the system can go down at any time. Here are a few suggestions for keeping a publicly available Linux machine for X86 safe.

1. Protect the Basic Input/Output System (BIOS). This is the first thing you need to do, as many of the other protections depend on this. Password protect access to the BIOS. Most modern ones will allow this. Also be sure that no one can open the case. Locks are available for many cases. In the event that you forget the password, you can disconnect the on-board battery or make a jumper connection on the motherboard and the BIOS will be set to default values.

2. Prevent booting from the floppy drive. Many BIOSes allow you to specify that only the hard drive can be booted first, forcing the computer to go into Linux or another OS on bootup without checking the floppy drive. This will not only prevent booting into DOS but may also prevent a boot-sector virus or two from infecting the hard drive.

3. Use Linux only. Booting into DOS or Windows can cause trouble, especially if they intend to cause harm to the computer. Booting into Linux will minimize this risk, since they cannot run any DOS programs.[4]

4. Don't use LILO unless you have to. LILO can boot off another device if told to (and if you have a Linux boot disk). Putting the Linux kernel on the MBR of the first hard drive can help prevent other OSes from being loaded inadvertently.

5. If necessary, disconnect the reset and power switches. This may force you to have people nearby who can power-cycle in the event of a crash.

6. Don't give out the root password. This goes without saying, but just in case. . . I said it.

7. Be on guard. These steps will not make your computer bulletproof but should help prevent major damage to Linux systems.

8. Disable the CTRL-ALT-DELETE in /etc/inittab. The line you'll want to look for is probably similar to this:

```
ca::ctrlaltdel:/sbin/shutdown -t3 -r now
```

---

[4]If this is the case, you should also take DOSEMU off the Linux system.

Once you have your machine secure against reboots, you can set the machine up in a lab for public use.

2.8   Summary

In this chapter, we covered the following:

- LILO is used to start the kernel up. There are a few different ways to install it on your hard drive
- The kernel, on bootup, displays a number of messages regarding the drivers and devices it finds.
- Back up your system often, and keep emergency diskettes handy in case of any problems.
- The init process is process 1. Killing it will reboot your Linux machine
- Even though the X86 architecture is not very security conscious, there are steps you can take to secure a Linux setup.
- The init process is always process 1. Killing it is the same as telling Linux to shut down.

User Administration 3

Administering the human side of your network—the users.

There is more to administration than making sure that the system itself is running properly. You must keep the users of the system running as well.

3.1 Adding Users

As you've probably discovered by now, the user account and information are stored in two files:[1] /etc/passwd and /etc/group. The /etc/passwd file stores usernames, encrypted passwords, real names, and other user information. The /etc/group file stores group information and lists the other groups of which the user is a member.

There are several methods you can use to add a user. The first, and probably the most difficult, is to make an entry in the /etc/passwd file

---

[1]More than two if you're using shadow passwords.

(and `/etc/group` if necessary) for the new user. The passwd field looks something like this:

```
markk:OQLpOZwXo.shE:500:500:Mark F. Komarinski:/home/markk:/bin/tcsh
```

As you can see, there are seven fields separated by colons. In order, these are the username, encrypted password, User ID (UID), primary Group ID (GID), real name, home directory, and login shell.

To enter a new user, simply add your own line. Replace the entire encrypted field with an ° or some other character. Be sure the UID is unique. Now, create the home directory you entered, copy files from `/etc/skel` to the home directory, and chown all the files in the home directory to the new user. Once the user exists, give the user a password by using the command as root:

```
passwd bob
```

Assuming that bob is the `userid` you created, this will put a valid encrypted password in the passwd field, and the bob user can now log in. The first thing the new user should do is change their password.

If that seems a bit complicated, there are two other methods you can use. First, RedHat comes with a `usercfg` that will allow root to create or delete users from the system. It does all of this automatically. The downside is that it's X based, which is not much fun for automated scripts and the like. The third option for creating users is the `/usr/sbin/adduser` command. The only option required by the program is the username you wish to create. The program will then create the user, move files around, chown, and so on. Both `adduser` and `usercfg` create groups and assign unique UIDs based on the last UID used above 500.

Groups

Groups and GIDs are used to collect logical groups of people together. For example, engineering would have files they'd want to share among themselves, but not necessarily with sales. Or accounting would want to share files with each other, but not with the rest of the company. The three levels of access for Linux files are user, group, and world. User is for the individual user who owns the file. The group is the group the file and user belong to, and world is everyone else. If you belong to the eng group (engineers) and want anyone else in the eng group to read a file, make sure the file belongs in the eng group:

```
chgrp eng README
```

Then, set appropriate permissions on the file:

```
chmod 660 README
```

This particular chmod command gives read and write permissions to the owner (you) and anyone else in the eng group. No other users have access to this file.

The chmod command actually uses four octal numbers (0-8) to specify permissions:

Ownership	User	Group	Others
0—no setting	0—no permissions	0—no permissions	0—no permissions
1—save text image	1—execute	1- execute	1—execute
2—set GID	2—write	2—write	2—write
4—set UID	4—read	4—read	4—read

The ownership settings are rather special, in that they give some extra functionality but are also security holes. The "save text image" means that once the program has finished running, it will save the text portion in memory to decrease the amount of time it takes the program to load later on. This can quickly eat up memory if many programs have this, but if you use some programs a lot, this may be helpful.

The set GID means that once the program runs, set the group ID of the user to be that of the file. If a program is in the sales group and has its GID bit set, then when I run that program, I will be in the sales group only within that program while it is running. Some E-mail programs use the set GID to lock files in the `/var/spool/mail` directories. The user becomes part of the "mail" group while the E-mail program is running and can write to `/var/spool/mail`.

The setUID is the same as the setGID but works with user IDs instead. Some programs, like network snoopers, require the use of devices or functions that can be run only by root. By setting ping to be set UID root, everyday users can run the ping program. If you set a program to be set UID, be careful, what you're doing. If the program creates a new shell process, it will have the UID of the owner of the file. If the owner of the file is root, this can lead to common users getting root access very quickly. All the user would have to do is start a shell, and the new shell will be running as root.

The /etc/skel Directory

This directory contains a "skeleton" user. That is, it contains files that you can use as a base for other users. In most cases, it contains setup files for X, /bin/bash config files, and a .login. You can add to or change these files as you like, but remember that existing users will not have these changes taken into account. Only new users will see them. If you want to have common settings for all users, you can use the /etc/.login, /etc/csh.cshrc, and so on.

3.2   Deleting or Disabling Users

If you want to disable a user account (that is, prevent the user from logging in again), replace the password in the /etc/passwd file with an * or some other character. Since the * isn't a valid encrypted password, there is no password that will allow you to log into that account.[2]

To delete an account, remove the entire line from the /etc/passwd file. The user will cease to exist to the system, and root cannot su to that user.

The differences? If you disable an account, the account technically still exists. That user can still receive mail,[3] has a home directory (that other people can access if the permissions are correct), and has all the rights of any other account. The user just can't log in. When an account is deleted, the system will bounce any mail that comes to that user, and all files owned by the former user will now be owned by the UID that the user had. Also, any accesses to the home directory (cd ~bob, for example) will not work.

When to Disable and When to Delete

So, when should you disable an account and when should you delete it? It depends on what information you want to keep. If you're an Internet Service Provider (ISP) and the customer cancels, you may just want to delete the account. If you're in a business and an employee quits, you'd probably want

---

[2]The root user can still use "su" to enter that account, as su does not ask root for passwords.

[3]A deleted user can still have an entry in /etc/aliases to forward mail to another system.

to make the account disabled for six months to give everyone else time to transfer files to other users, or to back up the account to tape.

The best criterion for this is: If the user has data in their home directory that others would want or need to access, disable the account. Once the files needed by the disabled account have been moved to other locations, delete the account. If the account has no information needed by other users, back up the home directory and any other files the user owns and delete the account.

3.3 Using Shadow Passwords

There are a few advantages to using shadow passwords instead of using `/etc/passwd`. One is that encrypted passwords are not stored in a location where just anyone can read them. The `/etc/shadow` file contains the encrypted passwords for users and is readable only by root. Thus, only processes running as root can access the passwords. Another advantage is that `/etc/shadow` stores more than just the passwords. It can also store data, such as the last time a user changed his or her password. To maintain a good security level, you should have users change their passwords at least once every six months or so, or immediately if there is the possibility that the password was compromised.

The disadvantage to using shadow passwords is rather large—most Linux programs assume you're not using them. This can cause a major headache while compiling programs. Also, many installations do not give shadow passwords by default, meaning that you'll have to put it in post-installation.

3.4 Interaction with Users

This section is more for the human side of interaction. The way you interact with your users determines how they will interact with you. The first thing to remember is that your users will probably not know as much about Linux as you do. They may need simple concepts or programs explained to them. Giving them a lot of low-level gibberish makes you look cool, but it probably won't answer the user's questions.

As an example, you could say, "Well, sendmail is thinking your mailhost is foo when it should be bar, so I'll have to go change the `/etc/aliases` file on the NIS server to make it point to the right server." Or you could say "The mail isn't in the right location. I'll try and move it." If you knew absolutely nothing about computers, which would make you feel better? Don't let your sadistic side get the better of you, no matter how tempting it is. Just read your Dilbert cartoons and snicker.

One other important thing you should do is keep your users informed. If you need to shut down the server, be sure to give everyone at least a few minutes warning before you do it. If you have to take the server down for maintenance, do it near the end of the day and give everyone a few hours to get their work done. Just dropping people off the server may cause them to lose files and work. Also be sure that your backups work and test the backups frequently so you can be sure that you can restore them if needed.

Some writers have the notion that the people you're assisting in your day-to-day activities are not really your customers—they're just the people you work with. We see it differently. Your primary job, if you're an Manager of Information Services (MIS) person, is to make sure that the people you're helping are able to do their jobs. If they can't do their jobs, then you won't have one to do. So it would be fair to think of the people you're helping as customers.

As such, you have to be nice to them and should be ready to drop what you're doing to make sure they can keep doing their jobs.

3.5 RPM

The RedHat Package Manager (RPM) is used by RedHat, Caldera, and other RedHat-based distributions. It allows for upgrading or installing an entire application with a single file and a single command. The package is precompiled (or can be compiled by you if you choose). All the information about the package is stored on the system, making it easy to verify what files are used by a specific package and easy to upgrade a package to a newer release. Packages can have dependencies, so that if package B needs to have package A installed first, you'll be notified of this. Even if you're using a different distribution, you can install RPM and install packages. Note that RPM won't help in this situation with packages already installed.

Using RPM

The command you'll be using for just about everything is *rpm*. The only other command is the *glint* X-based application. Glint graphically displays all the packages on your system in a hierarchical format and will allow you to see the available packages on a CD-ROM or other directory for installation. Packages are available from the RedHat FTP site, or from a RedHat CD-ROM, or many Linux FTP sites. Once you get the .rpm files, you can install them using the -i option to rpm or using the upgrade option (-U)

3.6   Summary

- `/etc/password` and `/etc/group` contain all the user information on the system
- File permissions are based on user, group, and everyone
- Be nice! Your users are your customers

Shells 4

Interacting with the Linux system via the shell.

The Linux shell is the primary interface to the Linux kernel. It starts your applications, lets you run commands, and is a programming language as well.

When you log into a Linux system or start an xterm, you're using a shell. When the kernel boots and it runs the `/etc/rc.local` or `/etc/rc.d/ init.d` scripts, it's running a shell. In DOS terms, the shell would be the command.com file. The shell is what runs the commands you use. The shell can provide additional functions like filename or command completion, monitoring your mailbox, or monitoring for other users logging in.

There are two primary types of shells that Linux uses. First is the sh (for just plain shell) which has a very bare-bones functionality but is easy enough to use to create rather powerful programs[1] that you can run. The second is csh (for C shell) which has more user features, just a history and command

---

[1] Also known as shell scripts.

and filename completion, and is a bit more complex for building shell scripts. There are other shells available, such as ksh, ash, and bash, but they are variations or extensions of sh or csh.

4.1   Common Features

Both shells are available for login by users by changing the entry in the /etc/ passwd file. If you install new shells, change the /etc/shells file to add the name of the shell. If a user has a shell that is not in the /etc/shells file, the user will not be able to log in. Another method of changing a user's shell is using the chsh command. A regular user can run this to change their own default shell.

By adding a #!/bin/sh or #!/bin/csh as the first line of a shell script and setting the shell script executable (chmod +x file), the contents of the shell script is run through the shell. So, a file called whome.sh that is set executable and has the contents

```
#!/bin/sh
whoami
id
```

would have the following output if run:

```
[markk@wayga ~]$ ./whome.sh
markk
uid=500(markk)gid=500(markk)groups=2(daemon),100(users),500(markk)
[markk@wayga ~]$
```

Note that you can replace the /bin/sh with /bin/csh if you want since the whoami and id commands are regular UNIX commands. The only place where a shell script to use one type or another is when you get into things like loops or other features specific to shell scripts.

Wildcards

Wildcard expansion is a method where a character or small group of characters match a larger group of items in a set. In csh and sh, the ° character means one or more characters, and ? represents one character. Using this, all the files in a directory can be listed as just °. All files that have only two characters can be represented as ?? (since each character can be represented with one ?). The wildcards can be used at any point in representing a filename.

For example, all the files that start with the letter *a* can be represented as a*
and all the files that end in *.txt* can be represented as *.txt*.

History

The bash and tcsh programs have the ability to keep a running history of the
commands you have run. The bash shell can store a history across logins,
which allows you to see what commands you ran before you logged out.

The history is stored as a "sliding window," so that if the history command
size is 50, and you run 51 commands, command number one is forgotten, and
the first entry in the history file is command number two.

Environment Variables

Environment variables store information used by the shell (such as the PATH
variable) or information used by specific applications (such as Netscape or
man). Here are some of the common variables that get set on login on a typical system:

- PATH—Contains a search path for applications. The shell starts on the
  left side of the search path and searches every item listed in the search
  path until it reaches the end, or finds the application.

- HOME—Has the location of the user's home directory, as it's defined in
  the /etc/passwd file.

- MANPATH—Used by the man program to search for man pages. This
  typically contains /usr/man, /usr/local/man, and /usr/X11R6/man
  but may include diretories where other manual pages are located.

- TERM—Terminal type, which should relate to an entry in the /etc/
  termcap file.

- MAIL—Contains the location of a user's mail spool file, typically /usr/
  spool/mail/*user*. In some cases, this can be set to /var/mail/*user*.

- DISPLAY—Contains the host, monitor, and X server for X applications
  to display on. See the chapter on X for more information about how the
  DISPLAY variable works.

- EDITOR—Contains the program used as a user's default editor. Usually set to /bin/vi.

Pipes and Redirection

The shells have the ability to redirect the output of one program and send it either to another program, or to a file. If you send the output of a program to another program, it's called a pipe. If you send the output to a file, or take input from a file, it's called redirection. To simplify how this works, there are three main types of input and output for a program:

- STDIN—Standard Input, which is normal input (input from the keyboard, or a pipe).

- STDOUT—Standard Output, which is normal output from a program or comes out of a pipe or redirection.

- STDERR—Standard Error, which is similar to STDOUT but comes on a different channel so it doesn't corrupt the data in STDOUT.

Commands get piped when a command string contains the | character. So, this command

```
ls | more
```

would pipe the output from the `ls` command to the `more` command. Many commands (such as `more`) will resort to taking information from STDIN if no options are given. In our case above, since `more` has no files to list, it just takes STDIN.

If there were an error in the `ls` command (for example, the directory did not exist), the error message would get sent out on STDOUT. The error would not get sent through the pipe to the `more` command.

Redirection is done in a few different ways. If you take input from a file, the character used is <, and if you send output to a file, the character is a >. You can think of it as the arrow pointing toward the command. You can duplicate the functionality of the pipe using a temporary file:

```
ls > temp.file
more < temp.file
```

The first command sends the output of the `ls` command to the `temp.file` file. That file is then used as input to the `more` command. There are ways to redirect STDOUT, and that is different for each type of shell.

Note that if a temp.file existed before, it will be overwritten by this.[2] If you want to append data to a file, you can use >> instead of >, and the output from the program will be appended to the end of the file.

Filename and Command Completion

Normally, sh does not allow for filename completion, and csh needs to have a variable set for it to be turned on. Both the bash and tcsh shells have filename completion turned on by default. Hitting the TAB key will complete a command if it's the first word on the command line and resorts to filename completion if it's the second or later word in the command line. Command completion searches the entire PATH for the name of the command, and if more than one command matches this, the command will be matched up to where the two program names differ. Hitting CTRL-D in tcsh or hitting TAB repeatedly in bash will display the available choices.

4.2 sh

The typical sh on Linux systems is really called bash (Bourne again shell). It's based on sh but has some features from csh and ksh in it.

When bash starts up on login, it reads the `/etc/profile`, followed by `~/.bash_profile` or `~/.profile` if available. This contains startup information such as setting the path or other settings. The `/etc/profile` is a global setup file, while the `.bash_profile` or `.profile` is local to each user.

When you log out, the `.bash_logout` file is run.

When a new shell is started (for example, if a program starts a shell, or xterm starts up), the ~/.bashrc file is read. In this instance, this is called a non-login interactive shell.

Environment Variables

To set an environment variable under bash, merely enter the variable you want to set, an equal sign (=), and what you want to set the variable to. For example, if you want to change the TERM variable to vt220, enter the command

```
[markk@wayga ~]$ TERM=vt220
```

---

[2] Unless you have the noclobber option set, in which case you won't be able to overwrite (or clobber) an already existing file with redirection.

You can examine what variables are set with the set command. Variables with multiple entries (like PATH or MANPATH) get separated with colons, like this:

```
PATH=/usr/local/bin:/bin:/usr/bin:/usr/X11R6/bin:/home/markk/bin
```

The bash program sets a few other environmental variables that you'll want to pay attention to:

- BASH_VERSION—Contains the version of bash that you're running
- HISTFILE—Stores what file will have the history when you log out.
- HISTFILESIZE—Lists the number of commands that are stored in the history file. This should be less than the following (HISTSIZE).
- HISTSIZE—Lists the number of commands stored in the history.

For Loops

A for loop runs through each entry and changes to the next entry each time the loop is started. That didn't make sense? Take a look at the following bit of code:

```
for i in *.doc
do
        ls -la $i
done
```

This would do something similar to the command ls -la *.doc, only a bit slower. The for loop sets the variable i to the first file matched by *.doc and then does an ls -la on that file. The i variable then changes to the next file matched by *.doc and does an ls on that as well, and so on until all the files matched by *.doc have been listed.

While Loops

While loops check against a test. If the test is true, the contents of the loop are executed until the condition of the while loop is false. This can typically be the existence of a file, or the value of a variable.

```
while [ -f /var/spool/mail/markk ]
do
        echo "Mail exists in /var/spool/mail/markk" >> ~markk/mail.file
        sleep 30
done
```

This little program checks for the existence of the `/var/spool/mail/markk` file. As long as the file exists, the file `~markk/mail.file` will get a line added to it, and the program sleeps (waits) for 30 seconds before starting over. If the `/var/spool/mail/markk` file doesn't exist the next time the while loop runs, the loop exits.

In case you're wondering about the [ ] that you see in the while, it is a replacement for the test command. The test command can test on various conditions (existence, ownership, permissions) of a file. In our case, the -f means to see if the file exists. The man page for the test command will give more information about the kinds of tests that you can use. This will also work with tcsh or other shells.

4.3   tcsh

The tcsh shell is the Linux replacement for the csh shell. On startup, the tcsh shell reads the `/etc/csh.cshrc` and `/etc/csh.login` files. Once done, tcsh reads the `~/.tcshrc`, or if that file cannot be found, `~/.cshrc`, followed in both cases by `~/.login`. In a non-login interactive shell, the `/etc/csh.login` and `~/.login` files are not read.

On logout, the `/etc/csh.logout` and `~/.logout` files are executed.

Environment Variables

The tcsh shell has the idea of environment variables, plus variables specific to tcsh, which are not really part of the environment. Multiple entries in a variable are separated by spaces and encoded in parentheses, so, the path would look like

```
path (/usr/local/bin /bin /usr/bin /usr/X11R6/bin /home/markk/bin)
```

Environmental variables intended to be read by other programs are set with the `setenv` command. The `setenv` command is similar to environmental variables under bash, in that multiple entries are separated by colons. Setting variables is like this:

```
setenv TERM vt100
```

Note the lack of an equality statement. The first argument to setenv is the variable, and the second argument is what to set the variable to. Running setenv by itself gives a list of any set variables and what they're set to.

Here are some simple tcsh settings:

- autologout—After a certain amount of time (the option to autologout) of inactivity, log out the user. If a second number is included in the setting, the terminal will lock after the second number of minutes.
- history—Contains the number of commands stored in the history. Note that this is similar to HISTSIZE in bash.
- mail—contains the location of the mail spool directory (or multiple ones) and prints "You have new mail."
- watch—Contains a list of user/terminal pairs that get monitored by tcsh for a connection. You can replace the user or terminal with any to match all users or all terminals. If a match is made, the shell prompts you with a note saying who logged in and the terminal they logged in on. set watch=(any any) monitors all users on all terminals

For Loops

For loops under csh are functionally the same as under sh. The loop iterates through all the items in the list until the list is complete. The command is slightly different (called foreach) and the syntax would be

```
foreach i (*)
      ls -la $i
end
```

While Loops

While loops are also the same as under sh. As long as the starting condition is still true, the loop reiterates. The *break* command will allow you to break out of the loop completely, and the *continue* command will break out of the loop, but start processing at the while command again. If you use either of these commands, they have to be made within that loop.

```
while ([-f /var/spool/mail/markk])
      echo "Mail exists in /var/spool/mail/markk" >> ~markk/mail.file
      sleep 30
end
```

Using shell scripts allows you to combine the power of UNIX applications with a programming language that is almost guaranteed to be on every UNIX machine. This makes shell scripts extemely portable.

4.4   Summary

- Environment variables store information about you
- The shell can be used interactively or as a programming language

Networking with Linux 5

Let your Linux box connect to other machines using PPP and Ethernet.

One of the biggest benefits of Linux and UNIX is the built-in TCP/IP networking. This networking gives you E-mail, remote connections, and World Wide Web (WWW) access.

In order to connect your machine to the network, you'll need either an Ethernet card or a modem and a PPP provider.[1] Once this is done, you'll have to reconfigure the Linux kernel to take advantage of the networking hardware. There are more networking options available in Linux than just those for the Ethernet card and Point to Point Protocol (PPP), but these are the two most common methods. For example, you could use PLIP (Parallel Line IP) or ATM or Frame Relay or AX.25.

---

[1]This can be your Internet Service Provider (ISP), employer, or university.

5.1   TCP/IP

The Transmission Control Protocol / Internet Protocol (TCP/IP) is the way that UNIX machines talk to each other. This is also the primary way of connecting to and using the Internet.[2] The entire TCP/IP world (as it's defined right now, anyway) is based on a 32-bit number. This allows for about four billion hosts[3] to all be on the Internet and talking to each other. In order for us humans to figure this out, these 32-bit numbers are referenced by four 8-bit bytes, also known as an IP address, for example, 192.33.4.10. For the further sanity of the human race, these IP addresses can also be referenced as names (ns.psi.net) to make it easier for us to use. Note that these two addresses are not the same. Linux prefers using numbers, and we humans prefer using names. The middle ground comes in the form of DNS (Domain Name Service) which allows for mapping IP addresses to domain names, and vice versa.

DNS works with a root name server, located in various parts of the world. When a user has their Web browser point to www.wayga.net, the machine asks the local DNS server to map that name to an IP address. The local DNS server first looks at the root name servers. These root name servers know that the nameserver for the wayga.net domain is 208.197.103.125. The DNS server then connects to 208.197.103.125 and requests the IP address for www.wayga.net. The DNS server at 208.197.103.125 responds by saying that www.wayga.net's IP address is 208.197.103.125. The local DNS server stores that IP address in its cache in case it's needed again and then provides that IP address to the user application. The user application completes the connection and up pops the Web page. The DNS servers really do more than this and provide for the first pass at mail routing, aliases for machine names, reverse DNS, and even give basic system and location information.

At an application or system level, TCP/IP has over 65,000 ports available for connecting. This allows for FTP, telnet, E-mail, WWW, DNS, and hundreds of other functions to happen all at the same time. When a Web browser connects to a server, Linux opens one of those unused ports and makes a con-

---

[2]Coincidence, or conspiracy? You decide.

[3]There are a few hundred thousand IP addresses that aren't used because they're broadcast or reserved numbers. Don't worry if you think that we're running out of IP addresses too quickly. IPv6 has 128-bit IP addresses (that's a 39-digit number for those of you without calculators).

nection to the server. The server monitors one specific port (port 80 for WWW), sees a connection request, opens an unused port on its side, and then tells the client what port is available for connection. Other important TCP/IP ports include port 25 (E-mail), port 23 (telnet), and ports 20 and 21 (FTP). A list of the known ports and their uses is kept in the `/etc/services` file. Note that for security reasons, ports lower than 1024 can be opened by root only. This is why the main Web server has to run as root, but its clients can run as another user.

TCP/IP has two main connection methods that you'll probably run into: UDP (User Datagram Protocol) and TCP (Telnet Control Protocol). UDP is a connectionless protocol. The packets are usually small, and interaction between the client and server really consists of a number of openings and closings of network connections. UDP is a bit faster and less resource-intensive than TCP but does not guarantee transmission of a packet. NFS is a program that uses UDP. TCP is a connection-based protocol. The client talks to the server, the port is opened, and the connection begins. When the connection closes, it should be because both programs have finished their need for the network. TCP does guarantee packet delivery, and most protocols (Telnet, HTTP, SMTP, etc.) use TCP, as the connections may be longer in time than UDP connections.

Ethernet

Ethernet was developed in the 1970s as a broadcast-style network. In the commonly used coax network, Ethernet cable was run in one long cable, and each end terminated with a 50-ohm resistor. Each machine that was on the Ethernet network hooked into this cable using a tap. In order for machines to identify themselves, each Ethernet adapter has a unique address (Media Access Connector or MAC address) assigned to it by the Ethernet adapter manufacturer. When an Ethernet adapter wants to talk to another Ethernet adapter, it sends a message containing its own MAC address, as well as the receiving MAC address down the entire Ethernet cable. If the receiving MAC address is on that run, it gets the message. Collisions occur when two Ethernet adapters try to transmit at the same time. If this happens, both adapters stop transmission, wait a random amount of time, and retransmit. Having too many collisions indicates a network that has very heavy traffic and is running inefficiently. A link that has a high number of collisions should be broken up unto two or more separate Ethernet runs.

Each Ethernet Packet has To and From Ethernet addresses (see Figure 5–1) , along with the IP to and from addresses, followed by the data and,

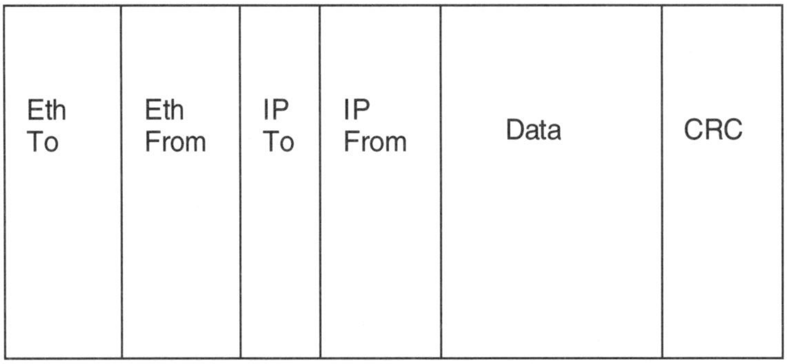

Eth To	Eth From	IP To	IP From	Data	CRC

Figure 5–1   Simple view of an Ethernet packet.

finally, some error checking data to verify the packet arrive complete. A typical Ethernet packet can be no larger than 1514 bytes. IPv4 takes up 40 bytes, and the Ethernet framing takes up another 18 bytes, leaving a maximum of 1456 bytes of data.

Even though all the other Ethernet adapters see that message, they do not answer or respond. The only message that all Ethernet adapters should receive is an Ethernet broadcast. Network monitors take advantage of this feature of Ethernet to give an overall view of that particular Ethernet run.

In order for a packet (say an IP packet) to get across a network to another Ethernet run, a router is used. The router doesn't look at the Ethernet header but instead looks at the protocol being used. If the router knows that a particular packet needs to be forwarded to another network, it forwards the packet.

What allows Linux (and TCP/IP) to make connections between an Ethernet address and an IP address is the Address Resolution Protocol (or ARP) cache. When the Linux machine starts talking on an Ethernet network, it starts asking (via ARP) what the MAC addresses for other machines on the subnet are. Here's how it works.

Linux first sends an Ethernet broadcast asking for a mapping from an IP address to a MAC address. The receiving end with that IP address responds with an ARP reply, giving the IP address and its MAC address. Linux then stores that MAC address in a cache for future use. The cache times out every now and then, so this may happen several times a day. Don't worry, though—there are plenty of 10 Mbps for everyone on the network. If a packet has to go through a router to get somewhere else, Linux addresses the Ethernet packet to the router (or gateway), and the router then picks it up and forwards it to another network.

In a reverse situation, the BOOTP protocol involves a Reverse ARP (RARP) that announces its MAC address, asking which IP address to use. For diskless machines, or even Windows machines using Dynamic Host Configuration Protocol (DHCP), this is the way that these machines can get themselves configured. A machine that has RARP or DHCPd running then responds with the IP address and other information (the gateway and nameserver for example).

Even though the Ethernet protocol is a standard, there are three main ways of actually implementing the physical layer. Thicknet is a 15-pin connection with very heavy gauge wire that is no longer in use. The best thing you can do with a thicknet connection is attach a transceiver on it to convert it to another physical layer.[4] Thinnet, or coax, runs one long wire which has all the Ethernet adapters adding taps or T-connectors along the wire to connect. Coax is very inexpensive to implement, but a wiring problem anywhere along the wire can cause failure of the entire network. Coax also requires termination on both ends to keep the Ethernet signals from reflecting and causing network problems. With the large number of wires and connectors that can be on an Ethernet run, your chances of failure for a large-scale installation increase. The last, and preferable, setup is RJ-45, also known as 10-BaseT. 10-BaseT costs more, since you have to buy a hub, and is harder to implement, since a cable has to go from the hub to each individual machine, but only the failure of a hub would cause more than one person to have network trouble at the same time. If a wire from the hub were to become disconnected, no other users would be affected.[5] The RJ-45 connection also has the capability of running at 100 Mbps instead of the regular 10 Mbps, and most new cabling installations use Category 5 (Cat 5) cabling which is required for 100 Mbps. Category 3 (Cat 3) is suitable for 10 Mbps.

Connecting to an Ethernet Network

To get yourself hooked into an Ethernet network, get yourself an Ethernet card. Most should work, but you may want to check out the Ethernet-HOWTO for a list of cards. For the most part, if it's from a major provider like 3Com, there is probably support for that card.[6] Install the card in your machine and reboot. If the kernel recognizes your card, then you're set for

---

[4]I lied a bit. Thicknet provides for electrical isolation in areas where you might have a ground loop domain problem. for example, going between different floors in a multistory building. Some 10BaseT hubs have this capability as well.

[5]Unless, of course, you are the disconnected user.

now. If not, recompile the kernel and be sure to add support for your particular Ethernet card. The first Ethernet card is usually designated eth0.

In order to add networking for this Ethernet card, you have to first initialize and set up the IP interface; then you have to set up routing for the interface you just set up. No, the two are not the same. The IP interface merely gives the kernel an IP address to work with. It still needs to know when a packet wants to go out and what interface it should use. Otherwise, you're likely to use the loopback interface, and your packets will get nowhere fast.

The /sbin/ifconfig program will register the Ethernet card with the TCP/IP services. The typical syntax is

```
/sbin/ifconfig eth0 netmask <addr> broadcast <addr> <IP address>
```

The netmask and broadcast addresses are given, followed by the IP address for that interface. The interface is automatically brought up if you give it a new IP address, so you don't need to explicitly tell the interface to start.

Now that you have that, you can get the routing set up:

```
route add default gw <address>
```

This sets up a route to your gateway (firewall, router, etc). This is set up to be a default route, so any packets that Linux cannot determine how to route will be sent to this address for further processing.

The RedHat network configuration is an excellent tool for setting up your network devices. Get your IP address, nameserver information, gateway, and netmask from your network administrator. If you're the network administrator, look further in this chapter for instructions on finding this information. Under the Names section, verify your hostname, domain, and IP address for your nameservers. The Hosts section lists what IP addresses and hostnames you have in your /etc/hosts file. This should contain at least your IP address and hostname. If you have other hosts you want to list here, go ahead and add them.

The Interfaces section lists which interfaces are available to you. The lo0 interface is the loopback interface and is used to route TCP/IP packets to itself. Think of it as a virtual Ethernet interface. Changing it will cause prob-

---

[6]Except the 3C501. If you find one, throw it out. Yuk. A standing offer in the Linux world early on was that the author of the Linux 3Com drivers would replace a 3C501 card with a 3C503 if you sent it to him just so there would be that many fewer 3C501 cards left on the planet.

lems with most other programs, including X. You can add the Ethernet interface and give the IP address and netmask. Don't turn on the "Configure
Interface with BOOTP," but you can turn on the "Activate Interface at boot
time." BOOTP is a protocol intended to dynamically assign IP addresses at
boot time. The interface should be configured at boot time, so that once the
machine starts, you can use the Ethernet.

PPP

The Point-to-Point Protocol (PPP) is the way to connect to the Internet or a
TCP/IP network via a dial-up line. As the name implies, PPP is designed to
work between two machines and two machines only. This makes it ideal for
dial-up applications, or even connecting remote locations via a leased line.
Many 56-Kb links use PPP to carry IP traffic over the line.

PPP depends on one machine running pppd server on one end of the
phone line, and a pppd client running on the machine dialing up (yours).
Unlike Ethernet, you have to configure the software differently, depending
on whether you're the client or the server.

PPP doesn't quite have the overhead of Ethernet, since no MAC addresses
are used. Also, some compression is added to the IP frames to boost the
amount of data that can be sent in a packet.

Like Ethernet, PPP can carry more than just IP traffic and can route IPX,
Appletalk, or DECNET along with IP over a PPP link. Linux does not really
take advantage of this functionality, but not many people need it.

PPP Client

Setting up a PPP client requires a modem, phone line, PPP server at some
other phone number, and PPP support compiled into the kernel. Check the
dmesg command to see if PPP support has been compiled in it. You can also
check the /lib/modules/ directory for ppp.o and see if it was compiled as a
module. If support is not compiled in it, recompile the kernel and reboot
using the new kernel.

The quick way of verifying that a PPP connection works is by doing something similar to the following:

```
pppd connect 'chat -v "+" ATDTphone CONNECT "" ogin: login word: pass-
    word' \
/dev/cua1 38400 debug crtscts modem defaultroute
```

The `phone`, `login`, and `passwd` are assigned to you by whomever is providing the PPP account. Also change the `/dev/cua1` to be where your modem is. Remember that `/dev/cua1` under Linux is the same as COM2: under DOS and Windows. The `chat` command is used to dial the modem, and provide the login and password information. Once chat returns success (that is, once it makes a successful connection), PPP takes over the line and starts a connection. The server and client negotiate settings like Maximum Transmit Units (MTU), compression, and a few other settings. This will take a few seconds, but once it's done you should be able to use the `/sbin/ifconfig` command to examine the network connections. If you see a ppp0 listed, you're ready to go.

If you want to use DNS, be sure to enter a valid DNS server that you can reach in the `/etc/resolv.conf` file. Be sure to add it as in the following:

```
domain wayga.net
nameserver 192.33.4.10
```

This sets the domain and the default nameserver. If you know of other nameservers, you can enter them here.

All this configuration can be filled out in scripts using the RedHat Network Configuration Manager. You merely have to enter the phone number, line speed, modem, login, and password. All the rest of the scripts are done for you.

PPP Server

In order to get the PPP server software running (which, coincidentally is the same software as the PPP client), you must have IP forwarding and PPP turned on. This allows Linux to act as an ARP proxy and answer ARP requests for an Ethernet address. If you're using a multiport serial card, you should have the drivers for that in the kernel as well.

Once this is completed, assign a bank of IP addresses that are not in use and will not be in use. These will be the addresses used for incoming connections, and there should at least be as many available as you have phone lines. Don't want to run out of IP addresses, eh?

Once this is done, create new accounts for each user that will be connecting via PPP. Many places use the name of the user with a P prepended to it. If my normal dial-in name were "mark," then my PPP dialup would be "Pmark" to signify a PPP connection. Have the user information in `/etc/passwd` look something like this:

```
Pmark:#56njvc893h:500:500:PPP user:/home/mark:/usr/local/bin/pppd
```

In the home directory of that user, create a `.ppprc`[7] file and add the following:

```
 -detach
modem
crtscts
lock
192.55.123.100:192.55.123.111
proxyarp
```

This gives PPP some initial settings to work with. The -detach says to not detach from the console. The modem says to monitor the CD (Carrier Detect) line and to terminate if CD drops. The lock will lock the device, preventing anyone else from using that serial port. The two IP addresses are the address of the server (waiting for the call) followed by a colon and the IP address to assign to the client when it dials in. The proxyarp allows the server to put the PPP client in its ARP cache and respond to packets that are supposed to go to the client.

Once this has been completed, set up getty to monitor the serial ports, and dial in to make sure that the static IP addresses work. The pppstats command can give a running total of packets in and out for the line.

If you choose to use dynamic IP addresses instead of static IP's to save on IP addresses, create a `/etc/ppp/options.ttyXX` file for each tty file that is attached to a modem. Replace the XX with the name of the serial port, for example, `/etc/ppp/options.ttyS0` for `/dev/ttyS0`. The content of the `options.ttyXX` file is the same as the `.ppprc` file listed above.

If your PPP clients are going to be Windows 95 machines and you're using the default "Dialup Networking" you'll need to add the scripting tool to Windows 95. It's included on the CD-ROM as `\Admin\Apptools\Dscript`. A slightly better version is included in the Windows 95 Plus! pack.

5.2 INETD

The inetd meta daemon is used to start programs automatically when a request comes in on a specific TCP/IP port. What happens is inetd monitors all the ports that are in its configuration file, and when a request comes in, it starts the application and returns to watching ports. There are two files that inetd needs to work: the `/etc/services` and `/etc/inetd.conf` files.

---

[7]You could presumably have the home directory for Pmark and mark in the same location, but be sure to have the `.ppprc` file unwritable by anyone but root.

/etc/services

The `/etc/services` file contains information about a TCP/IP port number, and a name for the specified port which is later used in the `/etc/inetd.conf` file. It's not often that you'll need to add entries to this, but some programs may have you do it. Here's a portion of an `/etc/services` file:

```
chargen         19/tcp          ttytst source
chargen         19/udp          ttytst source
ftp-data        20/tcp
ftp             21/tcp
telnet          23/tcp
smtp            25/tcp          mail
time            37/tcp          timserver
time            37/udp          timserver
rlp             39/udp          resource        # resource location
name            42/udp          nameserver
whois           43/tcp          nicname         # usually to sri-nic
domain          53/tcp
domain          53/udp
mtp             57/tcp                          # deprecated
bootps          67/udp                          # bootp server
bootpc          68/udp                          # bootp client
tftp            69/udp
gopher          70/tcp                          # gopher server
```

The first entry in the line is the service name. This is followed by the port number, and the protocol (usually TCP or UDP) and it is then followed by any aliases. As you can see above, the port where E-mail comes in is called the smtp port and it is located on port 25. Its alias is mail, so I could run a command like:

```
[markk@wayga ~]$ telnet localhost smtp
Trying 127.0.0.1...
Connected to localhost.
Escape character is '^]'.
220 wayga.ratatosk.org ESMTP Sendmail 8.8.5/8.8.5; Mon, 1 Sep 1997
   18:54:30 -040
```

and that telnet command would connect me to TCP/IP port 25 (where send-mail is currently running).

/etc/inetd.conf

The /etc/inetd.conf file takes the port information in the /etc/services file and tells inetd what ports to monitor. Here's a portion of a sample inetd.conf file:

```
# These are standard services.
#
ftp     stream  tcp nowait    root      /usr/sbin/tcpd    in.ftpd -l -a
telnet  stream  tcp nowait    root      /usr/sbin/tcpd    in.telnetd
gopher  stream  tcp nowait    root      /usr/sbin/tcpd    gn

# do not uncomment smtp unless you *really* know what you are
# doing.
# smtp is handled by the sendmail daemon now, not smtpd.  It does # NOT
# run from here, it is started at boot time from /etc/rc.d/rc#.d.
#smtp   stream  tcp nowait    root      /usr/bin/smtpd    smtpd
#nntp   stream  tcp nowait    root      /usr/sbin/tcpd    in.nntpd
```

The entries in this file are as follows:

- entry from /etc/services for what port to monitor.
- stream or dgram (tcp is stream, udp is dgram).
- protocol (tcp or udp).
- options (wait or nowait). Wait says to wait until the program has finished or returned before returning to watching the port. The nowait option says to not wait and return to monitoring the port. If nowait is selected, only one instance of a program will run at a time
- user to run as—this is usually root.
- path of the program.
- name of the program, and any options you'll want to add.

In the example from /etc/services, we made a connection to the mail port, but the inetd.conf example shows that smtp is not being monitored. What happened? For some high-throughput programs (httpd and sendmail are prime examples), you don't want to have a program constantly restarting since it takes a lot of time for a program to start initially. But, for a program that is already running to fork or spawn off a new process, the overhead is much less. Thus, it's better for programs like this to be constantly running and taking care of the connections itself.

Programs like telnetd or ftpd don't need a lot of startup time, so inetd can handle starting up new copies as it needs them.

5.3   Network Applications

Now that the network is set up, what are you going to do with it? Most of the
standard topics (Web, ftp, E-mail) have already been covered, but the rest of
this chapter will cover applications that work across the network for the benefit of everyone. DNS (the nameserver) and NFS (network file server) are
two such applications.

DNS

The   nameserver   is   the   program   that   matches   an   IP   address
(208.197.103.125) to a hostname (wayga.net). It also provides for matching in
the opposite direction as well, informing you that the machine that has the
address 208.197.103.125 is called wayga.net. Since one of the jobs of a
nameserver is to look up and cache DNS requests from client machines, it
can be used at one end of a slow link (between two offices perhaps) and
reduce the amount of DNS traffic across the link. It also has provisions for
forwarding E-mail addressed from one host to another and can provide backups for particular hosts in case one Web server is busy while another is idle.

In any instance where you're connecting to a TCP/IP network, you'll want
to use DNS[8] for hostname resolution. The setup of this is easily done by putting a few lines in your `/etc/resolv.conf` file:

```
domain wayga.net
nameserver 192.33.4.10
```

Modify the wayga.net to be your domain name and change the IP address
to be the nameserver provided to you by your ISP. This IP address is an
actual nameserver, and if you don't know your local nameserver, this IP
address should work in a pinch to get you up and running. You can also put
multiple nameserver entries in here, and it will search in order until it makes
a connection to a DNS server.[9]

If you plan on running named (the DNS server software) locally, then you
should change the IP address to read 127.0.0.1. Be sure to have a few other
IP addresses in there in case named goes down.

---

[8]Yes, even if you're using NIS.

[9]Note that the search stops after the response from the first DNS server. If the
first DNS server replies "host not found," the search stops there.

Should You Be a DNS Server?

You should use the DNS server only in the following cases:

1. You own a domain and want to control the DNS

2. You run a large network over a slow link

3. You have no connection to the Internet

For item 1, many ISPs will offer to handle your DNS serving for you, but if you're in an environment where machines change frequently, it may be easier to do it yourself than wait for the ISP to update their tables. For item 2, named can act as a cache to store frequently used hosts, and this will reduce some of the traffic. In item 3 . . . well . . . if there's no other DNS host on your network, someone should do it, and it may as well be you. If you don't match any of these three, you probably don't need a DNS server running.

If you expect to be the primary or secondary DNS server to the outside world (i.e., the Internet), you'll have to make sure the DNS host is registered with InterNIC or another top-level domain organization. See the chapter on interacting with Internet agencies for information on getting this set up.

Once you're ready to start serving DNS, you'll have to set things up on your machine to do DNS serving.

named.boot

The `named.boot` file contains configuration information to give to named once it starts. It really tells named three things:

1. What directory the configuration files are stored in

2. What primary DNS services it provides

3. What reverse DNS services it provides

There are a few other functions that named does, but it's a bit outside the scope of this chapter. A sample configuration file looks like this:

```
directory       /var/named
;
cache           .                       named.ca
;
primary         wayga.net               named.wayga
primary         a-muse.org              named.a-muse
primary         0.0.127.in-addr.arpa    named.local
```

In this case, the named.boot is doing all three things. The directory statement tells named that any reference to files is going to be in the /var/named directory. Next, it says that the cache file is going to be for all domains and is kept in the named.ca file. The three primary statements say that it is providing DNS information for hosts in the wayga.net and a-muse.org domains, and the information about those hosts is stored in named.wayga and named.a-muse, respectively. The third primary statement indicates that any reverse DNS requests on the 127.0.0 network (also known as the loopback device) are to be done looking at the named.local file.

named.ca

The `named.ca` file contains information about the root nameservers. If the local named program does not have the hostname information locally, it then starts looking for it in the root nameservers. Here's a section out of the wayga.net `named.ca` file:

```
.                       3600000 IN      NS      A.ROOT-SERVERS.NET.
A.ROOT-SERVERS.NET.     3600000         A       198.41.0.4
;
; formerly NS1.ISI.EDU
;
.    3600000 NS    B.ROOT-SERVERS.NET.
B.ROOT-SERVERS.NET.     3600000         A       128.9.0.107
;
; formerly C.PSI.NET
;
.                       3600000         NS      C.ROOT-SERVERS.NET.
C.ROOT-SERVERS.NET.     3600000         A       192.33.4.12
;
; formerly TERP.UMD.EDU
;
.                       3600000         NS      D.ROOT-SERVERS.NET.
D.ROOT-SERVERS.NET.     3600000         A       128.8.10.90
;
; formerly NS.NASA.GOV
;
```

DNS Database Records

Now let's look at the named.wayga file. This file has an example of many of the features you'll want in your files:

```
@                 IN      SOA     wayga.net. enry.wayga.net. (
                  1
                  3600
                  600
                  3600000
                  10800 )
                  IN      NS      208.197.103.125
                  IN      NS      208.197.103.21
wayga.net.        IN      A       208.197.103.125
galileo           IN      A       208.197.103.21
localhost         IN      A       127.0.0.1
wayga.net.        IN      MX      0 wayga.net.
                  IN      MX      10 galileo
www               IN      CNAME   wayga.net.
mail              IN      CNAME   wayga.net.
ftp               IN      CNAME   wayga.net.
plan9             IN      CNAME   wayga.net.
```

The SOA line indicates the Start Of Authority line. This line tells named which domain this file is working on. The SOA line is constant up to the point after the SOA. It then has the following information:

- machine name acting as the DNS server.
- contact name (replace the @ in the E-mail address with a period).
- open parenthesis.
- serial number, which should be incremented every time you change the file. Since this is the first revision of the file, it has a serial number of 1.
- refresh time in seconds, or how often to recheck the SOA record. The 3600 says to refresh once an hour.
- retry time, or when a secondary server should retry contacting the primary server if something goes wrong.
- expire time, or when the secondary server should flush its cache if it can't contact the primary server.
- minimum time to live. This defines how long other servers should keep the records in their cache before it should be flushed. If it's too short, named is spending too much time requesting addresses it should already know, and if it's too long, the wiring IP information may be reported if a host changes ISPs or even IP addresses.

- close parenthesis.

- NS (to indicate the nameserver).

- name of the nameserver host (that's the local host).

Once the SOA is complete, you can begin adding hosts. The entry has four sections to it:

1. Name of the domain or hostname. If the name does not end in a ., the domain name (in our case wayga.net) is appended. If the address ends in a ., it is assumed it is the Fully Qualified Domain Name (FQDN).

2. IN—This separates the hostname from the rest of the record.

3. Type of record. The record type can be any of the following:
   - A—directly maps a hostname to an IP address. All other records have to point to an A record

   - MX—mail exchanger. Lists what hosts will accept E-mail for that host or domain. Before the record contents, you can indicate a number for preference. In the case of wayga.net, the mail host is itself, but if wayga.net is busy or unavailable, galileo will accept the E-mail instead.

   - CNAME—also known as an alias, as you can see. Ftp.wayga.net, www.wayga.net, and mail.wayga.net are all pointers to wayga.net. Any DSN requests for these hosts will receive the IP address for wayga.net.

   - HINFO—may contain host information, but it's not used very much, as it can give potential crackers information about your machine.

4. Record contents. In the case of an A record, it's an IP address. For other records, it can be a hostname or system information.

Reverse DNS

If your machine is doing reverse DNS, the SOA is the same, but the records themselves are slightly different. First, as you can tell with the named.boot, the IP address is reversed. Instead of the 127.0.0 network, it becomes 0.0.127.in-addr.arpa. Reverse the network you're using, and use that as the domain in /etc/named.boot. Since the network for wayga.net is 208.197.103, the domain becomes 103.197.208.in-addr.arpa.

The records for wayga.net and galileo.wayga.net would look like this if we were doing reverse DNS:

```
21   IN   PTR  galileo.wayga.net.
125  IN   PTR  wayga.net.
```

As you can see, the hostnames need a . at the end, since reverse DNS can span physical IP addresses.[10] The record type is also different—PTR. The IP address needs only the portion of the network not already in the domain listed above.

Once this is complete, you can start named and verify your configuration with nslookup.

Configuring the Berkeley Internet Name Daemon 8.1 (BIND)

If you've decided to be a DNS server, be it a primary, secondary, or a mix of the two, you need to get (possibly compile) and configure BIND. It's very likely that named was installed when Linux was installed; if not you can retrieve it from the official distribution sites at `ftp://ftp.isc.org/isc/bind/` or any Linux distribution site.

As of version 8.1 the configuration file name and format have changed. Since the new version of BIND is or will be shipped with newer versions of every Linux distribution, we will go over the configuration of it.

The basic 8.1-style config file is named named.conf and lives in /etc. It has four types of statements: one controlling access, one describing the logging, one describing the more general options, and one or more describing zone(s) it is a server for. Comments in the file can be delineated using C or C++ style comment syntax.

BIND comes with extensive documentation, but we will try to detail the most important parts of it here.

The options statement describes what IPs to listen for and what port to use. Firewalls can complicate things and will likely require that you use a privileged port. 53 is the default port and can be specified in this statement. Lastly, the working directory for named specified here, /var/named, is fairly widely used. The zone files and any other files specified in various statements will live here in the absence of any pathing information. There are many

---

[10] As it is, wayga.net is part of someone else's IP network. That's why we don't do reverse DNS. If someone did a reverse DNS lookup on us, it would report a different domain.

other options which can be controlled from here; most of them have reasonable defaults (see the documentation for details).

The logging statement simply controls the verbosity of the logging and where log messages are send. Each category has various channels to which to send output and each channel can be customized with a channel statement. Logging can be controlled to a fairly fine detail (consult the documentation for the gory details).

Controlling what clients your server will answer queries from is done via the acl statement. If you have a lot of mobile users, you may need to be pretty loose with access to the name service.

Finally, the guts of the config file are the zone statements. They describe what zones the server serves, either as a master or a slave (we ignore the stub type; read about it in the documentation). A master is just that, the master authority for information in that domain (zone). A slave is a secondary disseminator of zone information, but it gets all the zone data from the zone master; no changes can be made at the slave. There is one special type used when specifying the root nameservers. It is called a hint because the named.ca really just supplies a list of servers, some of which will have the current list of root nameservers.

For a slave zone you must specify at least one master from which BIND can transfer the zone records. More than one can be specified. Only one will be the real master; the others will be other slaves which will presumably have up-to-date zone records.

Below is an example of a basic /etc/named.conf which will we use as a basis for some examples. Currently it will answer queries from any client.

```
options {
  directory "/var/named";
  /*
   * If there is a firewall between you and nameservers you want
   * to talk to, you might need to uncomment the query-source
   * directive below.  Previous versions of BIND always asked
   * questions using port 53, but BIND 8.1 uses an unprivileged
   * port by default.
   */
  // query-source address * port 53;
  listen-on { 127.0.0.1; 208.197.103.21; };
};


logging {
  category default {default_syslog; default_debug;};
```

```
  /* Uncomment to send debugging information to my own set of files */
  /*
  channel this_security_channel {
    file "named_security.log";
    severity info;
  };
  category security { my_security_channel; default_syslog;
  default_debug; };
  */
};

zone "." {
  type hint;
  file "named.ca";
};

zone "0.0.127.IN-ADDR.ARPA" {
  type master;
  file "named.local";
};

zone "103.197.208.in-addr.arpa" {
  type slave;
  file "named.208.197.103";
  masters {
    208.197.103.2;
  };
};

zone "ratatosk.org" {
  type master;
  file "named.ratatosk";
};

zone "wayga.net" {
  type slave;
  file "named.wayga";
  masters {
    208.197.103.125;
  };
};
```

The first thing you are probably interested in is restricting use of your nameserver.

There are 5 ACLs that named defines for you:

any	Allows all hosts.
none	Denies all hosts.
localhost	Allows the IP addresses of all interfaces on the system.
localnets	Allows any host on a network for which the system has an interface.

Defining your own is simple, the syntax is "acl *name* { *address list* }." Name is an alphanumeric string and address list is a list of IPs, IP prefixes, or the name of another ACL. It is possible to negate elements with "!."

For instance, to exclude machines on your LAN, you could define this ACL:

```
acl notlocal { ! localnets; };
```

It is important to keep in mind that the matches are checked against the list from left to right; as soon as a match is found, the rest of the line is ignored.Consider these two ACL entries:

```
acl first { 10.10.10/24 ; ! 10.10.10.128; };
acl second { ! 10.10.10.128 ; 10.10.10/24; };
```

Only the second one will work the way it was intended: deny the IP 10.10.10.128 name service. Since the IP prefix is tested first and matches 10.10.10.128 the denied IP is never tested. Thus the host you want to deny will be able to use your DNS server.

Using Your ACLs

Now that you have an idea of how to define ACLs we'll show you how to use them.

You may want to restrict what hosts can get (transfer) your zone record to only your trusted DNS slaves, one of which we have specified in an ACL statement.

```
acl trusted_slaves {localnets; 205.157.230.253; };

zone "ratatosk.org" {
  type master;
  file "named.ratatosk";
  allow-transfer {trusted_slaves; 208.197.103.125; };
};
```

Other Important Options

```
listen-on [port]
```

This option specifies what IP address and/or port to listen to. The default port is 53. You can specify IP prefixes as well.

```
listen-on port 7777 { 208.197.103.200; };
```

If no listen-on is specified, the server will listen on all prot 53 on all interfaces.

```
include
```

This statement is used to include other files which contain valid configuration information.

```
include "/etc/my_acls";
```

We've tried to cover the options you will most likely use. However, there are several potentially useful statements we haven't covered. You should spend some time looking at the documentation which also includes some features which will be implemented in future releases.

nslookup

The nslookup program interacts with the nameserver to give IP information about a host or domain. This program will also allow you to examine things like A, MX, or CNAME records. When run with an option of a hostname, nslookup will contact the local DNS host and return information on that host:

```
[markk@wayga named]$ nslookup wayga.net
Server:  wayga.net
Address:  208.197.103.125

Name:    wayga.net
Address:  208.197.103.125

[markk@wayga named]$
```

When run without any options, it puts you in an interactive mode, allowing you to enter hosts, set the kinds of queries, list hosts within a domain, and so on.

Entering a hostname from interactive mode will look up the host and return the results. The *set type=X* command will tell nslookup to report on only certain types of records (MX, PTR, A, CNAME, HINFO). Setting a type of ANY will search for all records.

```
[markk@wayga named]$ nslookup
Default Server:  wayga.net
Address:  208.197.103.125

> set type=ANY
> wayga.net
Server:  wayga.net
Address:  208.197.103.125

wayga.net          nameserver = 208.197.103.125.wayga.net
wayga.net          nameserver = 208.197.103.21.wayga.net
wayga.net          preference = 10, mail exchanger = galileo.wayga.net
wayga.net          preference = 0, mail exchanger = wayga.net
wayga.net
         origin = wayga.net
         mail addr = enry.wayga.net
         serial = 1
         refresh = 3600 (1 hour)
         retry  = 600 (10 mins)
         expire = 3600000 (41 days 16 hours)
         minimum ttl = 10800 (3 hours)
wayga.net          internet address = 208.197.103.125
wayga.net          nameserver = 208.197.103.125.wayga.net
wayga.net          nameserver = 208.197.103.21.wayga.net
galileo.wayga.net        internet address = 208.197.103.21
wayga.net          internet address = 208.197.103.125
>
```

As you can see, this is a bit more information than you got earlier. The server command will allow you to request information from another server. This is good for debugging, since you can now ask a remote server for information about the domain you just set up and make sure the information is correct. The last command that is rather important is the *ls DOMAIN* command, which will list all the hosts under *DOMAIN* Using this on the domain you have just set up will verify that all hosts are being listed.

NFS

The Network File System (NFS) allows a server to export a directory or an entire filesystem to other systems. This provides for not only getting the most out of hard drives, but can also allow a user's home directory to exist anywhere on the network, just as if it were local.

Setting up NFS for use is easy, as most Linux installations start up the necessary software at boot time. All that's left is to configure the NFS servers.

If NFS isn't started on bootup, all you need to do is fire up `rpc.mountd` and `rpc.nfsd` on startup. This can be in the `rc.local`, or in a script in the `/etc/rc.d/rc3.d` directory. The one other item that needs to exist is the `/etc/exports` file. The /etc/exports file lists what directories can be exported to other machines.

The `/etc/exports` file has a setup of the following:

```
directory    options
```

where *directory* is the directory to be exported, and *options* are any additional options to work on that export. The options are many and can provide different options per host. Any options not enclosed in a host are assumed to be for any other hosts. Options can be of the following:

- insecure—allow non-authenticated access.
- ro—mounts read-only (good for use with insecure).
- rw—mounts read-write.
- root_squash—prevents the root user from having any special access to the NFS drive by mapping UID 0 (root) to UID 65524.[11] This option is off by default
- no_root_squash—allows the root user to manipulate the partition as if it is local. This is turned on by default.
- all_squash—same as root_squash, but does it for all UIDs.
- no_all_squash—no UIDs are squashed (default).

Options can be prefaced with a hostname to apply that option to only that host.

```
/pub wayga(rw)
```

The wayga machine can mount the directory in read-write mode for all users (the default). The ro option means read-only.

```
/pub/foo wayga(noaccess)
```

---

[11]also known as the nobody user

The foo subdirectory is not accessible to wayga. The only thing that wayga will see is permissions for the foo directory, and an ls of it will return only "." and "..."

Remember that unless you have a firewall or packet filter up, all NFS access will be TCP/IP-wide unless you specify a host or group of hosts that can access that particular NFS directory.

From the NFS client, assume root power, and let's mount the /pub directory from above:

```
mount -t nfs wooba:/pub /mnt/pub
```

There are only a few changes in the mount command from mounting a hard drive or CD-ROM. The filesystem type is nfs, and the device name is replaced with a host:directory combo.

To have directories mount automatically on startup, you can enter them into the /etc/fstab file, or use the RedHat fstool to add the mounts. Remember to replace the device file with the host:directory combo, and use the filesystem type of nfs. Once the network is started, and NFS service has started, the NFS directories will mount.

One problem with NFS is that if the NFS server goes down, or the network connection between the client and server is broken, the client can effectively stop while trying to do file access. This can even include the situation where an NFS directory is in your $PATH. Running a command that searches through the path will cause your machine to appear to hang. There isn't a cure for it at this point. Just be sure that the server doesn't crash. Other network filesystems are in the works that will prevent some of these problems, but they don't quite work yet. The other important point is to make sure your networking is working correctly.

One additional program you may want to look at if you have a large amount of NFS drives is the amd program. This program is an automount daemon, and it automatically mounts and unmounts drives as needed. It's a bit outside the scope of this chapter, but you can download the program and give it a try if you have a lot of partitions to mount.

5.4 AppleTalk

To round out the list of Linux-supported networking/file sharing protocols, we turn to AppleTalk. Using Linux as an Apple fileserver has several advantages, including

- No limit on simultaneous users: Apple's AppleTalk sets a limit of ten concurrent users. To go beyond this limit you must upgrade to Appleshare, which isn't free.

- Versatility: The Linux server can also, as discussed earlier, serve disks (possibly the same disks) via NFS, SMB (Samba, used by Windows for Workgroups), IPX (Novell Netware), and NetBEUI (Windows NT).

- Additionally, you can take advantage of the superior remote access features of Linux which none of the popular non-Unix-based OSes can rival.

- Since Linux is truly multitasking and has less overhead than MacOS (at least without X running), performance will generally be better. This is true even under MacOS 8 since most of the enhancements were related to stability and the Graphical User Interface (GUI); even though the finder is multithreaded, its actual speed is about the same.

Some of the disadvantages are

- AppleTalk and the daemons that manage the file sharing need to write some "hidden" files (i.e., starting with a leading ".", MacOS will not see them) that tend to junk up the filesystem somewhat.

- AppleTalk and MacOS support a very loose file naming convention. Linux supports this admirably well, especially considering how restrictive traditional UNIX file naming conventions are. However, some characters must escape or be encoded somehow and thus filenames may look different when viewing them from the Linux side of things.

- There is no way to back up clients from the server (though backups for the clients can still be run from a Mac).

- There is no way to mount remote AppleTalk volumes on the Linux box. There is interest in doing this and some work is underway. It's likely that this will be possible some time in the not too distant future.

In addition to making disk volumes available via AppleTalk, it is also possible to make local printers available to your Macs or print to a network AppleTalk printer, possibly making it available to other, non-AppleTalk machines on your local area network (LAN).

In AppleTalk, there are two levels of access: guest and registered user. Being a guest user is basically like being the user nobody in UNIX: You have highly limited access to the server and typically can write only to areas that are world writable.

Registered users, on a Linux-hosted Appleshare server, authenticate using the user and password information in `/etc/passwd`, that is, they must have an account on the machine. If you don't want these users to have shell access, you can give them the shell `/bin/false`. This is analogous to what is done when setting up FTP-only accounts. If you would like to let your users change their passwords, you can give them the shell /bin/passwd. If you choose to do this, be sure to add `/bin/passwd` to the /etc/shells file so that it is a valid shell.

In the configuration files for netatalk, you define which directories are available at the two levels of access, including the home directory of registered users if wanted. For each instance of the AppleTalk daemon, you can specify a set of directories for guests and registered users to access.

The Netatalk homepage is `http://www.umich.edu/~rsug/netatalk/`. Linux-specific information can be found at `http://thehamptons.com/anders/netatalk/`.

Hardware Considerations

There are a few hardware caveats relating to Ethernet cards. Netatalk doesn't function on cards based on DEC's Tulip chip. Also, the driver for your card must support multicasting; the driver for Intel's EtherExpress doesn't do so.

Aside from these functional considerations, the best hardware investment is a good, fast disk. Spend the extra money to buy a fast disk and/or faster SCSI controller.

Typical Installation

The current full (non-beta) release is 1.3; the current beta is 1.4,which has proven very stable and has much better performance than 1.3. It is recommended that you use most recent 1.4 beta instead of 1.3.

Netatalk doesn't require any extra or exceptional software to compile and compiles easily under Linux. You will need to enable AppleTalk support in your kernel as well. It's safe to enable it as a module if you so desire.

Netatalk installs its various daemons and utilities under `/usr/local/atalk`. In particular, the `etc` subdirectory contains the configuration files: `AppleVolumes.default`, `AppleVolumes.system`, `atalk.conf`, and `rc.atalk`. As is the case for many network services, you will need to make a few entries in `/etc/services` as well.

Entries for `/etc/services`:

```
rtmp    1/ddp # Routing Table Maintenance Protocol
nbp     2/ddp # Name Binding Protocol
echo    4/ddp # AppleTalk Echo Protocol
zip     6/ddp # Zone Information Protocol
```

A sample `rc.atalk`:

```
echo -n 'starting appletalk daemons:'
if [ -f /usr/local/atalk/etc/atalkd ]; then
        /usr/local/atalk/etc/atalkd;        echo -n ' atalkd'
fi

if [ -f /usr/local/atalk/bin/nbprgstr ]; then
        /usr/local/atalk/bin/nbprgstr -p 4 `hostname|sed 's/\..*$//
   '`:Workstation
n
        /usr/local/atalk/bin/nbprgstr -p 4 `hostname|sed 's/\..*$//
   '`:netatalk
                                        echo -n ' nbprgstr'
fi

if [ -f /usr/local/atalk/etc/papd ]; then
        /usr/local/atalk/etc/papd;        echo -n ' papd'
fi

if [ -f /usr/local/atalk/etc/afpd ]; then
        /usr/local/atalk/etc/afpd;        echo -n ' afpd'
fi
```

`AppleVolumes.system` provides a filename for type mapping. Also carriage return to line feed mapping is controlled in this file. Typically altering file extensions for which this translation is done is the only reason you would need to edit this file.

`AppleVolumes.default` contains a list of directories and optional labels to be exported as Appleshares. If the label is present, it will be used to identify the volume in the chooser and desktop. A tilde (~) in this file will tell the server to present the user's home directory in the list of exported volumes.

A sample `AppleVolumes.default`:

```
# This file looks empty when viewed with "vi".  In fact, there is one
# '~', so users with no AppleVolumes file in their home directory get
# their home directory by default.
~
```

```
#
# Anonymous ftp area. Will show up as "FTP Area" in chooser.
#
/a/ftp "FTP Area"
#
# Data area. Will show up as "data" in chooser.
#
/usr/local/data
```

The `atalkd.conf` file, as you might imagine, contains the configuration information for atalkd. Entries in this file take the following form:

```
interface [ -seed ] [ -phase number ] [ -net net-range ] [ -addr
    address ] [ -zone zonename ]
```

If you have only one AppleTalk LAN and one interface on your server, you can leave atalkd.conf empty and atalkd will configure itself using information from AppleTalk routers on the network.

If you do have more than one network, AppleTalk will break them into zones. In this case you will want to use the atalkd.conf to tell your server what zone to present itself as being in. You can also configure atalkd to listen to multiple interfaces and route AppleTalk packets among them.

Minimal atalkd.conf for use with multiple Appletalk zones:

```
eth0 -zone "Production"
```

The zone is basically free-form.

Unless you are on a very large network, you can also let `atalkd` also set up its AppleTalk address. If this is not the case, you will have to assign one (or get one if you are not in charge of the assignment of these addresses). Addresses are specified by network and node:

```
-addr 45.10
```

In this example, the 45 before the period is the network, while 10 is the node on that network.

The `-net` option is used to specify which address range is covered in this zone. This option lets you set the address range which is automatically detected at server startup. If you have no zones, this number is irrelevant. The first number corresponds to the first network address of coverage in this range, and the optional last number corresponds to the last address covered in the address range. The address range should include netatalk's address number set with the `-addr` *net.node* option.

For example,

```
-net 106-110
```

The `-zone` option sets the name of the zone that `atalkd` should represent when talking on the net. This option, as discussed before, is merely a means of classification. It will be authoritatively broadcast if the `-seed` option is used and there are routers on the network whose zones don't conflict with that given after the `-zone` option.

Once you have config files set up, invoke the `rc.atalk` script:

```
# /etc/rc.d/rc.atalk
```

This will take a few minutes as netatalk scopes out the network, registers itself, and so forth.

Now, go to one of your Mac clients and open the chooser. Select your new AppleTalk server, select the volumes to attach to, and watch them show up on your desktop! (See Figures 5–2, 5–3 and 5–4)

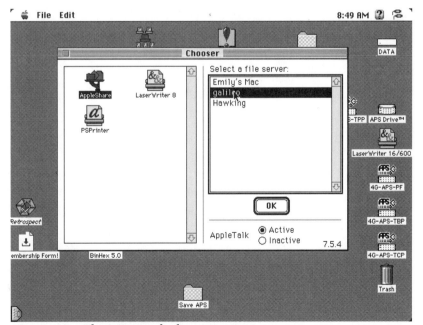

Figure 5–2   The Macintosh chooser.

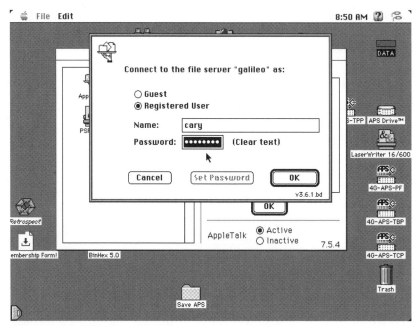

Figure 5–3   Selecting the server

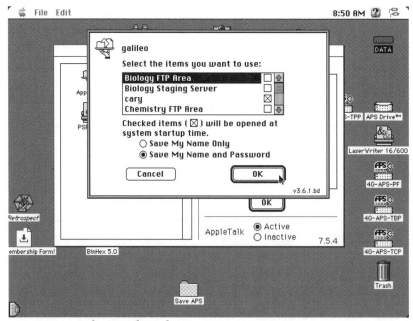

Figure 5–4   Selecting the volume.

Applesharing Your Printer

Making a printer available to your AppleTalk clients is very simple.

The netatalk printer daemon, `papd`, should be starting automatically when the rest of the atalk daemons start. You need to add an entry to `/usr/local/atalk/etc/papd.conf`:

```
Denna laserprinter:\
        :pr=lp:
        :mx#0:\
        :lp=/dev/lp1:\
        :if=/var/spool/lpd/lp/filter:\
        :sh:
```

Depending on the version of netatalk you have, you may have to reboot for the printer to be visible to your clients.

Printing to a Remote Appletalk Printer

It is also possible to print from your Linux box to a network AppleTalk printer. To do this, follow the instructions below.

Get your Appletalk zone using `getzones`:

```
# /usr/local/atalk/bin/getzones
biology
chemistry
```

If you are not sure which is your local zone, use the `-m` option for `getzones`.

Next you need to determine the name of the printer. You can use `nbplkup` for this:

```
# /usr/local/atalk/bin/nbplkup  :Laserwriter
                 galileo:LaserWriter            65280.247:128
        CANON GP200/215 PS:LaserWriter          65296.208:131
        LaserWriter 16/600 PS:LaserWriter       1.129:129
```

We gave `nbplkup` the argument ":Laserwriter" because we know we are looking for that type of printer. If the argument is left off, you will see everything in your zone.

Check the status of the printer you want to print to:

```
# /usr/local/atalk/bin/papstatus -p "LaserWriter 16/600 PS"
status: idle
```

Now test it:

```
# /usr/local/atalk/bin/pap -p "LaserWriter 16/600
   PS":Laserwriter@biology product.ps
```

If you are printing to a printer in your zone, you can leave off the zone name.

Assuming everything is working, the document should print out. Now you can go on to setting up /etc/printcap.

Here is a sample entry:

```
lp|Network LaserWriter|LaserWriter 16/600 PS:\
        :sd=/usr/spool/laserwriter:\
        :lp=/dev/null:\
        :pl#63:\
        :pw#85:\
        :mx#0:\
        :sh:\
        :sf:\
        :lf=/usr/adm/lpd-errs:\
        :if=/usr/local/atalk/etc/filters/ifpap:\
        :of=/usr/local/atalk/etc/filters/ofpap:
```

For more information on setting up remote and local AppleTalk printers see http://www.giub.unibe.ch/~eugster/appleprint.html.

5.5   Network Information Services (NIS)

The Network Information Services (NIS) is a set of programs for managing users and various network services from one master server. Recently an enhanced version of NIS, NIS+, has been introduced. NIS+ is more secure, works better in large networks, but is more difficult to set up.

NIS began life as the Yellow Pages. Yellow Pages however, is a registered trademark of British Telco so the name was changed. The original name's legacy is still around, most of the programs associated with NIS begin with "yp."

NIS stores its information in a set of directories and GDBM (GNU Data-Base Management) files rooted in /F/var/yp/F. NIS refers to these files as "maps." The maps are then made available to other machines in the NIS domain (not the same thing as a DNS domain!) via RPC (Remote Procedure Calls). NIS also allows for secondary slave servers. Slave servers get their maps from the master and answer requests if the master is slow or down, much the same way secondary DNS servers work.

The NIS maps are built from the various setup files commonly found in /etc: passwd, group, hosts, services, aliases, and so on. It is not necessary to use every map. Often only the password and group maps are used since most of the other files typically change infrequently.

One of the biggest problems with NIS was the security hole opened by broadcasting NIS requests—anyone could set up a server which would have a chance of answering the requests. Recent versions of ypbind allow the specification of the domain server either by IP number or name.

NIS Client Setup

It is most likely that your first encounter with NIS will be as a client. Setting up your Linux machine to be an NIS client is fairly straightforward.

First of all, you will need to know what information is being managed via NIS. We will assume a fairly typical setup of password, group, and host information.

You will need to add "nis" to your /etc/host.conf. Order is important. If you actually spend most of your time talking to hosts outside your LAN, you might want to put NIS last in the search order.

In the examples below, we've assumed /etc/passwd is fairly minimal, containing entries for the superuser, various daemons, and so forth, but no mortal user entries.

To append the whole NIS password map to the local /etc/passwd file add this line:

```
+::::::
```

You can customize access by adding additional lines starting with + or -. For example, deny the user "cary" access but allow all others (at least to the extent they have on any other NIS client), add this:

```
+::::::
-cary
```

The "+::::::" entry is not mandatory. Additionally you can control access by groups, using "@." This entry

```
+cary::::::
+rachel::::::
+@plan9::::::
-paul
-enry
```

allows access for "cary," "rachel," and the group "plan9." The users "paul" and "enry" (who are presumably in the aforementioned group) are denied.

It is also possible to override sections of the information in the passwd map entry or add users that don't exist in the NIS at all. For example, to give paul the shell `/bin/tcsh` and change Rachel's home directory (and allow only them access) and add a user surya, use entries like this:

```
+::::::
+paul::::::/bin/tcsh
+rachel:::::/local/home/rachel:
+:*:::::/bin/false
surya:IUg6jkhgT:506:100::/home/surya:/bin/bash
```

Finally, you will need to set up the ypclient programs and set the NIS domain name. It's likely that your distribution came with the NIS client (and server) programs. If not, you should be able to get them from any Linux distribution site.

Setting the NIS domainname is accomplished by running `/bin/domain-name` *nis domain*. You will also need to make sure the portmap program is running. Use the rpcinfo command for this:

```
[root:/home/cary]# rpcinfo -p localhost
   program vers proto    port
    100000    2   tcp     111   portmapper
    100000    2   udp     111   portmapper
```

If it's not in the list, run `/usr/sbin/portmap`, then `/usr/sbin/ypbind`. `rpcinfo` should then show something like

```
[root:/home/cary]# rpcinfo -p localhost
   program vers proto    port
    100000    2   tcp     111   portmapper
    100000    2   udp     111   portmapper
    100007    2   udp     637   ypbind
    100007    2   tcp     639   ypbind
```

At this point, your NIS client setup should be complete.

The nsswitch.conf File

The `/etc/nsswitch.conf` file determines the lookup order for all NIS information (unlike `/etc/host.conf` which is only for host lookups). The example below is self-explanatory.

```
#
# /etc/nsswitch.conf
#
# An example Name Service Switch config file. This file should be
# sorted with the most-used services at the beginning.
#
# The entry '[NOTFOUND=return]' means that the search for an
# entry should stop if the search in the previous entry turned
# up nothing. Note that if the search failed due to some other reason
# (like no NIS server responding) then the search continues with the
# next entry.
#
# Legal entries are:
#
#       nisplus              Use NIS+ (NIS version 3)
#       nis                  Use NIS (NIS version 2), also called YP
#       dns                  Use DNS (Domain Name Service)
#       files                Use the local files
#       db                   Use the /var/db databases
#       [NOTFOUND=return]    Stop searching if not found so far
#

passwd:        compat
group:         compat
shadow:        compat

passwd_compat: nis
group_compat: nis
shadow_compat: nis

hosts:         nis files dns

services:      nis [NOTFOUND=return] files
networks:      nis [NOTFOUND=return] files
protocols:     nis [NOTFOUND=return] files
rpc:           nis [NOTFOUND=return] files
ethers:        nis [NOTFOUND=return] files
netmasks:      nis [NOTFOUND=return] files
netgroup:      nis
bootparams:    nis [NOTFOUND=return] files
publickey:     nis [NOTFOUND=return] files
automount:     files
aliases:       nis [NOTFOUND=return] files
```

NIS+

NIS+ is Sun's successor to NIS. It has better security and handles large numbers of clients. Unfortunately, support for NIS+ under Linux is limited to the client side only, and it is still in the beta development stage. Unless you have a real need for NIS+, you are probably better off using traditional NIS.

If you need to set up an NIS+ client you will need a couple of things first. First, glibc 2.x; second, the NIS+ client programs. If you are running a recent Debian or RedHat distribution, you should have glibc 2 already. The NIS+ client programs can be found at `ftp://ftp.kernel.org/pub/linux/utils/net/NIS+`. You will need two files: `nis-tools-1.4.tar.gz` and `pam_keylogin-1.1.tar.gz`. Unpack and compile them.

Assuming your NIS+ server is set up to answer requests for your client (see your Solaris documentation for how to do this), you need to set the NIS+ domain name as you would for NIS and then run `nisinit`:

```
nisinit -c -H server
```

Edit `/etc/nsswitch.conf` making sure the only service after public key is nisplus ("publickey: nisplus"). Next start kerlogin (you will want to add this to your rc.local file).

```
keylogin -r
```

If your login makes use of PAM, you will need to install PAM keylogin (which you fetched from `ftp.kernel.org`). Next, edit the `/etc/pam.d/login` file to use `pam_unix_auth`.

```
#/etc/pam.d/login
auth        required        /lib/security/pam_securetty.so
auth        required        /lib/security/pam_keylogin.so
auth        required        /lib/security/pam_unix_auth.so
auth        required        /lib/security/pam_nologin.so
account     required        /lib/security/pam_unix_acct.so
password    required        /lib/security/pam_unix_passwd.so
session     required        /lib/security/pam_unix_session.soa
```

Lastly, edit your nisswitch.conf. Basically, you will want to replace nis with nisplus.

Setting Up an NIS Master Server

Once again, your distribution likely came with NIS server programs or you can fetch them from kernel.org or any Linux distribution site.

Compile the NIS software if you need to. Then `edit /var/yp/Makefile` to add or remove the maps you will be serving.

Now edit `/var/yp/securenets` and `/etc/ypserv.conf`. They are well commented and fairly self-explanatory. If you need more information, read the ypserv(8) and ypserv.conf(5) man pages.

Then start the portmapper if needed and then start ypserv. Verify that it is running:

```
[root:/home/cary]# rpcinfo -u localhost ypserv
program 100004 version 1 ready and waiting
```

Now run ypinit to generate the maps in `/var/yp` from the files in `/etc`:

```
ypinit -m
```

If you are setting up a slave server, run

```
ypinit -s master
```

And you're done!

5.6   Summary

- TCP/IP is the main protocol used by Linux
- Ethernet and PPP are the most common ways of using TCP/IP
- DNS provides name to translation
- NFS allows you to share information across a network
- Netatalk allows you to communicate over appletalk
- NIS allows you to distribute login information

Printing and Print Sharing

6

Getting the most out of a single printer across multiple machines.

Print sharing allows you to set up a single printer so that everyone on the network has access to it.

Print setup and sharing under Linux give you a number of choices. You can use the BSD-ish lpr, the lpr replacement LPRng, or just have Linux point to a remote printer on an AppleTalk, TCP/IP, or SMB network. Or have a computer on any of those networks and use the printer connected to your Linux workstation.

6.1 Connecting Printers to Linux

In order to use a printer under Linux, it must first be configured. First, make sure your kernel is compiled to use the parallel port device. By default, the parallel port is not set up in the Linux kernel.[1] Once you have a kernel with

---

[1] If you choose to use a serial printer, skip this stuff.

the lp active [you can tell by seeing something like `lp1 at 0x0378, (poll-ing)` at bootup or by using the `dmesg` command], you should be ready to print. Assuming your printer can handle plain ASCII (most do), you can send a text file to the printer by using something similar to

```
cat /etc/motd > /dev/lp1
```

This should print a copy of your motd file to the printer. If you get an error, you may want to see if the dmesg said something other than `lp1` (for example `lp0` or `lp2`) and try again. Once this is set up, we can get on with configuring the printer.

6.2   Serial vs. Parallel vs. Ethernet Printers

Using parallel ports is the obvious choice for driving a printer since there are no baud rates or stty settings to worry about, and the speed is much greater (parallel ports run at about 150 Kbps as opposed to 38.4 Kb for a serial printer). But there are limitations to the parallel port. The greatest of these is the distance. A parallel port can run only about 20 feet or so before the signal degrades too much and causes errors. A serial printer can run 50 feet at 38.4 K, and much longer if you choose to use an electrical interface like EIA-530 (a k a RS-422). Also, a serial cable can technically run through an RJ-45 (8-pin) wire, or three wires if you feel lucky. This is a big advantage over the 25 pins that the parallel port needs. Many low-end printers these days have only the parallel port connection, but most of the higher-end printers for workgroups or print servers have serial connections as well. Or they are options available after the purchase.

Then there are the ethernet connections you can have to a printer (see the remote printer section below). This is an okay idea for some printers, since ethernet runs through most buildings anyway. In a computer lab situation, where ethernet is running through the room anyway, and the server is in another room (or floor) this is an excellent idea. But the printer is also now using some of the ethernet bandwidth, first to get from the printer client to the printer server, then again to get from the printer server to the printer itself. It isn't a lot of bandwidth that you're using up, but now the "guys" playing Quake on the network have to drop from 54 frames per second to 53. You also have less control over the printer if the network goes down for some reason. Again, ethernet options are not available for the lower-end printers, but they are options for many high-end ones. Be sure that if you do get a network printer, there are drivers, or some other interface to allow Linux to talk to it.

6.3   Configuring the Printer

Linux uses the BSD style of printing. That is, there is a /etc/printcap file that has to be modified, and the commands are lpr, lpq, lpc, lprm, and so on. I prefer the BSD method, as it makes adding printers and modifying the printer setups very easy. Plus, most magic filters assume you have a BSD-style printcap. Here's a copy of the printcap for a HP LaserJet 4L connected to the parallel port on RedHat 4:

```
lp:\
      :sd=/var/spool/lpd/lp:\
      :mx#0:\
      :lp=/dev/lp1:\
      :if=/var/spool/lpd/lp/filter:\
      :sh:
```

RedHat has its own print filters installed. These filters will pretty much handle translating ASCII and PostScript into a format your printer can handle. In the case of the HP printer, this is PCL. To print other formats directly from the command line (lpr), you'll need a magic filter to convert from GIF to PS (for example) which then gets sent to the printer.

This printcap entry is really all one line. You can tell because in the Linux world, a line that ends in \ is automatically added to the next line. Each printcap entry is one line, but that line can be extremely long. The first line (the lp:) defined the name of the printer. You can add alias names for the printer by adding |<alias> to the name definition. Once the name is given, the options can be put in any order. Here are what the above options mean.

- sd—Spool directory. This is where the files that have to be sent to the printer are stored. This is usually /var/spool/lpd/<printername>.

- mx—You can set a maximum file size that can be sent to the printer. The #0 means that there is no maximum file size. The default maximum is 1000 blocks, which equates to just under 1 Mb.

- lp—The device name for output. The /dev/lp1 specifies a parallel printer, but you can also use a serial device if you wish.

- if—Input filter. Any file going to the printer gets piped to this command before being put in the queue. This is where the RedHat Print Manager comes in and does its work. This is where other magic filters get installed as well.

- sh—Suppress printing of burst pages. Burst pages list the user, the name of the file being printed, and the job number along with other information. Think of this as a fax cover page. In a small network, you don't need burst pages, but if you have about five or more people using the printer, it's a good idea to have it.

The printcap man page has a list of all the options, what they're used for, and the default settings. If you're using a serial printer, you will want to add the following settings:

- `br`—Baud rate to use. Any valid baud rate will work.
- `ms`—Stty settings to give to the serial port after opening and before sending data. This is usually to set up things like hardware flow control.

A sample line addition of an 8-bit connection using hardware flow and running at a rate of 38.4 Kbps is

```
br#38400:ms=opost,cs8,-parenb,-cstopb, crtscts\
```

6.4   Print Filters

Print filters are programs that convert from multiple file types to one that your printer can understand. In most cases, this will be either PostScript (really easy to do) or PCL (harder, but not by much). The reason PostScript is so easy to use with printers is because most of the higher-end printers were connected to UNIX machines, and therefore the programs were written to output in PostScript. Now that PCL is being used more often in the lower-end printers (like mine) and Linux is everywhere, you'll probably need some kind of converter. This is where the print filters come in. We've had some experience with `magicfilter`, which is a filter specifically for Linux, with much success. Other filters exist, such as apsfilter, and they all work about the same. On your machine, you'll need a number of programs installed (ghost-script. netpbm, jpeg at the very least, probably also TeX and the assorted dvi programs). During installation of the filters, the installation script queries your system to see what programs are available and then makes the best guess to get from one graphics format to another. For example, to print out a JPEG image, the djpeg program would convert it to GIF format; then the gs program would convert from GIF to PCL (or PostScript or whatever). If you expect to be printing files directly from the command line (`lpr -Plp wayga.gif`) or do not have RedHat, you may want to look at getting `magic-filter` or `apsfilter` installed.

Now let's hook that printer into a network.

6.5   Printers on the Network!

When the printcap is set up, you'll need to restart the printer daemon (lpd) which should already be running and will be once Linux starts. To inform Linux of the changes on the `/etc/printcap` file, you can send a signal HUP (1 for Linux) to the lpd process. This will cause it to reread the `/etc/print-cap` file and restart.

UNIX

Once lpd is running, enter the names of the hosts that you want to have access to your printers in the `/etc/hosts.lpd` (for printer access only) or enter them in the `/etc/hosts.equiv`[2] file. Once this has been done, your printer is available for access from other UNIX machines immediately. Set the "`rm`" option to the remote host, and have the "`rp`" option name the remote printer. The only other option that needs to be set is the "`sp`" option (local spool directory). For added security, the "`rs`" option, if set on the print server side, will accept only print jobs from users on the remote machine that have accounts on the server machine. That is, a user account of the same name must exist on both machines before the print job will be accepted. The Linux lpd monitors TCP/IP port 515(tcp) for activity from print clients.

SMB (Windows Networking)

The very best way to get a Linux printer seen on a Windows network is to run Samba. We'll get into Samba in another chapter, but we'll focus on setting up print services here. The important thing to know is that Samba should be configured to use the `/etc/printcap` file and use BSD-style printing. That is about all the configuration Linux needs to serve a printer to a Windows for Workgroups, Windows 95, or Windows NT machine.[3] Users will be able to use the standard Windows print management tools (print queues) to see the

---

[2]Using the hosts.equiv could be a security hole, especially if you're in a network of Linux or UNIX machines.

[3]You could also serve another Linux (or UNIX) machine running samba as well, but that would just be silly, but still in "the UNIX way."

entire printer queue, and even remove their job if they choose. Be sure to install a print driver under Windows for the kind of printer you have installed, as the print filter on Linux should just pass the data along to the printer.

To print from Linux to a Windows machine, the procedure is a bit different. RedHat allows you (via the printtool) to add a printer that is connected via Server Message Block (SMB), and it takes care of the rest. The Windows machine finds the data and sends them off to the printer. In these cases, the print queue commands (see below) will probably not work, as Windows has its own protocol for handling the queues.

As you can see, it would be much easier and simpler for a printer to exist on a Linux server.

6.6   Managing Print Queues

Now that the printer is connected and working, people are going to try sending print data to it. At this point, it's time to put on the "print master" hat and get to work.

The print queues are FIFO (First In First Out) queues, so the first one in line gets to have access to the printer. If one job gets stuck, or the printer runs out of paper, the queue will begin to fill and you'll be hounded by users desperately trying to find their printouts. Not to worry.

The commands you'll want to know about are the `lpc`, `lprm`, and `lpq` commands. The `lpq` command shows what's in the queue and gives the current status of the printer, as best as `lpd` can figure that information out. Some printers will be able to tell `lpd` that they are out of paper, or that the connection is down, and these errors will show up in the `lpq`.

The `lprm` command will remove jobs from the queue. Only root and the person who submitted the print job can remove a job from the queue. If an accidental print job is 3 Mb in size and is currently tying up the queue, it may be best to remove the job. As root, you can remove all the jobs owned by a particular user with the command `lprm user`.

The `lpc` command is the "lp control." It can activate and deactivate queues and printers, rearrange jobs in the queue, and get a status of any printers listed in `/etc/printcap` (to paraphrase the man page).

Lpc can be run on the command line (`lpc restart lp`) or be run interactively, submitting many commands to various printers. Here's a list of some of the more important lpc commands:

- `disable { all|printer }`—Disable the named printer. New jobs cannot be added, but printing will continue.

- `down { all|printer }`—Disable the named printer completely. No new jobs can be added, and printing stops.

- `enable { all|printer }`—New jobs can be added to the queue (reverse of disable)

- `restart { all|printer }`—Try to restart a print daemon. Sometimes the lpd process will die or get stuck, and this will try to restart a new daemon.

- `status { all|printer }`—Get a status of the printers. List whether or not queues are up, and whether or not printing is enabled.

- `topq printer [job..] [user..]`—Print the jobs listed at the top of the queue

The lpc man page has more on the commands available, but these should get you started with the queue administration.

In the worst case scenario where the lpc commands do not work, you can use the `/etc/rc.d/init.d/lpd.init stop` command to stop the lpd program altogether. The `/etc/rc.d/init.d/lpd.init start` command will start lpd up.

For more information or help on how the print services work, check out the Printing HOWTO and the Printing Usage HOWTO.

6.7   Summary

Here's a quick review of what was in this chapter:

- Serial, parallel, and ethernet printers all have their relative advantages, depending on what your printing needs are.

- Linux uses the `/etc/printcap` file for controlling how the lpd program talks to the printer.

- Linux can talk to printers across the network, and Samba allows Windows machines to network with a Linux printer.

- The lpr, lprm, and lpc programs are used to manage the printers and print queues.

E-mail 7

Sendmail, mailing lists, E-mail clients, and POP/IMAP (remote connections).

This chapter shows you how to set up sendmail, set up simple mailing lists for customers, clients, or groups of people, review some of the E-mail clients available, and set up remote connections using POP (Post Office Protocol) and IMAP(Internet Message Access Protocol) mail standards.

E-mail (electronic mail) was one of the first methods for communicating over what is now the Internet. E-mail allowed short messages to route across various machines. In those days (1987) you often had to manually specify all the machines (or hops) an E-mail message would have to route through to get to the end host. With TCP/IP as the communication method, things are a bit smarter in that you don't need to know how to get to the end host—as long as some machine along the way knows how to route the E-mail for you. As an aside, the technical name for the E-mail that you get on the Internet is known as Simple Mail Transfer Protocol (SMTP). There are a few other protocols that work with SMTP, such as POP and IMAP, but we'll get to those later. You can find more information about SMTP in RFC 821.

The primary program that is the Mail Transport Agent (or MTA) is sendmail. There are others available, but sendmail is pretty much the standard for most Linux installations. You may have seen that really thick book with a bat on it that gets you into the nitty-gritty of sendmail. It gets really nitty-gritty.[1]

The upshot of all this is that you don't always need it in order to set up a simple E-mail server. The one thing you should know about sendmail is this: Always be sure you have the latest version. Each version of sendmail, while patching various bugs, seems to have a security problem with it. Seems like you need to upgrade your sendmail software more often than the Linux kernel.

Enough of that. Let's get to the typical sendmail options you'll see on startup. Most Linux installations have sendmail kick in on bootup. RedHat (being SYSVish) has an `/etc/rc.d/init.d/sendmail.init` script which runs on start-up. My installation starts the actual command like this:

```
echo -n "Starting sendmail: "
daemon sendmail -bd -q1h
echo
touch /var/lock/subsys/sendmail
```

As you can see, the sendmail program starts with the `-bd` option and the `-q1h` option. The `-bd` signifies that sendmail should start up as a daemon and run in the background waiting for connections, much the same way that a Web server is always running, waiting for a connection. The `-q1h` means that sendmail should go through its queue at least once an hour and try to send any data in its queue.

There are a number of reasons that an E-mail message can be held in a queue. For example,

- If you have a dialup-only connection to the Internet, and you send a note while you're not connected.
- The remote host is not dialed in (same thing in reverse).
- The remote host is down for upgrades or it crashed.
- There is no connection to the remote host (the network is down).

In any of these cases, you'll want to make sure that your E-mail gets through. Leaving the E-mail in sendmail's queue allows you to do this. A

---

[1]If you have anything to do with setting up sendmail, get that book.

machine directly connected to the Internet or on a LAN can change this to ten minutes (-q10m), since you're more likely to be connected to the Internet all the time. In case you're interested in what's currently in the queue, the mailq command will list what sendmail has. The mailq program will also list the reason why an E-mail is stuck in the queue. If there is a lot of E-mail in the queue, you may have a network or configuration problem.

You can verify that sendmail is running by connecting to TCP port 25.

```
[markk@wayga ~ ]# telnet localhost 25
Trying 127.0.0.1...
Connected to localhost.
Escape character is '^]'.
220 wayga.net ESMTP Sendmail 8.7.6/8.7.3; Fri, 18 Apr 1997 00:26:18 -
   0400
```

As you can see, the connection works, and I'm getting some information about the host I connected to: status number, hostname, type of SMTP (Extended SMTP), the Sendmail program (instead of qmail or the like) version 8.7.6, and the current time and date that my computer thinks it is.

The configuration options for sendmail are typically located in /etc/ sendmail.cf. Examine the file if you like, but don't change anything unless you know what you're doing! Small changes can render your E-mail system useless. As always, back up files that you want to edit, just in case.

A few options you may want to note:

- OA—Can set another file that contains aliases. We'll get into this with majordomo

- Mlocal—Specifies what program will act as the Mail Delivery Agent (MDA). This can be something like /bin/mail or /usr/bin/procmail (we'll get to this later too!).

- DS—Contains a pointer to a "smart" relay host. If you have a very slow connection to the Internet or don't have DNS set up, you can specify another machine to accept all your E-mail and deliver it for you. For dialup links, you only have to send the E-mail once, and a machine that is permanently connected to the Internet can hold it in its queue.

- Cw—This option works if you have one Internet host that has multiple names (for example, wayga.net and ratatosk.org). This entry will allow you to specify which hosts you will receive E-mail as.

7.1   Using m4 Files

One option that many versions of sendmail have is the option to have your sendmail.cf file automatically generated. This will allow you to keep a small file that has most of the options you wish to use. When upgrading sendmail, you need to recompile only the sendmail.cf to have the latest updates to that file. The m4 macro language is excellent for doing this, and sources for various types of sendmail.cf files are included.

If you do decide to use the m4 files, be sure to download the source code for sendmail, as the RedHat 4.1 distribution does not include m4 files by default. The m4 processor is installed by default and is located in `/usr/bin`.

7.2   You Have Mail!

Once E-mail has arrived at your system, there are a few things that happen to it before you actually get alerted to new E-mail. First, sendmail checks to see if you have a .forward file in your home directory. If so, then sendmail will forward the E-mail to whatever address is specified in the .forward file. If you're using procmail and you have a .procmailrc file, sendmail will run procmail and follow the rules in it. After that, sendmail appends the E-mail to a file called `/var/spool/mail/<USER>` where `<USER>` is the username. This file does not need to be created when making a new user; sendmail will take care of that the first time the user gets an E-mail message.

Creating mail aliases allows incoming mail to get routed to a different user or program, even if there is no user account with that name on the system. This will have a larger impact once we get to managing mailing lists. For now, you may want to examine the `/etc/aliases` file to see what aliases are currently defined. This is a method of having a mail alias that really sends the mail to someone else, or a group of people. For example, a common `/etc/aliases` file may contain the following:

```
MAILER-DAEMON:  postmaster
postmaster: root

# General redirections for pseudo accounts.
bin:        root
daemon:     root
games:      root
nobody:     root
uucp:       root
```

```
# Well-known aliases.
manager:    root
operator:   root

# Person who should get root's mail
root:       mark
mfk:        mark
bren:       brenda
bdk:        brenda
```

As listed above, you see that there are a number of aliases listed, most of them pointing to root. In some cases (bin and nobody), the accounts exist, but no one should ever log into those accounts. In this case, any E-mail that gets sent to bin or daemon merely gets forwarded to root. Also note that post-master is set to root, as in most situations the person who administers the mail also administers the rest of the system. The MAILER-DAEMON is mostly for mail errors. These errors get sent to root as well.

Later on, you see a few user aliases. These aliases are set up so that anyone sending E-mail to "mfk@wayga..net" will go automatically into the mark account. There is no mfk account, but people can send E-mail to that address. The same is true of anyone sending E-mail to "bren@wayga..net" or "bdk@wayga..net." A small business could have E-mail aliases of mark.komarinski, mfk, m.komarinski, markk, mark.k, and any other unique permutation of the name in case outside customers forget an E-mail address. It is something that's often overlooked but is very important to keep in touch with customers.

Once the mail is delivered to the correct account, a process called comsat runs; comsat is what actually tells the shell that you have new mail. Once the shell gets that information, it may notify you of it. The biff[2] program tells you if you'll receive notification, and it also lets you turn it on or off. The y option to biff will turn mail prompting on, and n will turn it off.

Now that you've received the E-mail message, how are you going to read it? This is the job of the MUA or Mail User Agent. This is the only area the end user is going to interact with. There are dozens of programs available from the low-feature (mail) to the high-feature full screen (elm, pine, mutt).

What you use for mail reading is pretty much up to the user. For example, many people prefer pine over elm, but I find that pine has too many menu layers to get to your actual mail. If you plan on having many users, it's best to install a few MUAs aside from /bin/mail. Each MUA has advantages. My

---

[2]Why name the command biff? Turns out that's the name of the author's dog. Under UNIX, if you write it, you name it.

current preference is mutt, because it has the ease of use of elm, plus a lot more configurability and integrated Pretty Good Privacy (PGP) support.

7.3 MIME

When SMTP was first designed, it would handle only 7-bit (plain ASCII) data. Hence, the "Simple" in the protocol name. With things like JPEG images, sound files, application data, and compressed files, there had to be some way of sending this binary (8-bit) data through a 7-bit stream. The first method of handling this was via the uuencode program. This program would turn 2 bytes of 8-bit data into 3 bytes of 7-bit data. The file size was larger, but it would now squeeze through the 7-bit path that SMTP provided. Another problem besides the file size was that the remote side had to decode the data (uudecode). This turned into a tedious procedure, the sender encoding the data and manually including it in a mail file and the receiver trying to strip out all the mail headers, text, and signatures to get to the uuencode file and then decode it.

In the early 1990s, the Multipurpose Internet Mail Extension (MIME) was developed to do this, and it is used today on the Web for determining file types. MIME encoded the data such that a standard way of locating and decoding a file would be used. Once a filetype was detected, each individual user could have a file (.mailcap) that would list what filetypes you knew about, and what application to run once you found a certain filetype. For example, if a JPEG image were sent, the receiving side might start up the xv program. Another user might have it set up so the image is converted into PostScript and sent directly to the printer.[3] Most mailers today have the ability to handle MIME mail, and there should be little to no interaction that you as an administrator have to worry about, except for installing programs for users and occasionally editing the /etc/mailcap file (the default mailcap file for all users) to add any new entries you come across.

7.4 The .forward File

When mail comes in, the .forward file is checked. If it exists, the E-mail is sent to the address listed in the file. This is helpful if you have multiple

---

[3]This is a good example of "the UNIX way"—there's more than one way to do anything.

accounts on the Internet and want all the E-mail to come to one location. An example of .forward shows another feature of the .forward file—instead of an E-mail address, you can have a command. The vacation program, which isn't available in RedHat (but is on the CD-ROM), allows you to put a program in the .forward file. Each time E-mail comes in, the program is run. The vacation program stores the E-mail and then sends a custom message back to the E-mail sender notifying them that you're on vacation (or out of town, out of the office, out of your mind, etc). The sender then knows that the E-mail got through.

Procmail

If procmail is installed as the Mail Delivery Agent (MDA) on your system (check the Mlocal entry in your sendmail.cf to find out), then you can immediately use procmail to filter all your incoming mail. If not, you can put a reference to procmail in your .forward to run each time new mail arrives. Procmail is used to process mail as it comes in. This can include putting all E-mail from the "Plan9 MUSH Advisory Committee" in one mailbox separate from everything else, or filtering all that annoying E-mail you get from billg@microsoft.com by sending it all to `/dev/null`.[4]

If procmail is set up to be the default local mail handler, setting procmail up for use is easy. Create a .procmailrc file and start adding rules for procmail to filter. If procmail is not your local mail handler, you have three options:

1. Make procmail the local mail handler (the man page has the suggested changes you can make to the `/etc/sendmail.cf` file). If you're using m4 configuration files, add "FEATURE(local_procmail)" to your file.

2. Run procmail periodically or use cron to filter out an already existing mailbox. This still allows you to use .forward (in the event of vacation and the like), but the mail is not always sorted and you have to wait.

3. Put a reference to procmail in your .forward file. Note that this won't let you forward all that easily. In the .forward file, put a line in that looks like

```
"|IFS=' '&&exec /usr/local/bin/procmail -f-||exit 75 #YOUR_USERNAME"
```

---

[4]Anything sent to `/dev/null` is immediately discarded. This is called "the bit bucket." Thanks to the fact that Linux is a 32-bit OS, its bit bucket is one of the fastest around.

As you can guess, option 1 is the best, as it requires the least amount of effort on everyone's part.[5] Here's a copy of a sample `.procmailrc` file:

```
PATH=/bin:/usr/bin:/usr/bin
MAILDIR=$HOME/Mail        #you'd better make sure it exists
DEFAULT=$MAILDIR/mbox     #completely optional
LOGFILE=$MAILDIR/from     #recommended

:0:
* ^From.*mark
from_me


:0
* ^Subject:.*Flame
/dev/null
```

There are three sections to matching a line and performing some action on it, also called recipes. A recipe starts with a line that has at least a :0 starting. After the :0, you can include some flags (for example, H will scan only the headers). Pattern matching is done for any lines that start with an °. The rest of the line is sent to egrep[6] literally. If all of the lines match (the lines are ANDed together) then the appropriate action is taken. If not, it moves on to the next recipe.

There can be only one action line, and this is the one that does not start with an ° or :. An action starting with ! will forward the program to the specified user. An action starting with | will start a shell and pipe the E-mail to that program for processing. Anything else will be assumed to be a filename to append (or create if it doesn't already exist).

These two examples show that all mail that has a From line and ends in mark (which will be any E-mail sent by me) will be put in the ~/Mail/ `from_me` mailbox. The second example shows that all E-mail that starts with the word "Subject" and ends in "Flame" will be sent to /dev/null (the bit bucket).

The thing to know if you just want to delete mail out of hand is that you have to be absolutely sure that your logic is correct. For example, if you delete all mail that has the word "Flame" in it, then you can potentially lose messages with a subject such as "Flame broiled burgers free until 10 AM."

---

[5]Except the system administrator, who has to install the software and make sure that sendmail isn't busted. Oh wait. That's you. Scratch that.

[6]egrep = extended grep, and the syntax is not exactly the same as with plain grep

OK, so it's a poor example. You may want to store mail you want to delete for a while and examine it just to be sure you don't lose anything important.

7.5   Mailing Lists

Mailing lists allow larger groups of people to communicate via E-mail. In many cases, it is preferable to using USENET since

- Mailing lists do not need approval to be created.

Anyone with a machine connected to the Internet can create a mailing list on any subject. Getting members to subscribe to it is a different issue, however.

- Mailing lists can control who subscribes.

The mailing list administrator can make it so anyone can subscribe, or can make it so that the administrator is the only one who can add new members to the mailing list. The administrator can also remove offending members if a problem arises.

- Mailing lists can control content.

This isn't as bad as it sounds, since it is the alternative to the anarchy that is USENET. The administrator can set the list up to be open and provide a healthy discussion area (such as for developers working on a piece of software) or can set the list up such that the administrator has to approve each piece of E-mail that gets sent to the list (like the moderated USENET groups). The moderated lists are good for news releases, humor lists, or any other list where the amount of discussion should be low.

Majordomo

The best mailing list program in use has to be majordomo. Majordomo provides all the features listed above, plus adds a few other features, such as sending out regular digests, or archiving for future use. We'll get back to this later on.

The first thing that needs to be set up is majordomo itself, if it's not already installed. The source for it is located on the CD-ROM. You need to have perl 5 installed on the system (as well as gcc of course) in order to use it. First, create a majordomo user. Given the eight-character limitations of Linux's usernames, the username will have to be shortened to majordom. Thanks to `/etc/aliases`, no one ever has to know this. You should also create a home directory for the majordom user. This can be `/home/majordom` if you like, or `/usr/local/majordom` if you prefer, or anywhere you have space.

Su to majordom,[7] copy the majordom1.94.1.tar.gz file to the home directory, and uncompress/untar the file. Make any kinds of modifications to the majordomo.cf file; then just use the make command to create it. Once installed (which should be in the majordomo home directory) you need to make only one change to the `/etc/sendmail.cf` file. You should already have one OA (or O AliasFile) entries listed. Underneath that, put in[8]

```
OA/home/majordomo/majordomo.aliases
```

This sets up an additional file to handle aliases. This makes it easier for the majordomo administrator to add new mailing lists, and that person does not need root access in order to modify the lists.

Now on to creating the lists themselves. Let's create a (fictional) list called gastro. It will be an open list for sharing recipes, so anyone can join, and anyone can post a note to the group.

In the ~majordom/majordomo.aliases file (I'll call it the alias file from now on in case you choose to use the /etc/aliases instead) add the following:

```
gastro:         "|/home/majordom/wrapper resend -l gastro gastro-list"
gastro-list:      :include:/home/majordom/lists/gastro
owner-gastro:    mark
gastro-owner:    mark
gastro-request:  "|/home/majordom/wrapper majordomo -l gastro"
gastro-approval: mark
```

This sets up the basics. The list itself will be "gastro@host," the owner will be mark, and any requests to join the list will be sent to majordomo as well. Normally, users would send E-mail to majordomo@host to subscribe, but different mailing list software works in different ways.

Once the aliases are set up, you can initialize the lists using

---

[7]You set up a password for the majordom user, right??

[8]Note that this is a bit of security risk, as root should really be the only person who can create new aliases. If you want, leave this statement out and use /etc/ aliases instead of the majordomo.aliases file.

```
echo "config gastro gastro.admin" | mail majordomo
```

And the lists will have some default configurations put in. If you choose to change the defaults (and you should!) edit the `~majordom/lists/gas-tro.config` file. This has all the configuration settings for that particular list.

Now that your mailing list is set up, you should be able to E-mail to the list by just sending mail to "gastro@host" and the E-mail will be sent to all the subscribers of the gastro list. There are a number of extra features that majordomo has, and you should check out the Web site for more information and to get the latest updates.

One of the better known replacements for sendmail is called qmail. There are two reasons for its popularity: ease of use and security. This doesn't mean that qmail is best for everyone, since there are a number of changes in thought that your system has to go through to use qmail. It's also not perfect in a large installation (yet) also because of some of the ways that sendmail and qmail differ. The configuration for qmail is much simpler than sendmail, but it doesn't offer the "Swiss army knife" of Mail Transport Agents (MTAs) that many expect to see.

7.6 Qmail: Better Than sendmail?

Here's a few of the ways in which qmail and sendmail differ in methodology.

mail file location: Sendmail prefers to use `/usr/spool/mail/user` as a location for incoming mail. Qmail prefers to use *~user*/Mailbox as a location for storing mail files. This is for two reasons. First, putting the mail in the user's home directory provides for better quota checking and prevents overfilling a central location. Second, there are fewer security problems since there isn't a central location to store files.

Permissions: Sendmail runs almost always as root or with root privileges in order to write files, and so forth. Qmail runs as root only when necessary and otherwise runs as a qmail user which has no special permissions.

Mailing list integration: Sendmail has external programs to create and it administers mailing lists (majordomo and listproc). Qmail supports a method where individual users can have their own mailing lists and administer them themselves with no extra accounts or permissions.

Size: Sendmail is a monolithic MTA, where everything is done in the program itself. Qmail has a number of smaller programs to handle each
aspect of mail receipt, delivery, sending, and so forth.

Installing Qmail

After you get the qmail-1.01.tar.gz file from `http://www.qmail.org/` (or
newer version if it's available), untar and uncompress the file. This will create a qmail-1.01 directory with the source code in it. Review the INSTALL
file so you know what the full install procedure is. This procedure allows
you to build and install qmail without affecting the sendmail you probably
already have installed until you're satisfied that qmail is working correctly.
Qmail resides in the `/var/qmail` directory, so you'll need to create that
directory and remember that so you can monitor that directory. Next you'll
need to create users for qmail to use. Since security is a big component of
qmail, these new users will need to be created to separate qmail from the
root user and regular users.

   Now for the simple part. Enter `make` to build qmail. The compile should
take a few minutes to complete, and you'll be ready for the installation and
testing. The biggest problem you may run across is the fact that your home
directory and .qmail files cannot be group or world writable. This will show
up in the logs as something like

```
Feb  8 16:50:00 wayga qmail: 886974600.032889 delivery 10: deferral:
   Uh-oh:_.qmail_file_is_writable._(#4.7.0)/
```

In this event, just find the .qmail file it's referring to and change the permissions. You'll also want to check for other copies of the sendmail program
floating around the filesystem (like `/usr/sbin/`, for example) and change
those to use the qmail version. Also while testing, remember that mail is no
longer being delivered to /usr/spool/mail/*user*, but ~*user*/Mailbox.

   Once the testing and configuration are done (the INSTALL file is pretty
thorough on this), you can then tell your users about the changes and start
using qmail.

   A few notes you should know of if you're considering changing MTAs.

• Don't put this on your main server! If you're upgrading or changing
   software to something you're not used to, always use a staging machine.
   There are instructions in the FAQ file on how to upgrade slowly from
   sendmail to qmail with a minimum of fuss and trouble. This upgrade

path allows you to use both qmail and sendmail until you get the bugs worked out before you move to qmail.

- You may not want to put this on a connection that goes down frequently. One of the features of qmail is that it continually tries to deliver mail. If the Internet link goes down often, you could be in a situation where qmail is trying to deliver lots of mail at the same time. If it's enough mail, it could potentially chew up all your CPU resources.

- In addition to the /usr/spool/mail directory changing, the .forward file is ignored in favor of the .qmail file. The .qmail file has a number of features that can't be put in .forward, but programs that operate on .forward won't work anymore.

Once qmail is configured and working properly, you'll need to make sure that you can deliver mail to each user (check their mail file and the syslog output in /var/log to make sure mail is being delivered properly).

There are a few things that you will notice once qmail is installed. For the benefit of your users, you should warn them ahead of time.

- As previously mentioned, mail now gets stored in ~*user*/Mailbox instead of /usr/spool/mail/*user*. You'll need to make sure that the MAIL environment variable is changed (see /etc/profile). There are two problems with the /usr/spool/mail approach to delivering mail. First, it's a security risk. Second, the way sendmail does local mail delivery is prone to losing mail if the mail directory is mounted via NFS or if the server goes down while writing E-mail. The "Mailbox" format in qmail makes sure the E-mail is written to the disk before it reports success back to the main qmail program. If there is a locking problem or the machine goes down while a message is being delivered, it will get delivered when the machine restarts or the lock goes away.

- Qmail does not look in the .forward file anymore for forwarding E-mail to other users. The replacement file, .qmail, handles this. The nice thing about this is it allows you as a user to create your own simple mailing lists. For example, if I wanted to create a simple mailing list related to this book, I could create a .qmail-linux file in my home directory. That file then gets a list of the people I want to be on this list. Once this is done, any E-mail sent to enry-linux@wayga.net gets sent to the entire list. You can even have a .qmail-default to catch all enry-* E-mail that comes in. Note that this isn't a very full-featured mailing list system as it doesn't handle automatic subscribes or unsubscribes. This is where ezmlm comes in (see next section).

- Qmail also does not use /etc/aliases at all. There is a global way of setting up E-mail aliases, which is a bit easier to use. The alias user is used by q-mail to handle addresses that don't exist. For example, you could have ~alias/.qmail-markk contain the line

```
enry@wayga.net
```

to forward E-mail that comes in for markk@wayga.net to enry@wayga.net. A common use of this is setting up postmaster, abuse, or root aliases.

- The root user does not receive E-mail. Due to the number of security problems this could cause, it was determined that root should be aliased to someone else (like the actual administrators of the machine). This makes cracking a root account that much harder.

Ezmlm

The ezmlm package allows for easy mailing list setups. It has all the functionality commonly needed in mailing list applications: automatic subscribe/unsubscribe, moderated lists, and digest creation (handled by ezmlm-idx). Unlike many other mailing list applications, ezmlm is command based—there should be no need for the mailing list administrator to edit files. Another feature of ezmlm (and qmail) is that mailing list creation and administration do not require access to the root account.

By default, many of the ezmlm programs get installed in /usr/local/bin/ezmlm. The install instructions are in the INSTALL file (located in the ezmlm-0.53 directory) and are also straightforward. Once installed and tested, users can create their own mailing lists with the following commands:

```
ezmlm-make ~/list ~/.qmail-list user-list host
```

This creates the mailing list. The mailing list itself is contained in ~/list. This mailing list is not moderated in that anyone can subscribe and unsubscribe. If you want a private mailing list where only the moderator can add or remove members, you can add the -P option. Once the mailing list is created, you can just remove ~/list/public to create a moderated list or just create the file to create a public list:

```
ezmlm-sub ~/list e-mail
```

This subscribes the E-mail to list. The new member is subscribed to the list.

```
ezmlm-unsub ~/list e-mail
```

This unsubscribes E-mail from list.

```
ezmlm-list ~/list
```

This lists the members of list

Once a list is created, the user-list-subscribe and user-list-unsubscribe E-mail addresses are created for users to subscribe and unsubscribe. If the mailing list is moderated, these mail addresses will not work and the moderator will have to manually add new members. An extension to ezmlm (ezmlm-idx) provides for more moderation and archiving.

Ezmlm Files

Once a mailing list is created, here are a few files you'll find in the directory and what they mean.

archive/	Contains an archive of the mailing list. Messages are numbered from 1 on. If the "archived" file exists, no messages will be archived
archived	If this file exists, ezmlm will archive messages.
headeradd	Contains a list of headers that will be added to E-mail sent by ezmlm.
headerre-move	Has a list of headers that will be removed from E-mail that gets sent out by ezmlm.
key	This file has some random binary data to prevent forging subscription requests.
num	Contains the number of messages sent so far.
public	If this exists, users can subscribe and unsubscribe without the help of the moderator. If it doesn't exist, only the moderator can add or remove users
text	Directory containing files that ezmlm will send back as administrative messages. You can change these files if you want.

7.7   Remote E-mail (POP and IMAP)

POP (Post Office Protocol) and IMAP (Internet Message Access Protocol) are two of the standards for receiving E-mail from a remote machine. The best example of remote E-mail use is in an office situation where there is a Linux server, and Windows (or Mac, or other UNIX) clients also running on the network. The clients can receive their E-mail in a number of ways (Eudora, Netscape, PC-Pine, etc.) and still have one central mail server.

Each protocol has strengths, weaknesses, and assorted Mail User Agency (MUA) that support them. Both are typically installed in a Linux setup ready to run. Authentication of E-mail is done by the same user/password scheme that is used to log in. One of the advantages of using POP or IMAP is that little user setup is required. You can typically install and run the program without any trouble.

POP

POP (RFC 937 and RFC 1225) was one of the first methods for retrieving and sending E-mail to/from a remote machine. The protocol is rather simple, and the commands are the same as the regular UNIX /bin/mail program. You can get, send, list, and delete mail. That's about it. The good thing about it, though, is that you can pick up your E-mail at the office from home. The down side to POP is that the E-mail on the server is often deleted once it gets sent to you.[9] So while you can get your E-mail from work to home, you then have to send the E-mail back from home to work, or else you won't have any E-mail at work. Netscape and most PC-based Internet E-mail programs handle POP.

IMAP

IMAP (RFC 2060) was created to handle some of the deficiencies of POP. IMAP is designed to be a "client/server" setup where the server keeps the mail until the client requests that it be deleted. IMAP also allows a setup where you can download your E-mail to a notebook, delete messages, respond to messages, and so on and then sync back up with the server. This is

---

[9]To be fair, this is a problem with the applications that use it, not the protocol itself. POP can be set up to leave E-mail on the server, which can fill the server very quickly.

designed for laptops, which may not always be connected to a network. In POP, all the E-mail is downloaded at once, which is a bit of a problem for large messages over slow links. IMAP supports a mode where only portions of an E-mail (the headers) are downloaded. IMAP is also for more than just E-mail, since the protocol allows for transmission of other kinds of data, such as NetNews articles. Only a few programs (pine and Netscape) currently handle IMAP because the protocol is a bit newer than POP. A large list of available IMAP clients and servers is available at the IMAP Web site http://www.imap.org.

7.8   Summary

- Sendmail is the default way of sending E-mail
- You might benefit from using qmail
- MIME allows you to E-mail binary data from one person to another

Internet Agencies 8

If you're on the Internet, you'll probably have to deal with one of these groups sooner or later.

Even though the Internet appears to be an anarchy, there is a sense of order to it. Various agencies have been set up to give a bit of order to this apparent chaos.

Even if you get your connection via an ISP, you still have things that may require outside assistance, like registering your domain and tracking crackers if one should happen to attack your site. How do you keep up with security issues?

8.1 InterNIC

In the old days (early 1990s), domains were free for the taking. If you filled out your template and sent in the form, you got yourself a domain name. Everyone thought this would go on forever, but alas...

In the mid 1990s, the National Science Foundation (NSF) started cutting off funding to the Internet and allowed commercial organizations to begin using the Internet to sell and advertise. The response was an explosive growth in the number of domains being added. This got into the hundreds of thousands a year. To impose some order on this, and make up for some of the missing NSF funding, the InterNIC (http://www.internic.net) was created to provide for a top-level DNS domain and to register new organizations within the United States. The downside to this was a new Internet fee: $100 for the first two years, then $50 each year after. After paying this fee, you are entitled to have your domain registered in the InterNIC database and your domain can now be recognized by the rest of the Internet. This doesn't mean that InterNIC will give you anything else, like DNS services or an Internet link. You will just have your domain name registered and a pointer to a DNS server. You're still responsible for getting Internet service and a DNS server.

Now time for some clarification. InterNIC only handles the U.S. domains: .edu, .net, .org, .com, .gov, and .int. Other domains, such as .us or other country-based domains, are not registered with the InterNIC and you'll have to find out who handles your regional DNS service to get registered with them. Many of these have a fee, but some (like the .us) are free or have a smaller fee than InterNIC. To register in the .us domain, go to http://www.isi.edu. The .us domain doesn't give the kind of general quality that, for example, .com would give. For example, instead of wayga.net, I'd probably get something like wayga.wakefield.ma.us. but I could still build a domain under that such as ftp.wayga.wakefield.ma.us. In some ways, this is preferable to just a .com domain, since it allows you to specify a site (ibm.armonk.ny.us) directly. Foreign companies have slightly different subdivisions and may subdivide by location, type of organization (commercial, educational, etc.) or a combination of these. To find out the contacts for a particular country's top-level domain, check out http://www.isi.edu/div7/iana/domain-names.html.

One other thing to remember about country codes is that they may not be what you think they are. For example, .ch is Switzerland, not China. And .ca is Canada, not California.[1]

---

[1] And Washington University is in St. Louis, and Miami University is in Ohio, and Rome is in upstate New York.

Registering a Domain

The sample for domain registration is good for InterNIC, but other agencies will probably want to have the same information when you register. Either way, all the following information contains things you should already know.

You'll need to have a domain name first. Take one that isn't already taken (obviously) and make sure the domain you take isn't a registered trademark of someone else. Sure you can take mcdonalds.com, but their lawyers get paid more than yours, and there's more of them. The InterNIC does not take sides in these kinds of disputes, so don't think that just because you got a domain that you own it for all time.

There are a few choices when registering a domain. The .edu is for educational institutions (mostly colleges and universities—elementary and secondary schools usually get a state-based domain). The .com is for commercial organizations that don't necessarily provide Internet access or aren't necessarily based on the Web. The .org domain is for organizations, either formal or a group of people getting together (apache.org or linux.org for example). The .net domain is for groups that resell Internet access or provide access to other groups. And the .gov and .mil are for the government and military, respectively. This leaves you with three probable choices—.com, .net, or .org. Pick the one appropriate for your organization.

Next you'll need up to three people. One is the technical contact, one is the administrative contact, and the third is the billing contact. The technical contact is the person who typically registers the domain and is the Manager of Information Services (MIS) person. The administrative contact is probably your boss. The billing contact is the one who gets the bills. They can all be the same person if you wish. These names and addresses will be compiled into the database as well, giving a handle that you can use later at InterNIC instead of reentering your address, phone number, name, and so on.

The last important items are the primary and secondary DNS servers. Since InterNIC doesn't provide you with DNS service, you must enter the two hosts that will be able to provide IP addresses for your domain. Two are required so that one can act as a backup in case the primary is down or busy.

InterNIC also asks for information such as, "What does your organization do?" Fill in all the information requested and wait. In a few days, you'll get E-mail saying the domain was added. If you're changing a domain, the administrative, technical, and billing contacts will receive a request from InterNIC to verify the new information. This prevents one contact from changing the information without the knowledge of the other two, and it prevents a cracker from changing the domain information (for example if microsoft.com were to point instead to linux.org). This is more a denial-of-service attack and was common until InterNIC requested verification.

whois

The whois database is a hook directly into the InterNIC hosts and allows you to see domain information and get information on the people who run the domains.

The whois database not only lets you see information about a domain, but also about people. For example, since I own the "wayga.net" domain, I have an entry in the whois database (MK146). Looking up this information would give my name and E-mail address. Back in the early days, this was a great way to find someone's E-mail address. But since there are millions of people on the Internet now, the only people in the whois database are domain administrators.

Using whois is easy. Just type something like

```
whois wayga.net
```

The original version of whois looked at an inappropriate whois database (nic.ddn.mil which is for military use only). The Linux version of whois should point at the right server name, but if it doesn't, you'll have to replace whois with

```
whois -h rs.internic.net wayga.net
```

After the whois command, you can list names or domains and get results from the InterNIC database on who owns a particular name or get contact information for the administrators of that domain. This is especially helpful if you're trying to track a cracker in your system and know what domain they're coming from. You can then contact the administrators of the domain and alert them.

8.2   CERT

The CERT Coordination Center was founded in 1988 to coordinate security problems on the Internet. It was founded after the great Internet Worm in the late 1980s and is located at Carnegie-Mellon University in Pittsburgh, Pennsylvania. If you don't know anything about the Internet Worm, I'd suggest getting either *The Cuckoo's Egg* by Cliff Stoll, or *Cyberpunk: Outlaws*

Samba 9

How to let your Linux machine serve files and printers to Windows machines.

Microsoft Windows uses a protocol called SMB to do most of its networking. Guess what? Linux can talk SMB.

There are two ways to do this. First, you can compile the kernel to handle SMB natively. This is more efficient, but it only allows you to mount Windows share drives. You can't do any file serving or print serving.[1]

The other option is called Samba, developed mainly by some nice folks in Australia. TCP/IP and SMB work quite nicely together. In fact, they work so well together, one could piggyback a packet of SMB data within a TCP/IP packet.[2] This relationship is one that Samba uses to get Windows machines to

---

[1]Yet. The kernel keeps changing and growing. If it does add support, hopefully the concepts will be the same as Samba, so you don't have to throw out this chapter.

[2]Which itself is piggybacked on ethernet, or FDDI, or ATM, or PPP or what have you.

talk to Linux. The latest version of Samba can be found at http://lake.can-berra.edu.au/pub/samba/samba.html.

Let's quickly go through a small network.

9.1   Setting Up a MS Windows Network

This is actually easy, if you have Windows for Workgroups, Windows 95, or Windows NT. There are apparently DOS clients as well. So from here on in, we'll just say "Windows" to relate to all three versions of the OS, and you'll have to do some reading to match what I tell you to your particular version of Windows.

What You'll Need

First, get the ethernet cards and drivers loaded. Also install your backbone. The best available networking scheme for the money is 10BaseT, as there are fewer problems that can cause the entire network to go down. But it's more expensive; you have to buy a hub, switch, patch cables, patch panels, run one cable to each machine, and so on. But it is certainly worth the money.

If you want a cheaper ethernet, or you have a very small network, you can get the very affordable 10Base2. This is also known as "thinnet." All you have to be concerned about in a 10Base2 network is that both ends are terminated with a 50-ohm resistor. Thinnet has the disadvantage that if one section of cable goes bad, the entire network goes down.

You'll also need to make sure that each Windows user has an account on the Linux server. Their shell can be non-existent if you like, but the account and a home directory have to exist. If you want, make the shell something like */bin/false*. If you want users to be able to change their passwords, set the shell to be */bin/passwd*. Also be sure to add */bin/passwd* to the */etc/shells* file.

Once you have your network and you Linux box set up, get the software working. Windows will allow you to use the Windows networking option to create a simple network. Be sure to use the same workgroup name across all the machines.

What's a Workgroup?

A workgroup is something similar to a subnet, but not quite the same. A subnet breaks users up physically, as you need a router or bridge to get from one subnet to another. A workgroup is a more logical breakdown. For example, you can have accounting, manufacturing, and sales all on the same subnet, but all in different workgroups.

Once the software has been set up, you should be able to browse the network and see all the other machines at least on the same subnet as you.[3] If you can't, get the software to this point. If something's wrong, you'll usually get a somewhat cryptic explanation of the problem and how to fix it.

Install TCP/IP Stack

Windows 95 and Windows NT both come with a TCP/IP stack already in the installation. Windows for Workgroups has one available at the Microsoft home page (http://www.microsoft.com/). Download and install it on the systems. When Windows asks for a username and password, be sure to give the username that exists on the Linux machine and use the Linux password as well. Note that Windows for Workgroups and Windows 95 both have bugs relating to password security, and you should check out the Microsoft home page for patches to both OSes.

I'll assume you know how to set up a TCP/IP network. If not, check the networking chapter for information on how to do this. Once you have the TCP/IP stack loaded on all the Windows machines, try having them ping each other, or ping the Linux box. The Linux box should also be able to ping the Windows machines. If you don't have a TCP/IP network available, check the chapter on ipfw for information on creating your own internal network using Linux.

9.2 Installing Samba

Now that the Windows machines are set up, let's go to the Linux machine. Install the latest version of Samba in a convenient location. We use `/usr/local/samba`. Directories should be created underneath this one with the names `lib`, `bin`, and `var`. The `lib/smb.conf` file is the one you'll be editing most, and you should take a look at it and the man pages for it while compiling and installing.

Here's a sample copy of an `smb.conf` file:

---

[3]You won't be able to see outside your subnet unless your bridge forwards non-TCP/IP packets. A router probably won't forward SMB packets, since it deals with TCP/IP only. But since Samba piggybacks on TCP/IP, you can still connect to machines in other subnets.

```
[global]
   printing = bsd
   printcap name = /etc/printcap
   load printers = yes
   guest account = nobody
   log file = /usr/local/samba/log.%m
   admin users=ricks markk
   read prediction = yes
   dead time = 15
   workgroup=AURAGROUP
   mangled map=(*.html,*.htm)
 lock directory = /usr/local/samba/var/locks
  share modes = yes
  os level = 33
  domain master = yes

[homes]
   comment = Home Directories
   browseable = no
   read only = no
   create mode = 0750
   read size = 8192
   max xmit = 8192

[printers]
   comment = All Printers
   browseable = no
   printable = yes
   public = yes
   writable = no
   create mode = 0700

[pcsoft]
   comment = PC Software
   path = /vol/repository
   public = no
   only guest = no
   writable = yes
   printable = no
   create mode = 0666

[accounting]
  path = /home/bob/shared
  valid users = fred bob
  public = no
  only guest = no
  browseable = no
  writable = yes
  create mask = 0777
```

Much like the Windows system.ini, files are broken up into sections starting with a word in brackets; the smb.conf file does the same. The [global], [printers], and [homes] are the only three reserved section headers. All others are assumed to be share names available for use. The [global] section sets options for the entire program. For example, the mangled map option says that all files that get to Samba that end in .htm should instead be written to the Linux server as .html. This makes writing files in Windows and sending them to a Web server easier.

Other options of note include the following.

- log file—When smbd fires up, this is where it will write its log file. In the above case, the name of the log file is "log." plus the name of the machine. This gives unique log files

- dead time—After <dead time> minutes are up with no activity, the smb connection goes away. This is good not only to save resources on the Linux server but also allows Samba to recover when a Windows machine crashes. A good choice would be around 15 minutes or so.

- admin users—These users are as good as root. In fact, they have root privileges to all the shares. This should only be you or the person administering Samba here.

- workgroup—The workgroup to attach to. This should be the same name that you set earlier in Windows.

The homes section will put in the browse network section of the Windows home directory for the user. The user can then click or mount that directory, and it's their home directory on Linux.

Once Samba is installed on the network, you can test it by starting smbd and nmbd (which handle a function similar to DNS) and doing a network browse. You should see your Linux machine in the list of machines (see Figure 9–1).

9.3   Installing Linux Printers on Windows

Samba knows enough (via the *printing* = *bsd* and *printcap name* = */etc/ printcap*) to load in all the printers available in the */etc/printcap* and make them available to SMB clients. The Linux side does not require any changes, but you may want to make sure that the */etc/printcap* file is set successfully and you can print. Samba will also deal with any remote printers

```
┌──────────────────────────────────────────────────┐
│ 🖧 Network Neighborhood               [ _ ][ □ ][ X ]│
│ File  Edit  View  Help                             │
├──────────────────────────────────────────────────┤
│  🖳 Entire Network                                 │
│  💻 Cody                                           │
│  💻 Dingle                                         │
│  💻 Galaxy                                         │
│  💻 Orion                                          │
│  💻 Roxanne                                        │
│                                                    │
│                                                    │
│                                                    │
│                                                    │
│                                                    │
├──────────────────────────────────────────────────┤
│ 1 object(s) selected                               │
└──────────────────────────────────────────────────┘
```

Figure 9–1   Dingle and Galaxy are UNIX servers running Samba

as well. Any printer you can get to from Linux should be available from Samba (see Figure 9–2).

The Windows side may be a bit more complicated. More sophisticated print drivers that demand to talk directly to the printer may cause you some problems. My first advice is to get a printer that supports either PCL or Post-Script. This way, you can at least send data to the printer. Be aware that more printers coming out these days may be using the "Windows Printing System" which will work with no system except Windows. If you have a printer that accepts PCL or PostScript, you can install generic drivers in Windows to print to the Samba printers. I have had some success at using the Apple LaserWriter for a PostScript printer, and HP LaserJet 4 as a PCL printer.[4]

Once the printers and shares are configured, you can let your users loose on it. Be sure to keep an eye on the log files to monitor any problems if they show up.

---

[4]Your mileage may vary. Try other print drivers under Windows and see how well they work.

Figure 9–2 Listing of printers and share drives available from Galaxy.

9.4 Summary

- Samba is an easy way to share drive space and printers with Windows, Windows 95, and NT machines.

NetNews 10

Installing the INN program on your Linux machine.

Usenet News is an internationally distributed discussion system which supports many different topic forums called newsgroups.

Almost all topics imaginable are covered within the Usenet spectrum, and new newsgroups are added every day to keep up with popular demand. Usenet can be useful for research, recreation, or just finding people with common interests. For a much more in-depth description of what Usenet is from a user and historical viewpoints, refer to the "What is Usenet" FAQ (frequently asked questions) located at

```
ftp://rtfm.mit.edu/pub/usenet-by-group/news.answers/usenet/what-is/
   part1
```

and

```
ftp://rtfm.mit.edu/pub/usenet-by-group/news.answers/usenet/what-is/
   part2.
```

The history of Usenet begins back in 1979 when two graduate students, Tom Truscott and Jim Ellis, thought of using the UNIX to UNIX Copy software (UUCP), to connect machines for the purpose of information exchange among users. At first, traffic was handled by a number of shell scripts, but the first public software was Anews. Anews was small and not designed to handle more than a few articles per group each day. When the volume of readers and posters grew, Anews was rewritten and released as Bnews in 1982 and then rewritten again as Cnews in 1987. RFCs 850 and 1036, titled *Standard for Interchange of USENET Messages* detailed the format for the interchange of network News messages among USENET hosts, defining the format of news messages, transmission methods, and propagation methods.

All of the news server releases up until Cnews were targeted primarily at UUCP networks, though they could be used over different protocols as well.

With the growing popularity of other networks such as TCP/IP and DEC-Net, more efficient methods of news transfer had to be developed, and so the Network News Transfer Protocol (NNTP), was born in 1986. NNTP was designed as a "store and forward" technology, meaning that news articles are stored in a central database from which readers pull individual articles. Further technical details of NNTP are discussed in RFC977, *A Proposed Standard for the Stream-Based Transmission of News*.

At first, NNTP was available only as an add-on package to Cnews, but then the Internet News program, more commonly known as INN, was developed. INN combined the NNTP section with the news server itself, making installation and configuration easier than before. Originally, the INN software was written and maintained by Rich Salz up through INN1.4sec, released in the middle of 1993. At that point, Rich no longer had the time to maintain the distribution, and Dave Barr unofficially stepped in and took over maintenance and wrote the 1.4unoff versions of the software. In 1996, Rich turned over the INN source distribution to the Internet Software Consortium (ISC) with the understanding that they would take over maintenance and development of future INN releases. The ISC, mainly James Brister, merged the changes that had occurred in the unoff source offshoot and then added more features and bug fixes and produced version 1.5 and above.

Today, most sites on the Internet use INN as their news server software, but there are various newly developed servers such as Cyclone, Dnews, Diablo, and others. This chapter deals primarily with the INN software and how to install, configure, and troubleshoot it on a Linux system.

10.1 INN Pre-Installation Considerations

There are several things to consider before you actually install INN and start receiving news. INN is a memory- and disk-intensive piece of software, especially if the machine receives and stores a large number of articles. Determining the amount of memory and disk space needed and planning the layout of the filesystems ahead of time can save you a lot of headaches in the future.

Space Considerations

Usenet news can consume a large amount of disk space depending on how many newsgroups you carry and what hierarchy the newsgroups are in. Plan ahead to estimate how much disk space you will need for the logs, the actual news storage area, and the news binaries. Currently, a full news feed tends to take about 3 or 4 gigabytes of incoming news per day. About half of this is taken up by the alt.* hierarchy, with the biggest section under that being the `alt.binaries` hierarchy.

If you want to receive news, but don't have much space to spare, consider getting only a partial feed. You can restrict what is kept on disk by hierarchy or by specifying a group name. If you're interested in certain topics, simply accept those few newsgroups which discuss those topics. Ordinarily, unless running an ISP or service, most people will choose to accept only a partial feed just because there are so many groups with several hierarchies not even in a language that you can understand.

For larger installations, it is generally a good idea to keep the spool, logs, the binaries, and config files on separate partitions because of performance issues. The space utilized by the news binaries and config files should remain more or less constant and can be put on the same partition as other binaries, usually in `/usr` or `/usr/local`. The segments that will change drastically in size are the spool and the log file partitions. The log file partition must always be at least twice the size of the space normally used because INN makes multiple copies of the history file when expire, the cleanup program, is running. The spool area must be able to hold however many days worth of news that you desire to keep as well as being able to handle an occasional spike when the local machine or an upstream news provider is down for a period of time and then sends a large amount of backlogged news.

Memory Considerations

As well as being a big disk hog, INN can take a large amount of memory if you have a large number of groups. INN keeps the history database in memory, and when expire runs, it keeps the entire remove list in memory. If the machine does not have enough memory to run expire in a timely manner, it can get far behind in news because the news server does not accept new articles when it is running expire. In order to avoid a cycle of no news and then a flood of new news, make sure that the local machine will be able to handle the disk and memory load required.

Other Performance Considerations

There are various ways to tune your news system for better performance both at the hardware and software levels. On the software side, you can speed up reads by client software by using the NOV indexing scheme (overview database). For any large news installation, also keep the overview database on a separate partition. The number of reads and writes to the partition by desktop clients and the feeding sites make it a heavily used directory. Also certain expiring administrative newsgroups like junk and control can save the server space and make reads and writes faster for that hierarchy. There are several software tuning steps that will be discussed later in the INN configuration section.

On the hardware side, the speed of news transfers is greatly influenced by the speed of the bus, performance of the network card, and layout of disks and disk controllers. To achieve the best disk performance, spread out input/ output (I/O) across several smaller (2 to 4 gigabytes), high-performance SCSI disks on multiple PCI or EISA controllers. Make sure to configure the controllers for synchronous SCSI with tagged queuing enabled. Obtain the md toolkit, available from `ftp://sweet-smoke.ufr-info-p7.ibp.fr/public/Linux/` and enable the md driver to use RAID0 striping for the news spool and the overview database partitions. Be sure to mount the news disks as no_atime to eliminate the inode update for every file access even when the file's contents are unchanged. For Linux kernels before 2.0.29, this requires an INN patch, available at `http://thereisnocabal.news.erols.com/patches/ext2_no_atime.diff`, from Clayton O'Neill. Clayton has a number of other useful INN patches on his site as well.

10.2 Setup, Obtaining, and Unpacking INN

The first step to installing a news server is to format all of the partitions that will be used and mount them. Next, create the news user and news group or verify that they already exist. The news user and group should own all directories that the INN software resides in for a secure installation. The news user should have a locked password and the home directory should be wherever the news binaries will be installed.

Verify that PGP is installed, or see the chapter on security for instructions on PGP installation and use, and make a PGP key for the news user so that it may do secure automatic control message authentication. Also, if the news machine has an FTP daemon, make sure that the news user is in the `/etc/ftpusers` file so no ftp access is allowed.

Once that's set up, confirm that you're using the source code for the latest version of INN. The Slackware news package comes with the Reference Implementation of NNTP as well as INN. However, if you select "INN" for installation, it doesn't remove the NNTP entry in the `/etc/inetd.conf` and it must be removed manually. It's generally safer not to install the INN implementation that comes with the Linux distribution and to just obtain the latest INN version, 1.6 at the time of this writing, from ISC's Web site at http://www.isc.com/inn.html. Also retrieve any patches released for the same version of INN. Once the news partitions are set up and the INN distribution and patches are downloaded, move everything to the news source directory, such as `/usr/local/src/inn`. Become the news user (`su news`) to uncompress and untar the source archive by doing the following:

```
>su - news
(make sure the path is set correctly)
>tar zxf inn-1.5sec3.tar.gz
>cd inn-1.5sec3
> ls -a
```

This is the source tree for the INN distribution, which contains several Makefiles, README instructional files, and directories broken down into the following topics:

frontends: Programs that control the central server and feed articles to it

innd: The NNTP server itself

backends: Programs to transmit articles to other sites

expire: Programs that purge article files and databases

nnrpd: The NNTP server for client readers

lib: Library routines

include: Header files

samples: Prototype scripts and configuration files

site: Where user-editable site configuration files are stored before being copied out to the actual news directory for implementation

doc: Manual pages

config: Tools to aid in site configuration

Take this opportunity to apply any patches to the software, and be sure to look through the README files, FAQ, Install files, and other pertinent documentation before attempting to configure and install INN. Pay special attention to section 2 of the FAQ where it talks about Linux-specific tips and problems.

10.3 Compiling and Installing INN

Unlike many gnu utilities, INN has no autoconfiguration scripts, so all parameter settings must be done by editing the config files and setting the parameters by hand. INN has built-in steps, with the first section being the "subst" program, located in the config directory. In this version of INN, subst comes as a shell script or C source. Unless problems occur, using the shell script version of subst is usually easiest, but the C version is often faster. To test the subst program do the following:

```
>cd $INNSRC/config
>cp ../sample-configs/config.data-linux-<version number> config.data
>chmod 644 config.data
customize config.data
>make sh
```

If you receive errors and the shell script was used, compile the C version and try again. If all goes well, subst works fine and the true configuration can now be done by editing the global configuration file, config.data. The config.data file uses the "#" character as comment line and the file format is as follows:

```
<parameter><one-or-more-tabs><value>
```

Even if there is no <value>, the <one-or-more-tabs> is still required to avoid syntax errors.

The Linux version of the config.data file should provide a mostly accurate starting point for the compilation, but for detailed information on each section of the configuration file, refer to the INN installation notes. The configuration file is generally divided into the following sections:

- Make config parameters: Identifies the path to the C compiler and defines what libraries and command-line switches are needed.
- Logging levels: Identifies what log levels innd and other programs should log under. Be sure to put the correct log levels in the `/etc/syslog.conf` file.
- Ownerships and file modes: Defines the user and group ownership of files, the umask, and the mail contact for the machine.
- C library differences: Identifies what library routines the operating system will use as well as the value of some commonly used variable types and sizes.
- C library omissions: Library routines that may be missing from the OS.
- Miscellaneous config data: Defines various macros to be included in `$INNSRC/include/configdata.h`. This section greatly determines how the news server will act and is one of the largest sections.
- Paths to common programs: Defines where news binaries and general system programs like sendmail and shell utilities reside.
- Paths related to the spool directory: Defines where the news spool, incoming and outgoing, overview database, tmp, and bad articles should go.
- Execution paths for innd and rnews: Defines some paths to programs used by rnews and innd.
- Sockets created by innd or clients: Defines where the socket files reside.
- Log and config files: Defines where the INN configuration and log files reside.
- Innwatch configuration: Defines at what points innwatch should throttle and unthrottle the news server.
- Tcl filtering configuration: Defines if tcl support is included or not and where tcl header and library files reside.
- PGP control-message verification configuration: Determines if PGP authentication will be used and what the path to the PGP binary is.
- Local configuration: Defines the news user's home directory.
- Actsync configuration: Defines what host to synchronize to and how.

- Perl Configuration: Defines if perl support is included or not and where the perl header and libraries reside.

Once the `config.data` file is verified to be correct for the current system, compile the news software as an unprivileged user by doing the following:

```
>cd $INNSRC
>make world > make.log
```

Assuming all goes well, verify that things will be installed in the correct place by doing

```
>make -n install
```

Then, when confident that all is correct, become root and install the package by doing

```
>su - root
#mkdir -p <news spool directory>
#chown news.news <news spool directory>
#chmod 775 <news spool directory>
#cd $INNSRC
#sh ./makedirs.sh
#./BUILD
```

The `makedirs.sh` script will create the higher-level directories and give them the correct permissions, and the BUILD script will install all of the files as well as provide a small active file and build a corresponding history file. This initial installation must be done as root to ensure that all of the SUID scripts and wrappers have the correct ownership and permissions. The only files that should be changed at this point are the ones in the `$INNSRC/site` directory. So from now on, unless the SUID file source is modified, you should be able to do all makes as the news user. In the future, before making any changes, it is wise to preserve the original source files by doing a `make backup` first. Also make sure to add cron jobs for `nntpsend` and `news.daily` when feeds are finally set up.

10.4 INN Internals

Before trying to start INN and obtain newsfeeds, you should have a fairly decent understanding of how the news system works. There are many different segments to the INN software that control different aspects of how news is handled. Some of these programs run all the time and some only start when needed or if run by hand. To get an overall picture, we'll start by describing how INN operates under various conditions.

rc.news

After installing INN, create a script that checks the consistency of the last INN shutdown and then starts the news server back up and performs any other needed cleanup. This is usually accomplished by calling the script provided in `$INNSRC/samples/rc.news` from an `/etc/rc2.d/` file or by running it from `/etc/rc2` directly. The `rc.news` script will read all of the variables from the INN configuration, set the flags that it will pass to `innstart`, and check to see if the server was not shut down cleanly.

It will also ensure that if an expire was being run, the newsmaster will be notified or carries on with the old article removal, as well as verifying the existence of the active and history files. After it insures that everything is in a stable state, it starts the server and a process called "`innwatch`" to monitor the machine.

innwatch

The innwatch program monitors the load average, disk space usage, and number of used inodes on the partitions defined for news use. The innwatch program can be customized for site-specific parameters by modifying the "`innwatch.ctl`" file located in `$INNSRC/site/`.

innd

As described above, `rc.news` starts the main process, innd, which is the actual daemon that listens for and handles all incoming connections on port 119.

When started, the innd reads the `active, newsfeeds`, and `hosts.nntp` files into memory and then opens a socket on port 119 and starts logging article transmissions to the history file and connections to the set of files specified in the `/etc/syslog.conf` file.

Logging

Where INN logs is controlled by several files, "`/etc/syslog.conf`," the settings in "`config.data`" before compilation, and in the "`control.ctl`" file.

The `config.data` file generally tells INN what the default log directory is and at what level to log various types of messages. The `config.data` file also defines where the errors and general messages (like all incoming news) should be logged. The `control.ctl` file tells INN where to log things like `newgroup` and `rmgroup` messages as well as other cancel message types. See the section on control messages for more details. The `syslog.conf` entries tell INN where to log messages of varying severity. Common entries to the `syslog.conf` would look like the following tab-separated entries:

```
news.crit       /var/log/news/news.crit
news.err        /var/log/news/news.err
news.notice     /var/log/news/news.notice
```

This tells innd that it should send messages of the correct severity to the corresponding log file in `/var/log/news`.

The Active and History Files

The active and history files are the main INN databases that keep track of what articles are stored or were previously stored on the machine. The "active file" has one line for each newsgroup which contains the newsgroup name, the high and low watermarks for the articles currently stored on the server, and the status of the newsgroups. The newsgroup status is determined at the time of creation and can be one of the following:

> y—Local postings are allowed.
>
> n—Only remote postings are allowed.
>
> m—This is a moderated group and all postings must be approved.
>
> j—Articles are passed on and are filed to the junk newsgroup only if received.
>
> x—Articles cannot be posted to this group.
>
> =group.name—Articles are locally filed in the "group.name" group, somewhat like a symbolic link for a newsgroup.

Coupled with the active file is the `active.times` file which provides a chronological log of when newsgroups were created. Each line contains the name of the newsgroup, the time of creation, and, optionally, the E-mail address of the person who created the group.

Equally important is the file that holds the record of all articles currently on the server and those that were on the server but are now expired. The "history file" contains one line for each article with the tab-separated fields being a uniquely identifying Message-ID, date the article was received, and a set of space-separated entries identifying what newsgroups the article was posted to. The third field is empty if the article has expired.

Both the history and active files are always opened by the innd process and are updated any time the news server receives a new article or when articles are expired. If one of these files is ever lost or corrupted, they must be rebuilt from the existing data on the disk. This can be a long and arduous process depending on how many articles the news server retains at any one time.

10.5 NNRP

The innd receives two kinds of connections on port 119: NNTP (Net News Transport Protocol) and NNRP. NNRP is the protocol used by news reading software to grab a specific set of articles and to allow client posting. If the connection to port 119 tries to establish an NNRP connection, innd spawns off an nnrpd process. The nnrpd will check the client's address against the list of accepted addresses in the "nnrp.access file" and if a match is found, will allow the client machine the level of access specified.

nnrp.access

The nnrp.access file contains entries of five colon-separated fields with the pound sign (#) as a comment character. The first field of the entry is a wild-card expression that must match the client's hostname or IP address.

The second field specifies what privileges, read and/or post, granted to the client software. The third field, which can be left blank, specifies a username that must be used when the connection is established. The fourth field, which can also be left blank, is a password that the client must issue before any privileges are granted.

inews

If the client is allowed to post articles to the server, the client software usually uses the "inews" portion of INN. The inews program is installed on the client machine and allows it to post an article to the server. Inews reads the article, normally entered interactively with some editor, and possibly headers from a file on the client machine. It then adds headers to the article and does some rule-based consistency checking.

If the article passes, inews reads the local "inn.conf" file to determine which news server to send the article to. If an unapproved article is posted to a moderated group, inews will attempt to mail the article to the moderator instead, reading the "moderators" file or reading the "inn.conf" file as a last resort. If configured to do so, inews will spool the article locally if the server is not available, and "rnews" must be run periodically to flush the article queue.

rnews

The rnews program reads news articles stored in a local queue, typically by UNIX to UNIX Copy (UUCP), and sends them to the local news server as defined in "inn.conf." A UUCP batch file starts with a pound bang (#!) to indicate that multiple articles are stored in one file. If the pound bang is not present at the beginning of the file, then rnews interprets the entire file to be only one article.

NNTP

The innd process can also receive a request for the NNTP protocol on port 119. NNTP is the protocol used by other news servers to transfer articles in batch style. When such a connection is received, innd checks the hosts.nntp and hosts.nntp.nolimit files for the name of the connecting machine.

Authentication

To allow the feeding machine access to the news server, edit the $INNSRC/ site/hosts.nntp or $INNSRC/site/hosts.nntp.nolimit file and add the feeding machine's name on a line by itself. Comments begin with a pound sign (#), and blank lines and comment lines are ignored when the file is parsed. The first field of the colon-separated newsfeeds entry is the hostname or IP address of the machine to be fed. The second field is a password that the client machine must provide when first connecting; this field may be left blank and usually is. The optional third field is a wildcard-matched listing of newsgroups that will be accepted from the client site. Generally this file is just set up with entries that have the client hostname and a colon (news.uu.net:).

If the peer news server is authenticated, the news server will accept all the articles being sent. The innd takes each article separately, logging each to the "news" file in the log directory that was specified in the `config.data` file before compilation. The innd will try to match the newsgroup with one in the active file in memory. If the group name matches, innd will verify that it has not already received the article by checking for the unique article ID in the history file. If the article is new and accepted, the innd will modify the active file, increasing the high watermark of the newsgroup and the history file, adding the new article ID.

Control Messages

In the special case of an article with a special header called "Control:" innd will convert the first word of text to lowercase and parse it to determine what should happen to the message. If the argument is cancel, innd will take the next argument as the Message-ID and remove it from the news spool and history file. If the first argument is anything else, the innd refers to the parse-control script, which is governed by the "control.ctl file," to determine the next step in processing.

The `control.ctl` file includes entries with four colon-separated wildcard-matching fields, and pound signs (#) indicate comments. The first field indicates what kind of message the ruleset is for. This first field corresponds to the first argument on the Control: header line. Common message types are ihave, sendme, rmgroup, newgroup, sendsys, senduuname, and version but any can be made up. The second field indicates whom the message must originate from. If the control message is "newgroup" or "rmgroup," then the third field specifies the pattern of the groups being created or removed. If the control message is of a different type, then the third field is ignored. The fourth field of the control.ctl file is what action should be performed if the message matches the other criteria.

`Control.ctl` actions include the following by default, but any other shell scripts can be written and added into the parsecontrol program to facilitate customized control of article handling. In previous versions of INN, for instance, PGP verification of control messages was not default but had to be added in by changing the parsecontrol script to recognize another action and call an added script.

doit: The action requested by the control message should be performed.

doifarg: If the control message has an argument, this is treated as a doit.

action: If no argument was given, it is treated as a mail entry. This is used in the "sendsys" entries script so that a site can request its own newsfeeds entry by posting a "sendsys mysite" article without opening up the news server to sendsys bomb attacks.

doit=file: The action is performed, but a log entry is written to the specified log file. If file is the word "mail," then the record is mailed to the newsmaster. A null string is equivalent to `/dev/null`, and a pathname that starts with a slash is taken as the absolute filename to use as the log. If there is no prepended slash, then the directory is assumed to be the log directory defined in the config.data file.

drop: The message is completely ignored.

log: A one-line notice is sent to the errlog defined in the config.data file.

log-file: A one-line notice is written to the file "log" as described above in the doit=file definition.

mail: No action is taken except to send mail to the newsmaster.

10.6 Newsfeeds

The article will also be fed to the newsfeeds file to determine if it should be sent off-site or run through any local channel feeds. To send news out to another machine so that the articles posted by users reach the outside world, you must edit the `$INNSRC/site/newsfeeds` file and add an entry for the feeding machine. The newsfeeds file lets the newsmaster fine-tune what news will be sent out to which sites and has the potential to be very complex, so be sure to read the man page if anything fancy is being done with one of the sites. Briefly, each entry in the newsfeeds file has four colon-separated fields; two of the fields may have optional subfields, marked off by a slash. Fields or subfields that take multiple parameters should be separated by a comma. Multiple lines may be used to define a site, but each line except the last must have the "/" continuation character at the end.

The format of each entry is as follows:

```
sitename[/exclude,exclude,...]\
    :pattern,pattern...[/distrib,distrib...]\
    :flag,flag...\
    :param
```

The first field is generally the name of the machine that the machine will send articles to but can also just be a generic name unique to the newsfeeds file. If any of the strings in the "exclude" parameter match a machine in the Path header, the article will not be fed to the site. The patterns in the second field are wildcard matches for the articles or hierarchies that will be fed to the client machine, and the distrib patterns are a listing of matches for the Distribution article header. The third field is a set of flags that defines the kind of feed and various size parameters. Most newsfeeds set up to send out local posts have "Tf,Wnm" as the flags. See the man page for an in-depth discussion of what flags are available and what each does. The meaning of the fourth field depends on the type of feed defined in the third field. In most cases, it can be omitted.

nntpsend

To flush batch files for outgoing newsfeeds, you must add an entry for the feeding machine in "`$INNSRC/site/nntpsend.ctl`." The nntpsend.ctl file consists of four colon-separated fields that define how and where news will be batched for each site. The first field is the name of the feed specified in the newsfeeds file, and a corresponding filename should be found in the area set up for outgoing news batches. The second field should be the hostname or IP address of the site, and if the hostname is used in the newsfeeds file, these two fields should be identical. The third field, if not empty, specifies the default truncation size of the site's batchfile. If the third field is empty, no truncation will take place. The final field specifies the flags passed to the process that actually does the remote news batch flushing, "innxmit."

The nntpsend program is usually run from cron about every 15 minutes on a constantly connected server, but this can be changed to a much greater time span or can be run by hand as news whenever new articles are posted.

When nntpsend starts for each host, it copies the batch file to a working file in the "out.going" directory of the news spool. If one nntpsend process is already running for a host, another will not be started until the working file has been flushed or an error occurs and merges the working file with the batch file.

The Overview Database

If the newsfeeds entry was a channel feed instead of a feed to another site, the article is passed off to a local binary. Some common channel feeds include news to mail and mail to news gateways, but the most common channel feed entry in the newsfeeds file is an entry called "overview" which will look something like the following:

```
overview:*:Tc,WO:/news/bin/overchan
```

This feed takes every article and feeds it through the overchan binary, which takes pertinent information from each article and stores it in a database for fast preloading of articles by news clients. The overview database is structured to be somewhat like a mirror of the news spool itself and keeps all entries in a hierarchical directory structure ordered by group names. Each group has its own overview file within that directory structure. For instance, the overview file for comp.os.linux would be something like

```
/news/over.view/comp/os/linux/.overview
```

and all the articles for comp.os.linux would be stored in

```
/news/spool/comp/os/linux/<article ID>
```

The contents of the overview file are governed by the overview.fmt configuration file. By default, the overview file contains the following headers: Subject, From, Date, Message-ID, References, Bytes, Lines, Xref. The order of the lines in the overview.fmt file is important because it determines what order the headers will appear in the database. If the overview.fmt file is changed after news has already been accepted, the overview database must be rebuilt from scratch.

ctlinnd

One of the most important pieces of user interactive software in the INN distribution is the "ctlinnd" binary. The ctlinnd program is the main control mechanism for the innd. It is responsible for creating and removing groups, article canceling, connection status of the server, rereading the configuration files that innd keeps in memory, renumbering the active file, and much more. For diagnostic purposes, one of the most frequently used ctlinnd commands is "ctlinnd mode" which verifies that the server is running, what mode the server is in, and if it is receiving new connections. A full listing of ctlinnd's capabilities can be viewed by passing the -h flag to the program. We will cover some of the more commonly used ctlinnd arguments and leave the rest for the man page to explain.

Creating and Removing Newsgroups

The task that ctlinnd is most often used for is creating and removing newsgroups on the server. If automatic group creation and deletion are not done, the newsmaster must add, delete, and change groups manually using the following syntax:

```
ctlinnd newgroup <group> [flags] [creator]
ctlinnd rmgroup <group>
ctlinnd changegroup <group> [flags] [modified by]
```

In each case, the <group> flag is the name of the newsgroup to be added, deleted, or modified. The flags on newgroup and changegroup should match the fourth field in the active file as described above. If the group already exists and a newgroup command is issued for the same group, it's equivalent to issuing a changegroup command for that group. Both the [flags] and the [creator/modified by] arguments can be omitted, and the group will default to being "y," local posting allowed with no creator or modifying E-mail address listed.

Adding and Removing Newsfeeds

After modifying the newsfeeds file to add a new site to only feed, run the "ctlinnd begin <site>" command to start feeding the new site instead of reloading the entire server. It is also prudent to run "ctlinnd checkfile" to make sure that any changes made to the newsfeeds file were syntactically correct, and INN automatically does this when the newsfeeds file is reloaded. Any errors found will be reported to syslog.

If a site has been removed from the newsfeeds file but a batch file still exists for that site, running "ctlinnd drop <site>" will remove the site from the list of active feeds and flush out the batch file. Merely running a "ctlinnd flush <site>" will just clear out the batch file. If no site is specified, then flush tries to clean out all of the batch files and also writes the active and history files to disk, flushing the local server as well.

Reloading the Server

After modification of any of the following files, the news server must be reloaded for any changes to take effect: history, hosts.nntp, newsfeeds, active, overview.fmt. The reload command will also take an argument of "all" to reload all of the above files. If the argument passed to ctlinnd reload is history, then the history database is closed and reopened. If the argument is hosts.nntp, then the nntp access file is reread. If the argument is active or newsfeeds, then both the active and newsfeeds files are reloaded. If the argument is overview.fmt, then the overview format configuration file is reread.

In this case, the optional third argument to the ctlinnd command is the reason for the reload, and it is logged by syslog to the appropriate file. To reload the entire server because you added a new feeding site, for example, do the following:

```
ctlinnd reload all "added a new upstream feeding site"
```

Stopping and Starting Connections

Ctlinnd is also used to control who can connect to the server to read, post, and feed articles over NNTP. To allow or disallow client readers, use the command "ctlinnd readers <flag> <reason>" where the <flag> starts with either "n," for disallowing connections, or "y," for allowing connections, and the <reason> is the test fed to the client when it tries to connect. To reallow connections the <reason> must match the <reason> given at the time of disallowing connections or be an empty string. Similarly, issuing a "ctlinnd reject <reason>" command will reject any connection that would be handed off to nnrpd with the <reason> given as the explanation. To allow connections after a reject, issue the "ctlinnd allow <reason>" command where the <reason> must match that of the reject command or be an empty string.

To pause the server so that no new incoming articles are accepted, issue the "ctlinnd pause <reason>" command and reenable connections with the "ctlinnd go <reason>" command. When pausing the server, no existing connections are closed but the history database is closed and written out to disk. This is only used for short-term locking, as when replacing the history file. Doing a pause also sends a note to the readers command so that no new readers may connect.

To stop incoming articles and sever all current connections, use the "ctlinnd throttle <reason>" command. This is a more long-term lock which also closes the history base and sends a no to the readers command. To reenable connections, send a "ctlinnd go <reason>" command. Server throttling is normally done when expire is being run or when extensive work is being done on some critical part of the news system.

Expiring and Reporting

As mentioned above, expire is one of the news processes that shuts down all connections to the server. Expire is one of the clean-up jobs that is run from the script "news.daily" each night. The script news.daily is usually run once a night but can be run more or less often if desired, from cron as the news user.

Typically news.daily removes old articles from the news server, rotates logs, and sends reports but it can be configured to each individually. The news.daily program takes several keywords as arguments, but we will only discuss the more commonly used flags.

If news.daily is running more than once a day, the flag "notdaily" can be specified for one or more of the cron runs so that log file processing and rotation only get done once. The "norotate" argument only specifies that the news logs should not be rotated. If the logs are not rotated but a report is sent every time, you will see duplicate information in the subsequent reports. The argument "noexpire" can be used to specify that no old article removal should be done, and the argument "nomail" specifies that no reporting mail should be sent to the newsmaster.

Article Expiration

If expiration is being done, the "expire.ctl" file is consulted by the "expire" process to determine which articles should no longer be kept on disk based upon their age logged in the history file. The "expire" program itself oversees the removal of the articles and calls other programs that do the removal and updating of the history, overview, and active files. The "expirerm" program is a script that calls "fastrm" to remove the articles listed in the file specified as the argument. By default, expirerm uses the "expire.list" file in the news log directory.

The expire.ctl file tells the INN software how long to remember Message-IDs in the history file and after how many days articles in certain newsgroups or hierarchies should be removed. The news article removal can also be based on the type of group, whether it be moderated (M), unmoderated (U), or all (A) groups. The first field of the colon-separated entry in the expire.ctl file is the wildcard match on the newsgroup name. The second field is either M, U, or A as matches the description above. The third field is the minimum time the article should be kept even if its expiration header claims otherwise. The fourth field is the default number of days that an article with no overriding expiration header should be kept, and the fifth field is the date at which articles will be purged. To expire all newsgroups in the alt.binaries hierarchy quickly because of space issues, put the following line in the expire.ctl file:

```
alt.binaries.*:A:2:3:5
```

Several arguments to news.daily determine how and when articles are removed during the article expiration process.

The "expireover" argument tells INN that after the old articles have been removed from the spool, the overview databases should be updated to reflect the new status of the articles. If the "delayrm" argument is used, then the names of the articles to be removed are written to a separate file and then batched for removal by the programs "expire" and "expireover." The "expire-overflags='<expireover args>'" argument tells news.daily what flags to pass to the expireover process if the "expireover" argument is specified. If delayrm is specified, news.daily passes the "-z" flag to both expire and expireover to tell them to use batching mode.

Log Rotation and Reporting

While the expiration process is taking place, news.daily logs all of the output to a file. When the expiration is done, news.daily uses the "scanlogs" program and its supporting scripts to parse all of the log files that the news server has built up for the past day (or since the logs were last rotated). Very detailed information about the number of articles accepted and transmitted and any errors that occurred are printed up and added to the expire data and mailed off in a report to the newsmaster. As its final step, the news.daily process rotates the old logs into a separate directory and then unthrottles or unpauses the server so connections are once again accepted.

10.7 INN Configuration and Testing

Now that the system installation and a brief overview of the INN internals has been completed, you must configure how news is to be handled on a daily basis. This includes declaring whom the machine accepts news from and sends news to, what machines may have read and posted access to the server, how long articles are kept, how new groups are created, and more. Each aspect of daily operation is generally handled by a separate file, usually found in the $INNSRC/site/ directory. After everything in the site directory is configured, do a "make install" to put the files into the news etc directory.

The news administrator must first decide what newsgroups to carry and what kind of control to have over new group creation. Starting out with the entire Usenet hierarchy leaves much to be desired because many groups are in foreign languages, large binaries, or just generally unwanted topics of discussion. If the number of groups to be carried is reasonably large, the newsmaster can go out to a site like uu.net and obtain an active file and trim it down.

Obtaining a Usenet Feed and Exchanging News

Once an active file has been created with the desired groups, the newsmaster must obtain a feed from some other machine. Newsfeeds are generally obtained from a service provider, or perhaps a friend. Once a feed is found, the feeding machine will need to access port 119 on the new news server to pass news, and the new news server will need to be able to access port 119 on the feeding machine to pass news back. Make sure that no firewalls are in place between the two machines, and then change the news machine's configuration files to allow the remote machine to have access.

To add new news hosts, edit the newsfeeds, hosts.nntp, and nntpsend.ctl files as described above. If news is not being received by the remote machine, try opening a telnet session to the remote machine on port 119. If a denial message appears, the remote site probably does not have the local machine in its hosts.nntp file. If news cannot get from the remote site to the local site, check the local hosts.nntp file and all of the logs in the news log directory for any errors.

10.8 Common Error Messages and What They Mean (Taken from the INN FAQ)

When Innd Fails to Start

- inndstart: inndstart cant bind Address already in use

  Either another news daemon is already running or something else is using port 119. Try opening a telnet session to port 119 or using netstat to identify who or what is connected to the port. Also check in `/etc/inetd.conf` to see if there are entries there.

- SERVER cant dbminit <history file> No such file or directory

  The history file was never created. Run the BUILD script or run "makehistory" by hand.

- SERVER internal no control and/or junk group

  When the active file was created, the control group was not an entry. Either run the BUILD script again or add the following entries for the junk or control groups to the active file by hand and restart the server:

  ```
  control 0000000000 0000000000 y
  junk 0000000000 0000000000 y
  ```

- Can't set up communication (bind failure)

  This indicates that the permissions on the _PATH_NEWSCONTROL directory are set wrong. Try installing INN again using the BUILD script or by doing a "make install."

- SERVER bad_newsfeeds no feeding sites

  Before the news server is brought on-line, it must feed to at least one site. If you're just testing a channel feed or local posting, a dummy entry must be added to the newsfeeds file to make INN think that the machine will be sending news out.

- SERVER cant GetConfigValue <argument>

  This indicates that <argument> is not defined in the inn.conf file and should be. Testing the inn.conf file by running the "inncheck" script should also print a message explaining what is wrong.

- INND: PID file exists -- unclean shutdown!

  This message is printed when INN is restarted after being shutdown improperly. The rc.news script will do some sanity checking and janitorial tasks as described above. The server will actually start after INN cleans up after itself.

When Innd Was Running but Then Dies or Throttles

- SERVER cant fork /some/tool Resource temporarily unavailable

  This error indicates that the news server has run out of processes and was unable to fork off the requested process as a result. If the news user already has an unlimited number of processes (unlimit maxproc), then try increasing the number of processes in the kernel.

- SERVER cant remalloc xx bytes Cannot allocate memory

  This error indicates that innd wanted to grow its data segment to a size larger than is allowed for a process. As above, unlimit the amount of space that the news user can allocate (unlimit datasize) or rebuild the kernel with a larger max number of processes.

- Bad file number writing history file -- throttling

  This error generally indicates that the news server hit the space limit for a given file. The news user must have a ulimit of 0 (infinite) to ensure that the history and active files do not grow too large.

  ```
  <site> <article-id> 436 No space
  ```

  This indicates that innd could not create a directory for a new newsgroup. This generally indicates that the section of the news spool that the new group creation was attempted in has the wrong permissions and/or ownership.

- File exists writing symlinking article file—throttling

  This error happens when innd writes an article and then tries to symlink the crosspost to another hierarchy in which the article ID it tries to use is already taken. This generally happens only if the active database and what exists on disk differ from one another or if an older version of Linux MMAP is being used. To solve the former, rebuild the active database. To solve the latter, rebuild INN with MMAP disabled.

- Not a directory writing article file—throttling

  This indicates that there is a directory in the spool that innd thinks is a file. Normally this only happens after a crash and disk corruption when fsck guesses wrong at the file type. To correct this, remove the offending file.

- Server throttled No space left on device writing article file

  If this error occurs, either the machine is out of disk space or inodes. To see how much space is used, execute "df -k"; to see the inode usage, execute "df -i." If the machine has space but is out of inodes, the newsmaster may want to consider rebuilding the partition to adjust the size of an inode and/or adjust the size values for the block/fragsize.

- `innd: ME cant renumber ... lo too wide`

This error occurs when articles in the news spool have article IDs larger than what will fit in the active file article ID field. To fix this, you must shut down the news server and edit the active file by hand, adding another leading zero to the high watermark numbers for each group. To do this safely, do the following:

```
ctlinnd throttle 'repairing the active file'
perl -lane 'split;printf "%s %.10d %.10d %s\n", @F' active
   > active.new
mv active active.old
mv active.new active
ctlinnd reload "fixed active file"
ctlinnd go 'repairing the active file'
```

Non-Fatal Errors While INN Is Running

- cant read Connection reset by peer

  This means that the client closed the NNRP connection ungracefully and usually does not indicate a problem.

- Expire had problems removing articles

  Something went wrong when expire tried to remove old articles. To find out what happened, take a look in the expire.log in the news log directory. Expire will also report this error if it finds no new articles to remove, so depending on the expire times, this message may crop up during the first few days that a news server is brought on-line.

- Can't replace history files, cross-device link

  Expire reports this problem when it runs out of space trying to create two copies of the history file. The news machine should have enough room to keep up to three copies of the history file on disk at all times. If the partition that the history file is kept on is not big enough for this, you can expire in a different directory by specifying the expdir=<directory> as an argument to news.daily.

- Group not matched (removed?) <groupname>—Using default expiration

  This merely indicates that the newsgroup <groupname> was removed from the server and it is using the default expiration to remove articles from the spool. These messages should disappear once the default expiration date for the last article has been reached.

Other Common Problems

- All articles received get fed back to the provider.

  This generally indicates that the entry that is set up for the feeding site in the newsfeeds file does not match the name used in the feeding site's path. INN will not refeed news to any host that has its name in the Path: header. To correct this, modify the newsfeeds file so that the names match or add a distrib pattern match as previously described in the newsfeeds section of this chapter.

- The active file and/or history file gets deleted.

  Losing the history and/or active files can be rather devastating, especially if both are lost at once. Luckily, INN keeps a copy of the previous night's files in the news log directory filed under active.old and history.old. Copy the corrupted files out of the way and copy the previous night's files in their place. If backups of the files are not kept, the file(s) will have to be rebuilt from scratch. The active file is particularly a problem because it does not get moderation specifics correct a good portion of the time.

If the history file was corrupted or lost, run "makehistory -bu" to pick up any new articles that were added since the corruption. If the active file was lost or corrupted, it should renumber when INN is restarted. If it doesn't, issue a "ctlinnd reactive" to force INN to pick up the new high and low watermarks.

Where to Look For Help

If the FAQ does not have an answer for the problem that the machine is experiencing, there are other places to turn for help. Several web sites, newsgroups, and mailing lists include information about using INN on Linux and setting up a newsfeed.

Web Sites

```
http://www.isc.org/inn.html
http://www.oceanwave.com/technical-resources/unix-admin/news.html
http://wwwcis.ohio-state.edu/~barr/INN.html
http://thereisnocabal.news.erols.com/patches/
```

Newsgroups

```
news.admin.technical
news.software.nntp
the comp.os.linux groups
```

Mail Addresses

```
bugs@isc.org
```

10.9 Summary

For many users, getting access to NetNews provides a source of information on a large series of subjects. But many Linux setups do not have the spare disk space to handle a full feed. In this case, you may only want a partial feed to handle the newsgroups that would be most beneficial to your users. Plan ahead for the disk space and time needed to maintain a feed before getting a feed.

Setting Up FTP Services 11

Virtual, anonymous and more.

The File Transfer Protocol (FTP) is one of the most frequently used services available on the Internet. Setting up an anonymous FTP server is fairly straightforward. Other services, like virtual FTP hosts and ftp only accounts, are a little more tricky.

We'll cover how to set up all of these services in this chapter and then talk about a few client programs.

11.1 Anonymous FTP

This is the most common service: a single anonymous FTP server on a machine. Most Linux distributions will set up this up automatically. Typically the ftp root will be `/home/ftp`.

If, for some reason, anonymous FTP isn't set up on your machine, it is very simple to set up.

Setting Up Anonymous FTP

In the instructions below, ~ftp is the home of the anonymous ftp user as specified in the /etc/passwd file.

The FTP daemon, ftpd, recognizes the anonymous user and adjusts some aspects of the account. The root directory for access is set to ~ftp. This means that access is limited to the directories and files in ~ftp at best. Permissions can, of course, restrict access further. Because the file system root is changed, several directories and files need to be set up to allow a minimal level of functionality.

- ~ftp should be owned and only writable by root.
- ~ftp/bin should also be owned and only writable by root. It should contain the ls program (located at /bin/ls). ~ftp/bin/ls should be owned by root and have the mode ---x--x--x, chmod 111 ~ftp/ bin/ls if this is not the case.
- ~ftp/lib should contain ld-linux.so.1, ld.so and libc.so.5. These can be found in /lib.

If you want listings to translate user and group IDs into names, you will need to create ~ftp/etc. It should have mode 755 and contain passwd and group files that associate IDs with names. The encrypted password field is not used and should be empty. The only fields that need to be present are username, UID, and GID.

The upload and download directory ~ftp/pub should have mode 755 and be owned by ftp. This will allow others to upload and read from the directory. You can of course change ownership and permissions to allow the level of access you desire.

The user "ftp" should have an entry in /etc/passwd similar to this:

```
ftp:*:14:50:FTP User:/home/ftp:
```

FTP is a service controlled by inetd and, as such, requires an entry in / etc/services. Once again, this should be set up already, but if it is not, add an entry like this:

```
ftp `  21/tcp
```

11.2 FTP Access for User Accounts

When someone connects with a username other than `anonymous` (or its alias `ftp`), three conditions must be met for access to be granted. The username and (non-null) password combination must be valid. The username must not be present in `/etc/ftpusers`. The user must have a valid shell, that is, it must be listed in `/etc/shells`.

11.3 FTP-only Accounts

It is possible to set up user accounts that can be accessed only via FTP. These accounts behave similarly to the anonymous account and can coexist peaceably with it. Since the directory root is reset, you will need to set up the `bin`, `lib`, and `etc` directories as they are set up for the anonymous account.

To restrict particular accounts to FTP-only access you need to edit (or possibly create) the `/etc/ftpaccess` file.

The example below sets up two users, `ftpbob` and `jane`, as FTP-only accounts.

```
#
# /etc/ftpaccess
#
class all real,guest,anonymous *
class ftponly ftpbob,jane *

loginfails 5

readme README*    login
readme README*    cwd=*

message /welcome.msg  login
message .message      cwd=*

compress      yes         all
tar           yes         all
overwrite     yes         real
chmod         no          guest,anonymous
delete        no          guest,anonymous
rename        no          guest,anonymous
overwrite     no          guest,anonymous

guestgroup ftponly
```

The class line sets up groups of users and a host pattern to match against the remote host. The "*" matches all hosts.

The corresponding `/etc/passwd` entries are

```
jane:9pfhxXoQVw:518:518:Jane's FTP-only Account:/a/ftp/jane:/bin/false
ftpbob:I8Leijpehfp:518:518:Bob's    FTP-only    Account:/a/ftp/ftpbob/./
    incoming:/bin/false
```

The shells for the two users are both valid shells that will deny them shell access. The home directory will become the root directory for the ftp session. Additionally, the `ftpbob` account will be `chdir()`ed into `/a/ftp/ftpbob/incoming`.

You probably noticed that the ftpaccess file sets up a number of other parameters as well.

The "`real`" word is a keyword for any valid account, "`anonymous`" stands for any anonymous account, and "`guest`" refers to guest level access accounts.

The `compress` and `tar` entries tell `ftpd` when to allow on-the-fly (de)compression or (un)tarring.

The README and message entries set up patterns to search for files to be automatically displayed (message) when connecting and entering directories (README).

In the above example, low-access accounts (anonymous and guest) are forbidden from deleting, changing the mode of, or renaming files.

`loginfails` does what you expect it to do: Drop the connection after the specified number of failed login attempts.

11.4 Virtual FTP Hosts

Virtual FTP is frequently used by ISPs to set up FTP services for multiple domains on one server. The stock Linux `ftpd` does not support virtual FTP hosts. You will need to obtain `wu-ftpd` and the patches to enable virtual host support.

The source for `wu-ftp` can be found at `ftp://wuarchive.wustl.edu/packages/wuarchive-ftpd/`. You will need version 2.4 as it is the version the patches are made for.

The patches themselves can be found at `http://www.westnet.com/providers/multi-wu-ftpd.txt`.

You must use IP virtual hosting in order for this to work. See the chapter on IP and firewalling on how to set up your ethernet card to answer multiple IPs.

Save the patch into a file and then apply it in the source code directory of `wu-ftp`. Assuming the patch is stored in `wu-ftpd-patch` in the source directory, enter

```
# patch < wu-ftpd-patch
```

You will need to add a line or lines similar to `/etc/ftpaccess`:

```
virtual 10.10.10.200 /ftp/ftp-virtual1/ /ftp/ftp-virtual1/etc/
   banner.msg
```

The first argument to the virtual directive is the IP of the virtual host; the second is the root of the ftp area for that host; and the third is the location of the file containing the welcome message.

tftp

Trivial tftp is a very simplistic FTP service. It has no user validation and no ability to change directories or to list the contents of the directories. It can get or put files in binary or ASCII mode. That's it.

Some remote devices may require a tftp host for part of their booting process, but, in general, tftp is used fairly rarely and you will likely want to disable it in `/etc/services` unless you need it.

11.5 FTP Clients

There are two types of ftp clients: those which support user-based FTP and those which support only anonymous FTP.

Today, probably the most common way to access anonymous FTP sites is with a Web browser. These are typically the only clients that only support anonymous FTP.

There are also a number of other FTP clients ranging from the simple command line like the `ftp` program to full-screen clients like NcFTP to graphical clients like XFTP.

ftp

The ftp program is a command-line-based program. It is not particularly friendly but should always be available on any Linux (or UNIX system).

NcFTP

NcFTP is a full-screen (still ASCII) ftp client. It sports a number of features, including

- A list of shortcuts for FTP hosts including storage for username and passwords (if so desired) for each host (see Figure 11–1).

```
Xterm                                                              _ □ ×
                              Bookmark Editor

                                 Number of bookmarks:  24
 Open selected site:      <enter>   aeneas        aeneas.mit.edu
 Edit selected site:      /ed       biology       biology.com
 Delete selected site:    /del      chemplace     chemplace.com
 Duplicate selected site: /dup      ftp11         ftp11.netscape.com
 Add a new site:          /new      funet         ftp.funet.fi
                                    galileo       ratatosk.org
 Up one:                  <u>       linux         ftp.linux.org
 Down one:                <d>       ncsa          ftp.ncsa.uiuc.edu
 Previous page:           <p>       neosoft       ftp.neosoft.com
 Next page:               <n>       python        ftp.python.org
                                    ranger        ranger.range.orst.edu
 Capital letters selects first      ratatosk      ratatosk.org
    site starting with the letter.  redhat        ftp.redhat.com
                                    sunet         ftp.sunet.se
 Exit the bookmark editor: <x>      sunsite       sunsite.unc.edu
                                    tcp           ftp.tcp.com
                                    wayga         wayga.net
```

Figure 11–1   A list of shortcuts for FTP hosts.

- Automatic connection as anonymous (sends "anonymous" as the username and a string you supply as the password; the anonymous FTP password is stored in the rc file in your home directory).
- The screen is split into a command typing area and an output area (see Figure 11–2).

```
 Xterm                                                          _ □ X

Email linuxguys@sunsite.unc.edu with comments/complaints about this archive.

Please see HINTS for information on how to get most effective use out of
this archive.  HINTS was last updated on 17 March 1997.


> ls

!INDEX              MIRRORS.html        games/
!INDEX.html         NAMES               info.for.cdrom.vendors
!INDEX.short.html   NEW                 kernel/
00-find.Linux.gz    NEW.html            libs/
ALPHA/              NEW.logs/           logos/
GCC/                POLICY.html         lost+found/
HINTS               README              ls-lR.gz
HOW.TO.SUBMIT       X11/                ls-lR.html.gz
INDEX.whole.gz      apps/               science/
Incoming/           commercial/         search/
LICENSES/           devel/              system/
LSM-TEMPLATE        distributions/      utils/
MIRRORS             docs/               welcome.html
sunsite.unc.edu                                            /pub/Linux
 sunsite>
```

Figure 11–2 The screen is split into a command typing area and an output area

- Filename and command completion using the TAB key.
- Viewing of remote files with a pager like less or more.
- Support for wildcard expressions when putting or getting files.
- Support for ftp: URLs, for example, `ftp://www.snerdwump.org/pub/wump-1.2.4.tgz`.
- Batch operation.

XFTP

XFTP is an X/Motif-based FTP client. It supports handy things such as selecting groups of files for upload or download. It can also move files between other computers (i.e., neither of them need be running XFTP, though they both need to be running some form of ftpd).

Local and remote files can be viewed with a built-in pop view or with a user-specified viewer such as emacs, less, or more. Additionally you can specify a program to use for various graphic formats.

Finally, the interface allows for a large amount of user configuration.

A screen shot of XFTP is shown in Figure 11-3 on the following page.

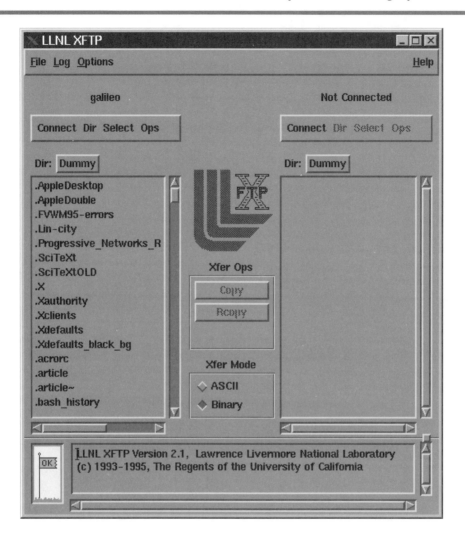

Figure 11–3   XFTP

11.6 Summary

FTP is an incredibly useful service, one of the few that has not been eclipsed by the Web. (Things like gopher, archie, and wais are all but dead now, replaced by Web equivalents.)

Most of you will, at worst, have to set up an anonymous FTP server and possibly make sure your users can access their accounts via FTP. This can be trivial if your machine was set up to handle FTP initially, as most Linux boxes are. You may have to create a few files and directories.

The trickier things to set up are FTP-only accounts and virtual FTP clients. Hopefully we've provided enough information to get you started

- Anonymous FTP is located in /home/ftp
- FTP clients give nicer interfaces to FTP

Applications for Linux 12

Linux can be more than just a server—there are a growing number of desktop applications.

This chapter is a survey of the more popular applications for Linux. These applications run the gamut from integrated office suites to symbolic math programs to emulators for running software from other operating systems.

12.1 Office Products, Word Processors, and Editors

In this category fall office suites, stand-alone word processors and spreadsheets, editors, and publishing tools.

Applixware

Made by Applix, Inc. (`http://www.applix.com/`), Applixware is probably the most complete and tightly integrated office suite available for Linux. It is still not as slick as similar products from Corel, Claris, or Microsoft, but it is making strides toward that goal.

Applixware is invoked by typing "`applix`" at a shell prompt. This brings up the main window (Figure 12–1) from which you can start Words (a full-featured word processor), Graphics (a drawing tool), Spreadsheets (a spreadsheet program), Presents (a presentation editor), Mail (a mailer that supports local or POP mail), and Builder (a tool for creating macros and custom Applixware applications).

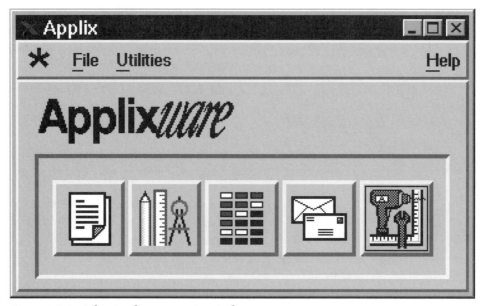

Figure 12–1   The Applixware main window.

Applix Words

As mentioned above, Applixware is very tightly integrated. Documents can be shared between applications and inserted into documents made by a different app (see Figure 12–2).

Staroffice

Staroffice is another office suite, but unfortunately it requires Caldera's OpenLinux and will not run on other distributions. It is made by Star Divi-

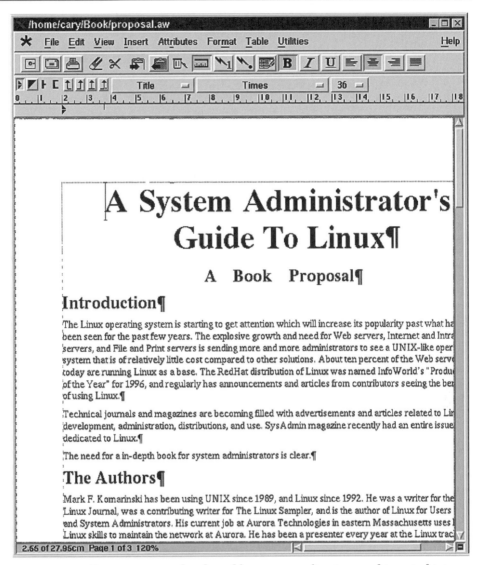

Figure 12–2 Documents can be shared between applications and inserted into documents made by a different app

sion (`http://www.stardivision.com/`), a full-featured office productivity suite that includes StarWriter (word processor), StarCalc (spreadsheet), StarDraw (graphics and presentation package), StarImage (image manipulation), StarGallery (multimedia tool), and StarChart (graphing and charting making utility).

WordPerfect

Corel's WordPerfect 7 (and previous versions) has been ported to Linux by the Software Development Corporations (`http://www.sdcorp.com/`) and WordPerfect 8 should be ported soon. WordPerfect is probably the most feature-rich word processor available for Linux.

The downside of using WordPerfect is that the rest of Corel's office products have not been ported with it, so it does not have a nice, well-integrated office suite to interact with. That said, Corel itself is porting its entire office suite to Java. This of course will let any machine with a Java virtual machine run it. For more information on Corel Office for Java, see `http://www.corel.com/javastrat/index.htm`.

Figure 12-3 is a screen shot of the 30-day evaluation version of WordPerfect 7.

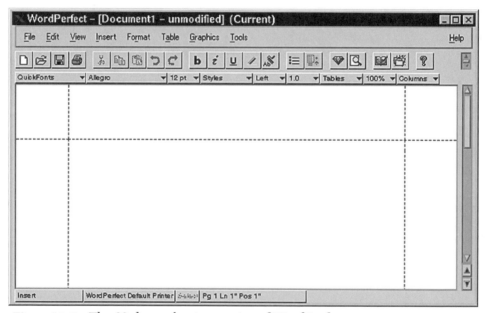

Figure 12–3   The 30-day evaluation version of WordPerfect

Plan

Plan is a freeware schedule manager. It requires Motif or LessTif (see below) to compile. It allows for sharing appointment information between users and various methods of notification (see Figure 12–4).

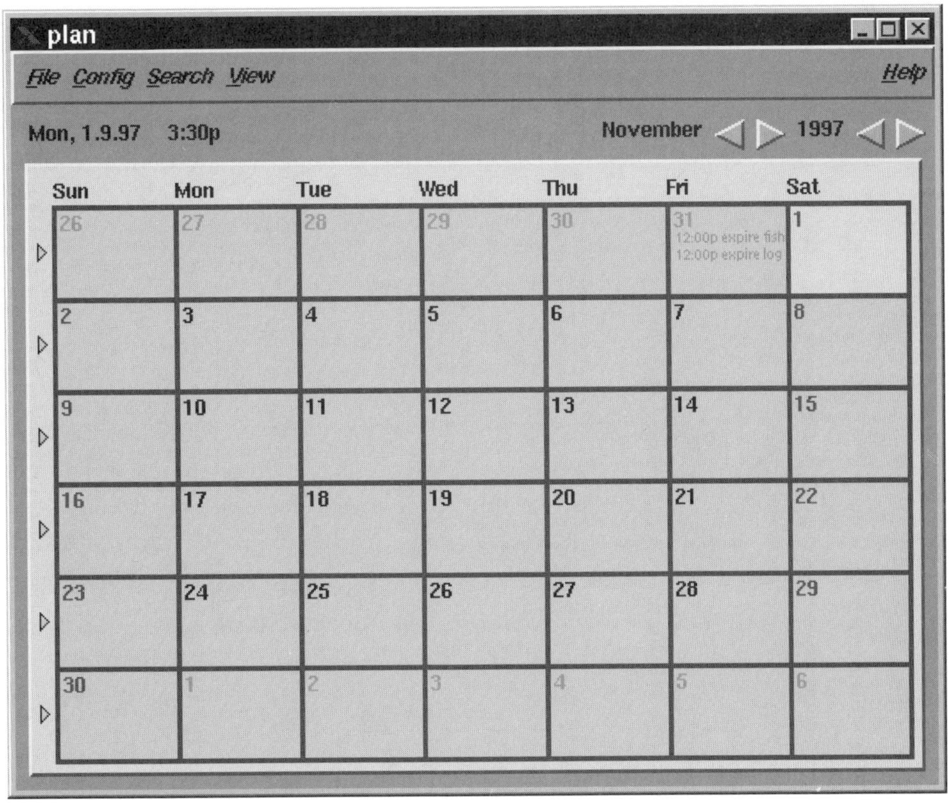

Figure 12–4   Plan is a freeware schedule manager.

NExS

The Network Extensible Spreadsheet is made by X Engineering Software Systems (`http://www.xess.com/`). NExS is a fully featured spreadsheet of with nearly 250 built-in functions, sheet sizes up to 32,767 rows x 4,096 columns, importing and exporting of tab-separated data or other spreadsheet formats, and C API (see from 12–5).

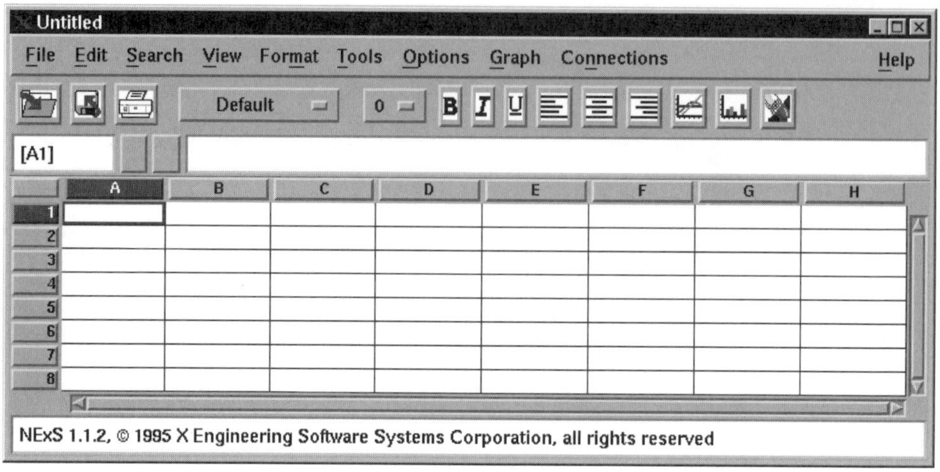

Figure 12–5   The Network Extensible Spreadsheet

TeX/LaTex

TeX is the original UNIX typesetting program. It is not a word processor and has no editing environment. TeX files can be created with any text editor. They are subsequently processed by TeX to create a formatted document.

Because TeX source is plain text and because TeX is free and has been ported to virtually every platform, documents created with it are completely portable.

When a TeX or related file is processed, the output is sent to a DVI (Device Independent) file. DVI is a flexible format that can be viewed with a simple, lightweight viewer or translated into other formats, for example, postscript for printing.

Over the years a number of extensions and utilities for TeX have been developed:

- LaTeX—by far the most common TeX extension. It is actually a set of macros to allow a higher level of interaction with TeX, which makes it easier to use. It provides specific modes for articles, books, and letters.

- BibTex—a bibliography and citation system. It will also allow you to build bibliographies for a particular document from a larger, possibly shared, bibliography.

- SliTex—specially designed for making overhead slides or large print documents for presentations.

- MakeIndex—a utility for creating an index for a TeX or LaTeX document. It supports up to three levels of indexing.

- HyperTeX—an extension for TeX that lets you create hyperlinked documents. The source then passes on the hyperlinking information to the `.dvi` file which can subsequently be translated into Acrobat format. (Acrobat is essentially an overlay for encoded, compressed Postscript that supports hyperlinking.)

- LaTeX2HTML—a utility for translating LaTeX source files into HTML files. It will create a hyperlinked table of contents, translate mathematical formulae into embedded GIFs, and properly handle references and footnotes.

TeX is supported by the Comprehensive TeX Archive Network. CTAN can be accessed at `http://www.tex.ac.uk/` where you can find information on LaTeX and other TeX extensions.

Xemacs

Xemacs (see Figure 12–6) is an enhanced version of GNU emacs for X. Xemacs is an incredibly full-featured editor. It has editing modes for dozens of types of files, including HTML, C, Perl, Python, C++, Makefile, TeX, LaTeX, and FORTRAN, just to name a few.

Additionally, Xemacs supports speech synthesis and voice control. This combined with the Usenet News read, Web browser, and mail reader make it an obvious choice for sight-impaired users.

Xemacs supports editing of multiple buffers in multiframes. Frames can also be split into subwindows either vertically or horizontally.

Xemacs can also be run in a screen mode. In this situation you will loose some functionality, mainly that relating to frames and pull-down menus.

Figure 12–6   Xemacs main window.

12.2 Drawing, Graphics, and Image Viewing and Manipulation

Xv

Xv is a shareware image viewer and translator. It supports GIF87, JPEG, TIFF (compressed and uncompressed), PostScript, PPM, PGM, PBM, Sun Rasterfile, TARGA, FITS, IRIS RGB, and PM (whew!). It can read; write;

edit colors and gamma corrections; process a number of algorithms (oil painting, edge detection, blurring, sharpening); and crop.

Gimp

The GNU Image Manipulation Program (http://www.XCF.Berkeley.EDU/ ~gimp/) is an image composition, authoring, and photo retouching tool. It is the closest thing to packages like Adobe Photoshop that are available for Linux.

It is very extensible and relies on an active user community to write plug-ins to extend GIMP's functionality.

Xfig

Xfig is a freeware drawing tool for X. It supports the drawing of interpolated lines, various polygons, grouping of objects, scaling, copying, and embedding text using many PostScript fonts. It ships with most distributions of Linux.

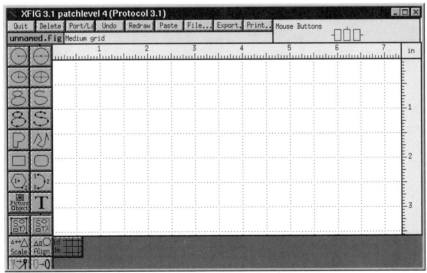

Figure 12–7 The xfig main window.

Xpaint

Xpaint is similar to xfig, but more oriented toward painting rather than drawing. It is free as well and ships with most Linux distributions.

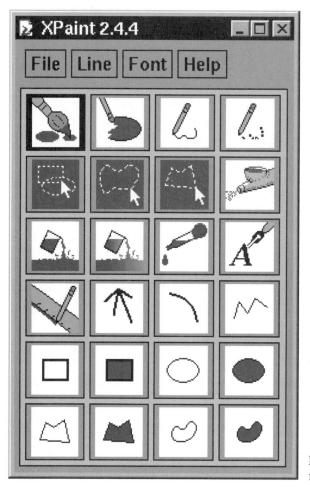

Figure 12–8   The xfig
main window.

Mapedit

Mapedit is an image map editing program from Boutell.Com, Inc. It can create client-side and server-side image maps. It supports GIF, JPEG, and PNG
image formats. It is very easy to use; even Windows users tend to find it easier to use than similar tools for Windows 3.1 or 95. More information can be
found at `http://www.boutell.com/mapedit/`.

12.3 Scientific Programs

Maple

Maple is a program for performing symbolic (as opposed to numeric) mathematical operations. The latest version has not yet been released for Linux.

Maple is a very powerful symbolic and numeric computation package. It also supports 2D and 3D plotting and animations. It has a scripting language for creating procedures and macros. The procedures can be exported to C or FORTRAN.

Figures 12-9 and 12-10 are a couple of screen shots from the demo version of Maple V Release 3.

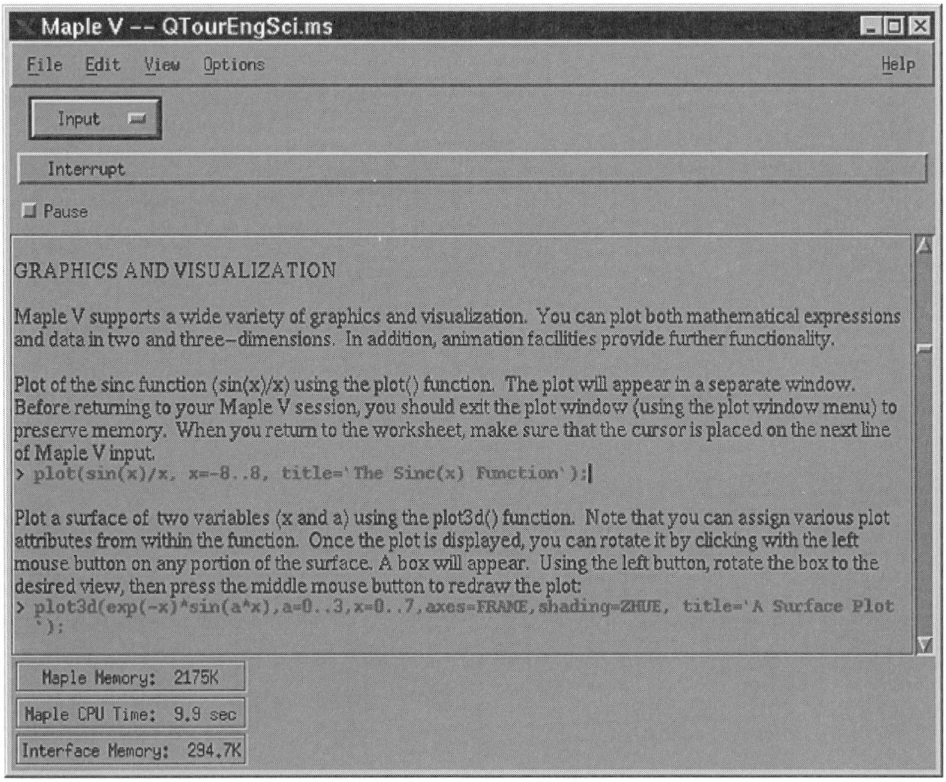

Figure 12–9   Screen shot of the demo version of Maple V Release 3.

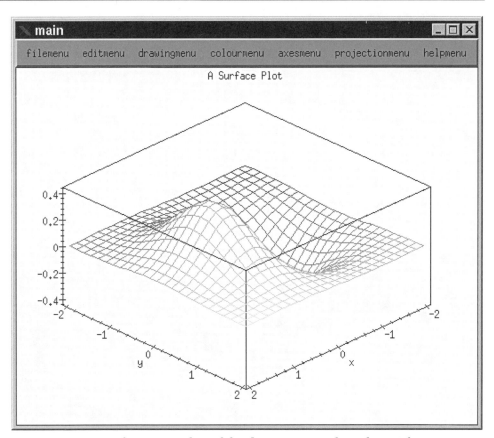

Figure 12–10   Another screen shot of the demo version of Maple V Release

Mathematica

Developed by Wolfram Research (`http://www.wolfram.com/`), Mathematica is a second symbolic manipulation package. One of the best features of Mathematica is that its kernel can be run on a separate machine from the frontend, allowing the frontend to operate independently on a client machine with other desktop apps while the kernel executes on a server machine with lots of RAM and a nice big CPU.

There is no demo or evaluation version of Mathematica available.

12.4 Emulators

Executor

ARDI (`http://www.ardi.com/`) makes a Macintosh emulator for Linux and a number of other platforms. A free, crippled demo is available. The list of completely and mostly usable software is quite long.

There is also an upcoming NeXTSTEP emulation version. Finally, students and educators can get discounts.

Executor is available in a fairly crippled demo version. It is just enough to let you know what is possible with it.

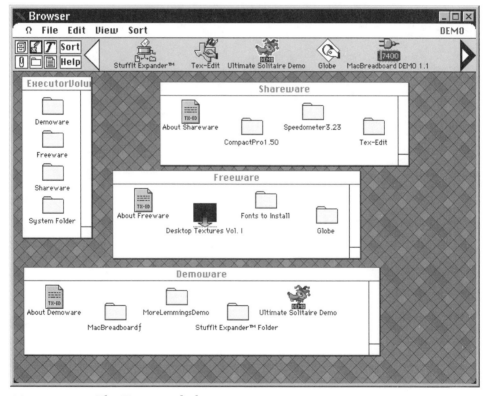

Figure 12–11 The Executor desktop.

Wabi

Wabi is a commercial MS Windows 3.1 emulator developed by Sun Microsystems. It has been ported to Linux by Caldera. It provides for cutting and pasting between applications, remote display, sharing of applications between users, Winsock networking, OLE (Object Linking on Embedding), DDE (Dynamic Data Exchange), access to serial and parallel ports, and many other features.

Wabi has a few limitations. It requires 8-bit color, so if you are running X with 24-bit color your server will need to support 8-bit pseudo-color. IPX/SPX connectivity is not available nor are virtual device drivers. See `http://www.caldera.com/doc/wabi/wabi.html` for more information.

WINE

WINE is a freeware Windows 3.1 emulator. Its home page is `http://www.qbc.clic.net/~krynos/wine_en.html`. In addition to running a number of popular Windows applications, WINE also ships a library that will allow you to build stand-alone applications from the Windows source code.

WINE is not as far along the compatibility road as Wabi is but significant progress is made with each new release.

Dosemu

A freeware DOS emulator. It can run on the console or under X in its own window. The best place to get information on Dosemu is the HOWTO which can be found at any Linux mirror site.

Acrobat

Adobe (`http://www.adobe.com/`) makes Acrobat Reader for Linux. It is available for free and, as far as we know, this is the only Adobe product for Linux.

LessTif

LessTif is a freeware clone of Motif. It is still in beta but a large number of Motif-based programs compile with it already. Additionally, precompiled programs which use the shared version of the library will run with it.

Some of the programs that can be run and/or compiled with Xmotif are

- Xemacs
- Plan
- Netscape Communicator 4 (dynamically linked with Motif)
- Xmcd (Motif-based CD player)

LessTif's home page is `http://www.lesstif.org/`; the source code, a list of compatibly applications, the FAQ, and much more can be found there.

12.5 Summary

As Linux's popularity has grown, so has commercial support for it, which in turn helps feed Linux's popularity. As we said at the beginning of this chapter, this is only a sampling of the applications available for Linux.

One of the areas that Linux is weakest in is graphical- and illustration-related applications. There are no applications that are on the level of Quark Xpress, Adobe Photoshop, PageMaker, or Illustrator. Many of these applications exist for other versions of UNIX so it should not be too difficult to port them to Linux (or other free Unices).

Linux Database Software

13

A cornucopia of DBMSs!

Linux has benefited in the realm of Database Management Systems (DBMSs) by being a UNIX-like OS. A number of software vendors have ported their Database (DB) servers to Linux. Better yet, a few have even been developed under Linux.

This chapter actually started as a section, but it got so big and DBMSs are becoming such an important aspect of computing, we gave it its own chapter. First, we will cover two very popular, lightweight servers in detail. Then, we have a less detailed listing of other native database servers. Finally, a couple of databases with partial Linux support will round out the chapter.

This is not an attempt to enumerate every database server for Linux. It is a list of the databases we've used and/or found interesting. For a more complete listing of commercial databases, see the Linux Commercial HOWTO.

Let's go over a few acronyms and terms for those who are not very familiar with the world of databases.

SQL—Structured Query Language, a language for performing queries on relational databases—Database Management Servers (DBMSs)

Key—A column or set of columns that organize a table. Often, but not always, keys will be unique; that is, a particular combination of values of the columns that make up the key must be unique (for a one-column key, this means each value in the column must be unique).

Schema—An interrelated set of tables and/or databases. Also a description of how a set of tables are joined via keys within each table.

RDBMS—Relational DBMS.

ODBMS—Object-Oriented DBMS.

13.1 MySQL and mSQL

These two servers are often mentioned together as they developed somewhat in parallel, and MySQL was initially based on mSQL. Both are used for similar tasks, as well.

mSQL

mSQL stands for mini-SQL, a shareware database server (free for non-commercial use). It supports, as its name suggests, a subset of the normal SQL specifications. Additionally, it has some extensions to SQL. Before we go any further, it is probably best to list what mSQL can't do, so you can decide if it's worth your while to use it for your particular application.

- There is no grants database or "logging in" to the database. Access is granted to users listed in `/etc/passwd` to read and/or write on a per database basis.

- Databases can be accessed locally via a UNIX domain socket or remotely via a TCP/IP socket. If you grant TCP/IP access to a database, you do so for all usernames, even though the username on the remote host is not necessarily the same person as on the local system. There is no method for finer-grained remote versus local access control.

- It does not support the Binary Large Object (BLOB) data type and is thus not really suitable for storing large blocks of data.

- It has no ALTER command. This means, for example, that once a table is created, columns cannot be added or removed or changed. While you may think that careful planning can minimize the inconvenience of this, don't fool yourself. Invariably, some outside force, be it a new product, new marketing strategy, or simple oversight, will force you to alter your carefully planned database schema.

- It is single-threaded, meaning it can process only one query at a time. As long as the load is not too heavy and the queries are not too complex, this shouldn't really be a problem though. What exactly is too heavy and complex will depend on your system and may require some experimentation on your part.

Despite these shortcomings, mSQL is still a very useful database server. For storing amounts of textual data that aren't too large, it is well suited. There are several other reasons you might want to use mSQL:

- It is lightweight, consuming only a small amount of system resources when simply running (as opposed to monsters like Oracle or Sybase which require many Mb of RAM simply to start up).

- Free for non-commercial use, and the shareware fee for commercial use is only $200.

- Large install base and widespread support on the Net.

- As a side effect of its popularity, most of the more popular languages have support for mSQL, including C (the native API is for C), Python, Java, Perl, Tcl, PHP/FI (a server-parsed scripting language which can be embedded in HTML).

- Two enhanced LIKE operators: RLIKE, which allows you to use the regular expression library and CLIKE, which is case-insensitive. Since there is a separate RLIKE that implements regex, LIKE and CLIKE do not need to do so and are thus faster than most other SQL operators which typically implement at least a subset of regex's functionality.

Lite and W3-mSQL

These two additional packages are a part of the standard mSQL distribution.

Lite is a scripting language designed for use with mSQL. Its syntax is similar to Perl. Its variables are dynamically typed, its arrays are dynamically sized, and its variable names start with a $. Its chief advantage over other languages is its tight integration with mSQL.

W3-mSQL is a Web interface to Lite that is embedded in HTML and server-side parsed. Also included is W3-auth, an access control package for

W3-mSQL. It supports users and groups and gives somewhat finer access control than the non-Web access control file. In some ways W3-mSQL is very similar to PHP, though it lacks support for other databases and is simply not as full-featured. See the chapter on Web serving for more information on PHP.

Differences between Versions 1 and 2

Version 2 is out of beta, but as of this writing, there are still a few bugs related mainly to stability. If you are happy with your mSQL 1 setup, you should probably wait a couple of patch levels (2.0.1 is the latest) or for 2.1.

If you are using mSQL 1, there are a number of reasons you might want to upgrade.

Joins in version 2 are *much* more efficient. Version 2 supports sequences, which were previously handled on the client side, and greatly enhanced indexing, which speeds lookups. Additionally, version 2 supports more data types than version 1, most importantly the TEXT type, a variable length character field.

Version 1 supports fairly rudimentary **WHERE** specifications, version 2 allows various **WHERE** clauses to be grouped with parentheses. Finally, the newer version allows for more flexible runtime configuration (as opposed to compile-time configuration) and supports more simultaneous client connections.

Some Other Notes

mSQL's author claims that it will manage up to 4 Gb of data but suggests that other system limitations will make such a large database impractical under mSQL. It's not entirely clear how this number is arrived at or, if this comes from a real-life example, to how many rows this corresponds.

Linux 1.3 or higher is required. Earlier versions do not have full mmap support which mSQL 2 requires. Additionally, you should have the kernel sources installed to ensure that you have all the necessary libraries and header files.

For an example of how to install mSQL, see the Web serving chapter.

MySQL

An increasingly popular free database server, MySQL, started off as an enhanced, free version of mSQL 1. It attempted to add a more complete set of the ANSI SQL specifications plus some enhancements. Today it implements nearly all of ANSI SQL and a bevy of additional features.

Like mSQL, it implements a regular expression like separately from LIKE to enhance performance. It is also fairly lightweight, though not as light as mSQL.

Here are some things that MySQL supports that mSQL doesn't:

- Expanded SQL, including things like an ALTER TABLE clause (allowing for columns to be added or dropped from a table after it is created), and embeddable functions which operate on all the data types.

- More data types, especially BLOBs (Binary Large Objects), and varying sizes of existing data types, for example, tiny, small, medium and large integer types.

- Usernames and passwords independent of the /etc/passwd. This is nice for CGI use. Rather than having to allow the user "nobody" read and possibly write access to the database, you can require a valid MySQL username/password combination that you can ask for on a form. The level of access a user has can be controlled on an operational (selecting, deleting, updating, reloading, or shutting down the server) database and host level.

- Optimized queries, including optimizations for joins (all joins are done in one pass).

- Multithreaded and able to handle multiple requests concurrently. This means that subsequent queries will not have to wait on a large, time-consuming query that was presented to the server first.

- Much looser licensing requirements—basically, unless you are going to sell MySQL, you don't need to purchase a license for it.

- Currently serving larger databases (as many as 50 million rows) than mSQL. This isn't to say that mSQL couldn't handle such a large database, it is just an empirical observation.

Some disadvantages to MySQL include

- Not as lightweight as mSQL.

- More complex access control system. This is probably the most difficult aspect of MySQL to master.

- Not quite as much support on the Net.

- Not as widely supported by various scripting languages.

The last point bears further elaboration. The C API for MySQL is very similar to that of mSQL, which has more widespread support. Because of this, it is fairly simple to port an mSQL application or module to MySQL. Also, the more popular CGI languages do have MySQL interfaces, including Python, Perl, Java, Tcl. There is also an ODBC API and support for MySQL in PHP.

In general, if you are frustrated with mSQL's limitations or licensing, you should definitely look into MySQL. If your favorite language doesn't have an interface and you know a little C, it is probably worth your while to port the mSQL module to MySQL.

Installing MySQL

MySQL is free in almost every circumstance, the one exception being that if you wish to sell it you have to purchase a license. Getting a legal copy of it for your use is simply a matter of FTPing the distribution. The source code is available, or if you choose, you can get a Linux binary distribution. Binaries also exist for Solaris and SunOS, as well as a growing number of other OSes.

MySQL's home page is `http://www.tcx.se/`, there are numerous mirrors: in the United States (`http://www.buoy.com/mysql`), Australia (`http://mysql.bluep.com/`), and many others all listed on the home page. Also on the home page are pointers to FTP for MySQL, the documentation home page, mailing list and contributed software.

Compiling and Installing MySQL

If you choose to compile it yourself, you will need a multithreading library. Under Linux you need the LinuxThreads library which comes with most recent versions of most Linux distributions, RedHat included. You will also need a C++ compiler, presumably g++ and libg++ under Linux. Note that libg++ is distributed separately from gcc/g++/gobj-c just as GNU libc is. Lastly you will need recent versions of gcc, at least 2.7.2; GNU make, at least 3.75; and libc, 5.4.12 or glibc, 2.0.2.

GNU autoconf is used, so there is the common sequence of configure, make, make install works. Useful options for the MySQL configure are

```
--prefix==/path/to/mysql/install/base
```

where to install MySQL

```
--localstatedir==/path/to/mysql/datafiles
```

where to keep the data files

```
--without-server
```

only compile client libraries and binaries

```
--enable-shared
```

build the shared library, `libmysqlclient.so`.

Other configure options can be listed with the `--help` option. You may also want to run an optional make check before installing.

We're not going to go into a lot of detail about how to deal with a troublesome compile since you can always fall back to a binary distribution. One thing to note is that unpacking the binary distribution and installing from the compiled source distribution will place things in slightly different directories. The binary distribution creates a directory named `mysql-<version>` and subdirectories for libraries, header files, and program files. Installing from the source makes mysql subdirectories in `/usr/local/lib` and `/usr/local/include`. This is important to keep in mind if you compile MySQL-dependent programs or modules.

Beyond making sure that you have the right versions of the tools needed to compile it, there is little to check. If you do run into trouble, the MySQL mailing list is probably the best place to ask for help. Information about it can be found in the FAQ at the MySQL home page or any of its mirrors.

Once you have it compiled, you can run the optional make check and then proceed to running the make install. This will install the MySQL in subdirectories of your install base as follows: binaries in `bin/`, the libraries in `lib/mysql`, header files in `include/mysql`, and the data area in `var/`.

Installing from a Binary Distribution.

Unpack the tarball where you want the MySQL directory to be created. It will create a directory named `mysql-<version info>-<platform info>`; you can create a link using ln or just rename it to `mysql`. The MySQL binaries will now be in `/usr/local/mysql/bin`, libraries in `/usr/local/mysql/lib`, header files in `/usr/local/mysql/include`, and `/usr/local/mysql/data` will be the home of the data files and subdirectories.

Setting Up the Grants Database and Other Data Files

The next step in our installation is to set up the grants database. Unless you've done some fiddling after the installation, you should just be able to run it and let it do its thing. What it does is set up tables for user access control. These users do not need to be system users, that is, they need not have /etc/ passwd entries.

The name of the grants database is simply mysql. It has three tables: db, host, and user. The db table lists access for the combination of user, database and host from which the user, is connecting. host controls access for the pairing of host versus database. Finally, user combines host, user and password.

To initialize the mysql database, you need to run mysql_install_db. If you used a binary distribution, in the directory created when you unpacked the archive, type

```
scripts/mysql_install_db
```

If you compiled from the source, run the above command in the top level of the source tree. This will set up root as a "superuser" when connecting locally, lock out remote users, and force other local users to be granted access on a per database level in the db table, set up db to allow any access to the test database or any database starting with "test_" to any user. It will also start the MySQL daemon, mysqld, for the first time.

Since the grants database is probably the most complex aspect of using MySQL, we'll give a few examples here. There are a few things to remember when manipulating the access tables.

- Passwords are stored encrypted.
- The tables are sorted, putting wildcard and "" entries last. The first match is then used. host is sorted first, then user, and last, for the db table, by database.
- The host table is consulted only if the host field in the user table is "". Then the privileges that are listed by the user table are logically ANDed with those in the host table.
- The results of the previous step are ORed (once again in the logical sense) with the user table.
- If there is no matching entry in db, the matching entry from host is ANDed with the matching user entry.

To start manipulating the mysql database, as root, enter

```
mysql mysql
```

If you installed from a binary distribution, you will likely have to specify the path to the `mysql` binary. If you installed from source, the binary will be in `/usr/local/bin`.

The following set of entries will thus lock out all local users unless they don't otherwise have an entry for a particular database in `db`.

```
INSERT INTO user VALUES ('local-
   host','','','N','N','N','N','N','N','N','N','N','N');

INSERT INTO user VALUES
   ('myhost','','','N','N','N','N','N','N','N','N','N','N');

INSERT INTO host VALUES ('localhost','%','Y','Y','Y','Y','Y','Y');

INSERT INTO host VALUES ('myhost','%','Y','Y','Y','Y','Y','Y');
```

In the above and the following examples myhost stands for the name of the computer where `mysqld` is running.

Now, to grant the user `cary` full access to the database `notebooks` we would add this row to the `db` table:

```
INSERT INTO db VALUES ('%','note-
   books','cary','Y','Y','Y','Y','Y','Y');
```

If we wanted to give all other users access to the data in `notebooks` but not let them modify the table:

```
INSERT INTO db VALUES ('%','notebooks','','Y','N','N','N','N','N');
```

To give the user `mark` full access with the password "osprey" from any host:

```
INSERT INTO user VALUES ('%','mark',pass-
   word('osprey'),'Y','Y','Y','Y','Y','Y','Y','Y','Y','Y');
```

To test your access control, you can use `mysqlaccess`. The syntax is straightforward:

```
mysqlaccess [host] [user] [database]
```

There are a number of options which control the amount and format of the output as well. The `--help` option lists them.

In general, it is easiest to give a user no access in the `user` table; simply set up their username and password. Then do all the access control in the `db` table. Of course, superusers have to be given full privileges in `user`. Also, if you want to give a user shutdown or reload privileges, you can do this only in the user table as well.

Now you may be a little worried about slinging your MySQL usernames and passwords over your LAN, or worse, outside it. This isn't as big a risk as you might think MySQL encrypts its network traffic to make it difficult to sniff out usernames and passwords. (Of course no decryptable encryption scheme is 100 percent foolproof. Cracking encryption is a matter of patience, cleverness, and lots of CPU power.)

You're now ready to start populating your database! Just a couple of final notes. When storing data in BLOBs or VARCHARs, MySQL doesn't allocate space in the table on disk until there are data there. This can substantially reduce the amount of disk space used by your data compared to servers where space for the entire VARCHAR or BLOB (or TEXT in mSQL) is allocated when the row is created, regardless of how much is actually stored in it.

Contributed Software for MySQL

- An Apache authorization module, useful if you have a large number of users to authenticate and lookups from the flat password file are becoming too slow.

- Another Apache module for storing your logs in an MySQL database.

- A module for running radius authentication through MySQL.

- Cyrillic language extensions (MySQL already supports German and Swedish in addition to English).

- A C++ API.

- An NSAPI (Netscape API) authentication extension (useful in the same situations that the Apache authentication module is).

xmysql: A GUI for MySQL

An X-based interface to the MySQL client, xmysql, exists and is available from the MySQL home page. It requires the Xforms library for compilation. Xforms can be found at http://bragg.phys.uwm.edu/xforms. It allows the user to choose tables and columns by pointing and clicking, doing a good part of the query building on its own. Of course it's likely that the user will have to enter some information in the **WHERE** clause.

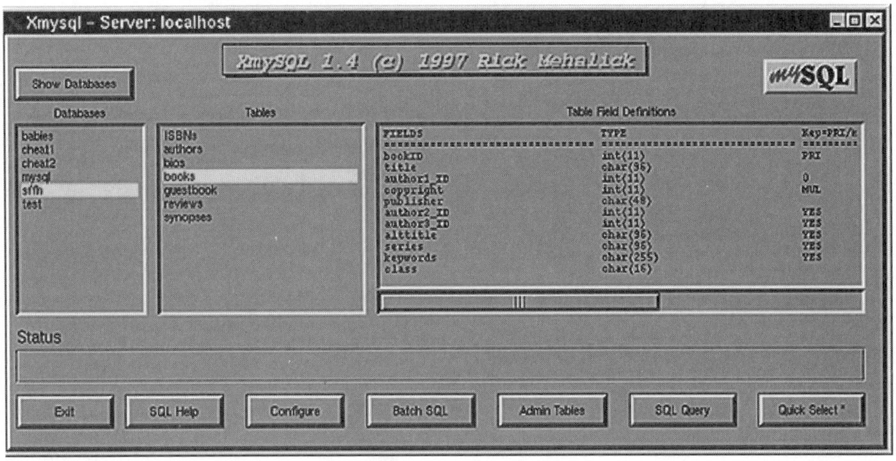

Figure 13–1   Startup screen for xmysql.

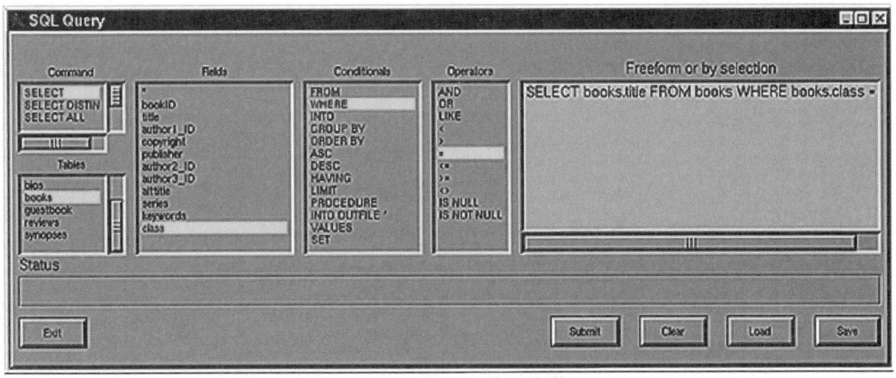

Figure 13–2   xymsql SQL Query window. The full query text is SELECT books.title FROM books WHERE books.class = 'horror.'

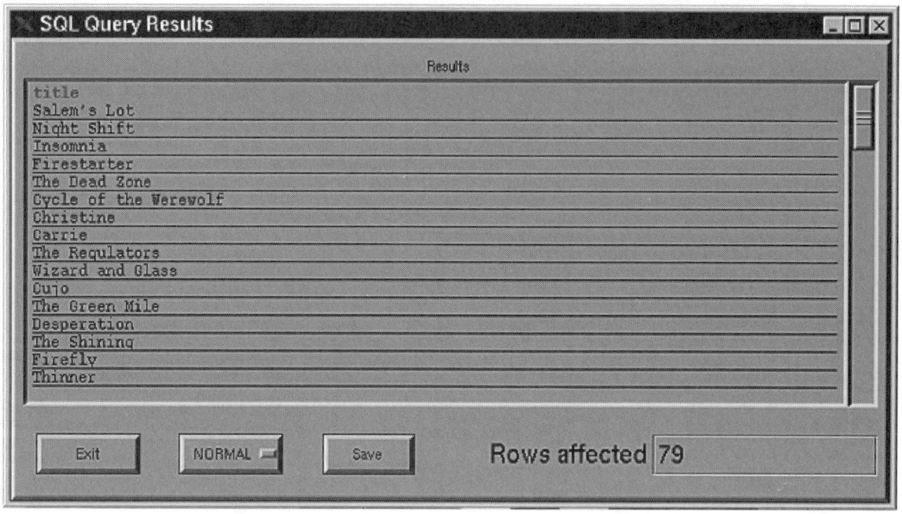

Figure 13–3   Results of the simple query from Figure 13-2.

13.2 Other Native Linux DMBSs

Freeware

PostgresSQL

Postgres has been around the UNIX world for quite some time. It is not purely relational and has some object-oriented features in its core. It's usually referred to as object-relational. In any event, in its most recent incarnation it supports nearly all of ANSI SQL plus some extensions, including embeddable functions. PostgreSQL also has APIs in C and Perl, Apache modules, and ODBC support. You can get more information from the PostgreSQL Web site: http://www.postgresql.org/.

Commercial

Solid

Solid Technologies sells its DBMS for nearly every UNIX platform, including Linux for the x86 and Alpha architectures. Support for Solid is available for Python, Perl, PHP, and, of course, C.

This SQL server is aimed at higher-end applications and larger businesses. A free evaluation copy is available. Client software for non-Linux/UNIX systems is available, too.

Solid supports a number of things you'd expect of a high-end database server:

- On-line backups (i.e., the server remains running and a "snapshot" is saved)

- Crash and power failure recovery to last checkpoint

- Fine-grained access control (at a similar level to MySQL's)

- Open Database Connectivity (ODBC) support

- Automatic crash recovery

- Symmetric Multiprocessing (SMP) support

Solid's manuals are available on-line in HTML.

Solid is designed to require a minimal amount of administration. It is easy to set up and more or less runs itself. System requirements are minimal: a couple of Mbs of disk space and a Mb of free RAM.

Pricing for Linux is considerably less than other systems. As of this writing, Solid Technologies is offering the desktop version (single-user, only UNIX socket connections) free for Linux.

Information on Solid can be found at `http://www.solidtech.com/`.

Empress

Empress is one of the first commercial databases for Linux. It is a relational database, like Sybase or Oracle. Empress supports these features (among others):

- Multimedia support
- Check pointing and rollback
- BLOBs (Binary Large Objects)
- Shared libraries and a C API
- Interfaces for Tcl/Tk, Perl, and FORTRAN (!)
- A GUI builder for quick building of graphical interfaces to Empress applications
- Two-phase commit

- A CGI pass-through for processing Empress HTML SQL (EHSQL). ESQL is embedded into a document and then parsed by the CGI and passed on to the client browser.

Personal Empress for Linux is available also.
More information on Empress can be found at

```
http://www.empress.com/.
```

Texpress

KE Software is a Canadian company that makes an object-oriented (as opposed to relational) database, along with numerous support applications and modules. It supports relational, free text, and multimedia data types.
Texpress also supports

- Massive datasets
- Object-Oriented (OO) features including inheritance.
- Extensibility. You can define methods on objects in the database. Methods can be defined for data display, validation, assignment, and branch expression. This effectively lets you write stored procedures and then associate them with a particular object or class of objects.

Texpress's design actually favors more complicated queries, processing them equally as fast, if not faster, as simpler ones. It also supports massive datasets with ease. As database applications become more and more common and complicated, these are important features to consider.

Texpress's object-oriented design typically means that data can be stored and presented in a more natural fashion, and it handles less structured data better than a relational database server.

More information on Texpress can be had at `http://www.kesoft-ware.com/`.

Essentia

Essentia is another database that incorporates some non-traditional technology. It employs what its developer, Intersoft, calls RISE, Reduced Instruction Set Engine. The communication interface is kept small and well defined. It supports both relational- and object-oriented models of data management.

Essentia also supports these features:

- Journaling and consistency checking.
- Database versions—allows you to go back and examine previous states of databases.
- Incremental backups.
- Mirroring.
- Shadowing—data to be modified are copied to a shadow and not committed to disk until a checkpoint is cleared.
- Locking at the row, table, and schema levels.

More information on Essentia and Intersoft is at `http://www.inter-soft.com/`.

13.3 Other Databases with Partial Support

Sybase

While there is no server for Linux, Sybase has made client libraries available for free. They're somewhat dated and in `a.out` format, but if you need them they're better than nothing.

Oracle

While not supported by Oracle, it is possible to run the Santa Cruz Operation (SCO) version using Intel Binary Compatibility Specification (IBCS) compiled either as a module or into the kernel. However, Oracle is complicated and expensive. It's likely that your substantial financial investment could be better spent on a database that has support for Linux such as Solid or Texpress.

13.4 Summary

As you've noticed, even if you only skimmed this chapter, Linux has a fairly large and rich set of databases available for use, ranging from the very lightweight mSQL to the freeware MySQL to larger commercial database servers like Empress, Solid, and Texpress to Oracle running in SCO emulation.

All of these servers have different strengths and weaknesses. If you find that one of the smaller free or shareware database servers isn't fulfilling your needs, nearly every commercial server listed here offers free or low-cost personal editions and/or trial versions of their larger packages.

Take a few weeks to *really* evaluate these before shelling out what could be a substantial amount of money.

Programming Languages 14

So many languages, so little time.

Aside from everything else that Linux does, it provides for some extraordinary programming languages to make repetitive tasks, or ones that don't seem easy to fix, very easy to fix.

The number of extant programming languages is quite large. There are literally scores, maybe hundreds, depending on how you choose to split a few hairs. A large portion of these, and nearly all of the more popular ones, have at least one implementation under Linux. To attempt to give even a brief summary of all of them would be a small book in and of itself. We have tried to cover the most important ones, those that we or others we know use and ones which are especially interesting. You may, of course, use any language that suits your need, and not all languages are appropriate for all situations.

In this chapter we take a break from the format in the other chapters. Two of the sections are written explicitly from a singular viewpoint: Perl and Python. Each of us has our own reasons for using the languages we use for a particular task. Mark still doesn't understand why Object-Oriented Programming (OOP) is so cool and downloads endless extensions to Perl, and Cary recognizes the usefulness of Python and does nearly all his programming including large amounts of Common Gateway Interface (CGI).

14.1 C

```
http://www.fsf.org/software/gcc/gcc.html
http://www.accu.org/
```

Neither of us are big C programmers. We know enough to hack C up a little and write small programs, but C is such an important language, in a UNIX-like system, it is rightly placed first in our list. The kernel and most of the everyday commands and tools you use are written in C. If you don't know C now, in the course of compiling and installing software, you will at least become a little familiar with it.

GCC is the "native" C compiler for Linux. It supports everything a good compiler should: optimization, debugging, ANSI C support, POSIX compliance; and more than a lot of compilers that are shipped with or are available for some commercial OSes (SunOS 4 in particular had a very lame compiler, but it was enough to compile the first stage of gcc to bootstrap your way up to a full gcc compiler which is all we ever used it for).

C is the most popular compiled language for high-performance, general programming. Because it is compiled, it is typically faster than an interpreted language like Perl or Python. C is also a fairly low-level language. This typically leads to longer development times for software. On the other hand, because it is a low-level language, it is possible to tune code to achieve very high performance.

Because C compilers exist for virtually every OS and platform, it is usually possible to port a C program to other platforms. Architecture or OS-specific libraries obviously complicate this process greatly (GUI libraries especially), but frequently analogs exist on the target platform.

When it comes right down to it, C is the foundation for all the other languages discussed here in that their compilers and/or interpreters are or were (some of the compiled languages can compile their own compilers) written at least partially in C. While nearly all of them offer high-level methods or functions for accomplishing various tasks, a proficient enough C programmer can write a program to do it just as fast if not faster.

The reason people use higher-level (often interpreted) languages is that the development time for applications is typically much shorter, and for the smaller tasks often addressed by higher-level languages, the performance trade-off is more than acceptable. This is not to say that larger applications can't be written in an interpreted language. Grail is a Web browser written in Python (using its Tcl/Tk interface and the tkinter module) which has acceptable performance. Additionally, Hotjava is a browser written in Java, a byte-compiled language; it too has decent performance. While neither is as feature-packed (or bloated) as Netscape, both have support for HTML 3.2 plus frames among other things.

14.2 C++

http://www.accu.org/

C++ is an object-oriented, compiled language whose roots lie in C (as its name suggests). It is not as popular as C, mainly because both it and OOP are younger than C. C++ and C mix very well together: It is easy to link object files from either language and thus mix the two languages within an application. VRweb, a VRML scene viewer, and MySQL, a freeware database server, are two applications that do this.

GNU's g++ is the C++ compiler most commonly shipped with all Linux distributions.

To dispel a common misconception, knowledge of C is not necessary to learn C++. While it is certainly useful to know C before learning C++, it's no more a necessity than knowing Basic before learning FORTRAN. They're two separate languages.

For applications where an OO language is better suited or desired, and the performance of a compiled language is necessary, C++ is the most popular choice. It is more and more frequently used in GUIs, databases, and other applications where classes and inheritance occur naturally and an OO approach is a more efficient way of coding it.

14.3 Perl[1]

http://www.perl.com/

To begin, my primary job isn't to be a CGI programmer. There is CGI work involved, but I have a lot of little things that I work on, and I'll describe some of them and how Perl has helped me get each job done.

---

[1] Written by Mark

My primary job is in technical support, and we use a database program called Remedy to provide our call tracking. One feature I wanted to add was the ability to have E-mail that comes in or out to be automatically added to a call. This involves a few steps:

1. Make sure the Subject: line for a call has a four-digit number. This would be the call number.

2. Extract that four-digit number.

3. Take the body of the message and the sender and add it to the call.

The first two items are actually easy, since Perl was designed with some rather powerful pattern matching capabilities. Searching the Internet gave me a group of people who gave a Perl interface to Remedy. This interface allowed me to log in to the Remedy server, modify the database to add the new entry, and then log out. The total size of the program was under 100 lines of code, and most of it was re-used from a sample program that came with the interface.

Another project is to monitor the phone system and make a listing every day of the number of incoming calls and the average length of each call. Someone else wrote a program to get the information and dump it in a file. All I had to do was open the file, read through until I hit that day's records, and then add up the times. Since Perl is made for string manipulation, I can pull out the hours, minutes, and seconds of the call, convert it all to seconds, and then build a total number of seconds of incoming calls for the day. I can then divide that by the number of calls, divide again to get hours, minutes, and seconds, and dump that into another file. Add a cron process to do this every night right after midnight, and there's the program.

My third example of why I like Perl has to do with our router to the Internet. Our current Internet link (56 Kb) is not all that big, and slowdowns are becoming more frequent. There has to be a way for me to find out how much of my bandwidth is being used during a day, and there is, using the SNMP network management tool. Sure, I could probably write a C application to talk directly to the router and pull the information out. But I don't like C and the thought of malloc() and free() disturbs me. Good thing there's (you guessed it) an SNMP interface to Perl—a 20-line Perl script to talk to the router and query it every few minutes for how many bytes it transmitted and received and then divide that into the time that passed. Let that run for a few days, use a graphing tool like gnuplot to give me a graph, and now I have a reason for getting a T3. Well, maybe not a T3, but something faster anyway.

Last, I have my CGI work. Most of the work on our Web site is on our internal network (some call it an intranet). This allows us to have a common repository for information—how the phones work, what drive letters are which NFS mount, even schedules listing when people will be out of the office. This last one requires the CGI work. I have a SQL database program called PostgreSQL which (you got it!) has a Perl interface. Perl also has a CGI interface, so I can build my form and CGI script all into one compact (under 200 lines) file. In one instance, a user can enter their name, what day they'll be out, and why they'll be out. This information then gets entered into the database. In another form, a person can enter data and query the database.

Why Perl over other languages? I've known Perl for a few years and gotten used to how quickly you can write a program and get it working. Plus you don't have to worry about all the memory, pointers, include files, and compiler problems that seem to be in C. I wouldn't want to write anything big in it, but my job typically doesn't require large programs. They're mostly small programs, and probably smaller in terms of line count than a comparable C program. Why not Python or another language? I don't need the OOP that Python provides. Other scripting languages (such as sh or csh) have all the functionality built into Perl already, but Perl has the form of a real language and is something I'm much more used to, coming from my Pascal and M days.

14.4 Python[2]

```
http://www.python.org
```

Now, unlike Mark, at least half of my job is CGI programming and ironically, I don't use Perl. I say ironically since anyone who has looked into doing CGI programming has undoubtedly noticed that most of it is done in Perl. In fact, it can be difficult to find a book that concentrates on writing CGI in any other language, but they are rumored to exist.

I used to be a huge Perl fan, but I didn't know any better then. I was actually just happy to be writing CGI. I discovered Python on my own near the end of my tenure in grad school and wanted to learn it, but never really had the time or didn't think I did. Finally, about six months and two jobs later I decided to finally learn another language. I really wasn't happy with Perl. I

[2]Written by Cary

looked into Tcl and then Python again and decided to give the latter a whirl. I wrote my first "real" Python program, a CGI script, about a year ago and haven't looked back since.

Python is an object-oriented scripting language written by Guido van Rossum. It is dynamically typed, supports multiple inheritance, user-defined types, high-level dynamic types, and classes. As alluded to above, it is often compared to Perl, as the two are frequently used for similar tasks. It is younger than Perl, and as a result, its usage is less widespread. Despite this, Python has a large number of contributed modules for tasks ranging from HTML generation to database interfacing to complex numerical calculations.

In general you can use Python for any task where you could use any other scripting language. Python has a very clear syntax and is more extensible than other interpreted languages, with the possible exception of Tcl. It has also been shown to scale better than the average interpreted language. As an example of this, a Web browser has been written in Python using the Tkinter GUI interface. While not as high performance as compiled browsers, it is certainly tolerable. It is at least as fast as the HotJava browser, which is the most similar browser, being interpreted byte codes while Python is interpreted text.

Since it was designed as an object-oriented language from the ground up, the OO orientation is a very clean one, unlike the somewhat ad hoc OO of Perl 5. Also, development of Python on other platforms has taken place more or less concurrently so Python is extremely portable.

Why do I like Python so much? Several reasons. First, the syntax is remarkably clear; my Python programs are much easier to read than in any other language I've used (FORTRAN, C, Basic, LISP, Bourne, and C shell). Second, program development is at least as fast as it was under Perl, usually faster. Third, I have discovered that I much prefer the OO approach to programming; inasmuch as any programming language can be said to work as my chaotic mind thinks, OOP comes closer than the "old-fashioned way," plus Python is consistently OO. Lastly, longer programs are much easier to develop and maintain.

Large CGI programs are uncommon, but certainly not unheard of. Most of the CGI I do is either a few dozen lines of code (for simple applications like reading data from a database or mailing form variables) or a couple hundred lines for more complicated stuff like inserting or updating a database or building GIFs with libgd. Now about that occasional big CGI application.

This CGI script processes the new and renewing subscribers to the Web sites at my place of employment. It started off as a collection of small Perl scripts which checked, minimally formatted, and mailed the form variables to a Mac, where they were processed by Leads!, a front end to 4D (a Mac DB I'd never heard of until I started the job). Needless to say, this was not the most robust way to populate our customer database. At the time, we had one subscription site and about a half dozen types of subscriptions.

Since I started my current job, the number of subscription sites has tripled and the number of oddball marketing deals that are made has gone from zero to a half dozen or more, depending on whether I'm counting or someone from marketing is doing it; there has been an almost geometric rise in the number of different subscriptions. What started as a collection of hacked, canned Perl scripts is now monolithic CGI of over 1,200 lines. It verifies and cross-checks as many as 40 variables; determines whether renewing members are adding sites, users, or both; inserts and/or updates as many as six tables in our membership database (at the moment split over two DBMSs, though not for long); and prints out a nice membership certificate suitable for framing. Despite the ad hoc manner in which the group and later single script developed the code, it is still easy to read and understand.—something that can rarely be said of a 1000+ line shell or Perl script.

As much as I like Python, there are a few things about Perl that I miss. Chief among these is the regex implementation in Perl. It is wonderful. Fortunately, the next version of Python will have expanded regex capabilities which should rival Perl's. Another is the lack of string interpolation. Since Python doesn't use a $ or other symbol to distinguish variable names, this is difficult or impossible to do. I'm finding I don't miss the latter too terribly much these days, but I'm eagerly awaiting enhancements to Python's pattern matching abilities.

There has been a fair bit of interest in making a compiler for Python, but this is not so straightforward, as Python is not a statically typed language (i.e., there are no variable declarations and a variable need not be of a constant size, and worse, a given variable name could represent a different type in various parts of a program depending on what is assigned to it, though this is not particularly good programming style).

Python and GUIs

Several windowing toolkits exist for Python's various UNIX implementations. The most popular is tkinter which provides an OO interface to Tcl/Tk. Tkinter provides the broadest cross-platform support, since it has been ported to Windows 95/NT and MacOS. There is also an extension for using the Athena and/or Motif (or Lesstif if you have that instead) widget sets. With version 8 of Tcl/Tk promising a more native look and feel, Tkinter will likely become the GUI tool of choice for most implementations of Python.

Python on Other Platforms

Thirty-two-bit ports of Python exist for Windows 95 and NT (Pythonwin) and MacOS (for both PowerPC, and Motorola 68K-based Macs). WPY is a 16-bit Python for Windows 3.1 and OS/2. Additionally, a separate port exists for DOS. All of these ports, except DOS (for obvious reasons), have support for their OS's native windowing classes.

14.5 Lisp and Scheme

```
http://www.cs.cmu.edu/Groups/AI/html/cltl/cltl2.html (Common Lisp)
http://www-swiss.ai.mit.edu/scheme-home.html (Scheme)
```

Lisp is a venerable language; its origins lie in the earliest days of artificial intelligence research in the mid-1950s. Machines like the IBM 704 and the PDP-1 (yes, one not eleven) are associated with it. As computer technology progressed, Lisp was implemented on more and more architectures; no two implementations were completely interoperable so Lisp and its dialects became splintered. In the early to mid-1980s the Common Lisp specification was hammered out and an ANSI standard adopted.

Today, Common Lisp sports functions with variable numbers of arguments, a large library of utility functions (it is four decades old!), and an object-oriented programming facility. As you might guess, since it was developed for AI, Lisp also has a very sophisticated condition-handling system.

Scheme is a much simpler dialect of Lisp. It has its own separate specification, about 50 pages in length, which lays out a conceptually elegant language. Interestingly, the Scheme specification is shorter than the index of "Common Lisp: The Language."

14.6 Java

```
http://www.blackdown.org/
```

Sun's Java, well, what can we say? It's all the rage and not entirely without cause. Its architecture-neutral design (including its GUI tool, the AWT) promises unparalleled portability. Like C++, it is an object-oriented language. Its popularity has given birth to large numbers of contributed extensions (classes) and a great deal of support on the Net.

Java is different than the other languages here in that it is meant to be completely platform-neutral. Java code is compiled into platform-independent byte-code files that can then be run on a virtual machine. Once a virtual machine (VM) has been implemented on a machine, it will (in theory) run any "pure" Java program or applet. Sun has a program for certifying applications as "100 percent Pure Java."

Java support can be compiled into the Linux kernel, allowing programs to be executed directly from the command line. Applets can be invoked this way as well, as long as Java binary support has been compiled directly into the kernel and not as a loadable module by setting the execute bit on the HTML file that references the applet class.

The feature that originally won Java much of its popularity is that the VM could be implemented in a Web browser and applets could be executed in the client VM served up by a Web server. At first the applets were mainly "gee whiz" things such as simple animations or moving text, clocks, and simple games like tic tac toe.

However, because of the enormous amount of contributed code and additional tools and specifications, such as Java DBC (Database Connectivity), "real" applets (and applications) are much more easily realized.

Information on Java for Linux, including where to download the latest developer's kit, can be found at the URL listed above. It should be noted that a native (as opposed to running the Solaris one in emulation) Java Development Kit (JDK) for Linux/SPARC is now also available.

APIs for interfacing Java to virtually everything imaginable exist. A search through your favorite application's contributed software list will likely turn up a Java API.

14.7 Tcl/Tk

```
http://www.sunlabs.com/research/tcl/
```

The Tool Command Language and Tk toolkit are the inventions of John Osterhout. Tcl is both a scripting language and a C library. Tk is not a separate language but an extension to Tcl for interfacing to X; it is also available as a C library. Tcl and Tk have been ported to MacOS and Windows, making them a good choice for cross-platform application development. However, interfaces for it exist for other languages as well, most notably the Tkinter module for Python.

Tcl by itself is actually not a particularly good scripting language. What it is designed for is "gluing" together other languages and programs. It is arguably the most extensible language listed here with the possible exception of Python.

Recently, Sun's Research labs and Tcl/Tk have adopted each other and are continuing development under the name Sunscript (this is the name of the research group; Tcl and Tk will retain their names).

The new release, version 8, promises an unprecedented level of native look and feel for Tk across X, MacOS, and Windows. This should make it very popular for building cross-platform GUIs. Those familiar with Tcl and Tk may recall that the last full releases of them were 7.6 and 4.2, respectively, and then wonder what happened to versions 5, 6, and 7 of Tk. Sun has synchronized the version numbers and apparently plans to release subsequent versions concurrently.

Because of Tcl's popularity, it has interfaces to several databases (MySQL, mSQL, Sybase) and even a Netscape plug-in. Additionally, Tcl is, as of 7.6, year 2000 compliant. The Sunscript group is working on various projects and applications for Tcl/Tk programming, including a commercial grade Tk GUI builder, an on-the-fly compiler, and maintenance of the current, native look-and-feel ports to MacOS and Windows.

Tcl's extensibility has allowed for several extensions to both it and Tk. Extended Tcl (Tclx) provides additional functionality with the idea of creating a more stand-alone scripting language. ObjTcl is just what you might guess it is—a Tcl extension that allows for the use of object-oriented programming techniques within Tcl. Tix is a set of extensions for Tk written in Tk. TkPerl is an interface to Tk for Perl5.

One of the most useful Tcl extensions is Expect. It is a tool for interacting with other command-line driven programs which require user interaction. Thus it is possible to automate any number of tasks which might otherwise require a much more complicated solution for automation.

14.8 SQL

The Structured Query Language (SQL) is the language used to talk to relational databases. In reality, it is a set of standards to which DBMS vendors add their own extensions. Because implementations of SQL differ so much, we didn't include a link for SQL; instead, we suggest you consult the documentation for your particular DBMS flavor.

In general, SQL's syntax is fairly simple and English-like. Some implementation feature functions can be embedded in query statements, full regular expression support, or even nearly full-blown programming languages. Others may support very little beyond being able to select, delete, insert and update.

14.9 Other Languages

There are literally scores of programming languages, certainly more than we have space to cover in any detail here. Those languages described above are among the most popular on Linux and many other platforms, but many other languages bear mentioning as well.

Many readers have surely noticed we left out some old standbys.

Oldies but Goodies

FORTRAN

```
http://www.fortran.com/fortran/
```

FORTRAN is a venerable language designed mainly for numerical calculations. Its most common incarnation on Linux is in the form of g77, a FORTRAN 77 compiler. The latest specification is FORTRAN 90, which is not as common as FORTRAN 77. Few compilers for FORTRAN 90 exist and no free ones exist for Linux.

BASIC

```
http://www.Uni-Mainz.DE/~ihm/basic.html
```

Not as old as FORTRAN, but still popular for its simplicity; Microsoft's Visual Basic and VBScript have played a large part in keeping it popular. It has had and continues to have many different incarnations both interpreted and compiled. Only recently has a BASIC compiler become available for Linux.

Pascal

```
http://sun01.brain.uni-freiburg.de/~klaus/pascal/fpk-pas/
```

Pascal is a language that has always been popular among computer scientists, both to teach good programming techniques and as a general purpose programming language. Free compilers exist for Linux, and one ships with most of the distributions.

COBOL

`http://www.cobol.org/`

Despite the fact that nearly everyone we know laughs at it, as of a couple years ago, more lines of COBOL code have been written than any other language. Its usage is almost completely confined to financial-related applications, but there are an awful lot of banks, finance companies, and people interested in everyone else's money. It is not a language well suited for general programming tasks, but a free compiler exists and is shipped with some Linux distributions.

Of More Recent Vintage

Most of the languages we discuss next are somewhat newer than the previous ones. Also, few of them are included in any Linux distribution. Regardless, these are useful and powerful tools which you may wish to consider using in place of the more common languages.

Smalltalk

`http://st-www.cs.uiuc.edu/`

It is one of the fastest growing languages on the planet. Its usage is estimated to be growing at around 60 percent a year. It is a very high-level general programming language, which typically translates into a short development time. Its syntax is easier to read and the language itself is also easy to learn.

Smalltalk is about as purely object-oriented as it gets. Everything is an object, leading to very consistent methods of handling things. Smalltalk advocates claim that it was "designed with the human being in mind."

Icon

`http://www.cs.arizona.edu/icon/www/index.html`

Icon is another high-level language, very high-level in fact. Its roots are in SNOBOL, though in its current incarnation, there is little resemblance.

Beyond having very powerful and extensive string and data structure processing features, it does not specifically address a particular problem set. Its syntax is similar to C but with a much higher level of semantics.

It is well suited for systems programming, though as a high-level compiled language it is certainly useful and used for shorter but compute-intensive tasks. Similar to Smalltalk, it was designed with the programmer in mind. This may not be as friendly as the Smalltalk slogan, but the point is clear: Icon's high-level design allows for rapid development of applications.

As an aside, the name Icon is not an acronym and it was chosen for the language before the term's usage to refer to window manager "icons."

Rexx

```
http://www.rexxla.org/
```

According to its creator, Rexx is "a procedural language that allows programs and algorithms to be written in a clear and structured way." Rexx's syntax is not particularly unique or unusual. It was designed to be a generic macro language which can be used with another application. When its parser encounters a function that it doesn't recognize, it asks the application to handle it. This way, if Rexx is used as the macro language for multiple applications, users need to learn only one macro language and the functions for each application, which presumably will be known from the normal use of the application.

Eiffel

```
http://www.eiffel.com/
```

Eiffel is a commercial, OO, compiled language designed for rapid development of clean reusable software. There is a strong emphasis on mechanisms and techniques to promote reliability and low bug rates. Although it is commercial, sellers and resellers frequently offer large discounts for personal, student, or educational use. Some companies offer prices considerably below their other UNIX prices for Linux versions of Eiffel.

If you want to develop in a fully OO, commercially supported, compiled language, Eiffel may be for you. Or if you can live without the commercial support, you may want to look into the next item in this list of languages.

Sather

```
http://www.icsi.berkeley.edu/~sather/
```

Sather's roots are in Eiffel. Early beta versions of it were nearly subsets of Eiffel 2.0; however, a major release later, both languages have gone their own ways. Sather was and is developed at the University of California, Berkeley, and as you might expect of a language developed at an educational institution, it is freeware.

Sather has garbage collection, multiple inheritance, is strongly typed, and its code can be compiled into C code. Its public license is very liberal to encourage users to contribute to its library.

14.10   Summary

We've literally just skimmed the surface of the scores (at least) of programming languages that are "officially" available and can be compiled for, or easily ported to Linux. Certainly, we've tried to cover the most popular languages and those that come with most Linux distributions. More likely than not, one or more of these languages will meet your needs as a programmer. If not, a search on your favorite Web search engine will turn up collections of links to programming languages for you to try out.

Web Serving 15

Various Web servers and extensions for Linux.

How to install and configure Apache-derived Web servers under Linux as well as popular modules, extensions, and key configuration directives are explained and some examples of their use are given.

With the phenomenal rise in popularity of the World Wide Web (WWW), everyone wants a Web page, be it a small personal home page where you can pull out your soapbox or a large corporate Web site where a company can distribute information (everything from press releases to hardware driver updates to troubleshooting guides), market themselves, or sell their products on-line. Linux has proven itself to be a robust, high-performance Web server on everything from a 386 to a DEC Alpha. Still, as with nearly any application, there are hardware and software issues to be considered.

A Note on Other Information Services

The Web's popularity has forced many other information services into the background or, in some cases, into obsolescence. Notables include Gopher, WAIS and Archie. Consequently, we make no effort to cover them in this book and refer the curious to either the Web or any of a number of texts covering "Internet information services."

15.1 Web Server Software

There are a number of Web servers (HTTP daemons) available for Linux as both commercial and/or free- or shareware. Additionally there is the choice of using a secure server versus a non-secure server. The difference between the two is the use of SSL (Secure Sockets Layer, a protocol for encrypting/decrypting data sent via a network socket). Secure servers use it, insecure ones don't. Typically, non-SSL servers are free- or shareware, while those employing SSL are commercially developed and cost several hundred dollars.

   In addition, a Web server can be forking or non-forking. Traditionally, HTTP daemons fork off child processes to handle incoming requests. Each child can typically handle a hundred or so requests, but it handles them serially; this means that heavily loaded Web servers may need to have a large number of child processes, each of which takes up additional RAM and CPU. In a server with a large httpd binary (especially a secure server) this can cause problems. The alternative is to have a server which multiplexes incoming connections internally. Typically this approach has yielded severs with impressive performance.

   Now RAM has been and looks to remain inexpensive and CPU performance has been increasing by leaps and bounds, so one may be inclined to question whether a multithreaded server is worth the effort. However, it has certainly been one of the main aims of Linux to get as much out of a computer's hardware as possible, which obviously means writing efficient software. This said, there are no non-forking servers which equal the extensibility of the best of the forking servers. It seems likely, though, that soon the extensibility of servers like Apache and the multiplexing of servers like Boa will be combined.

Encryption, the Web, and Uncle Sam

Until recently there were no Web browsers which supported encryption stronger than 40-bits, mainly due to U.S. export restrictions (based on the rather silly idea that no one outside the United States could make stronger encryption). With these restrictions gradually loosening and strong (128-bit) encryption now available on Web servers sold inside and outside the United States, browsers are appearing which support stronger encryption. Within the United States, it is possible to get enhanced versions of Netscape's browser which use 128-bit encryption. For more information on encryption and security, see the chapter on security.

Below is a sampling of secure and unsecure httpd servers.

Non-SSL Severs

- Apache (`http://www.apache.org`)—currently the most popular Web server, hands down. Loaded with features, it is also fast, free, and extensible.

- Boa (`http://www.boa.org/`)—a very new, very fast Web server, freely available with source code. Unlike Apache, it does not fork off child processes to handle additional clients; it multiplexes all connections internally.

- W3C httpd (formerly known as CERN httpd) (`http://www.w3.org/pub/WWW/Daemon/`)—the first Web server, ever. No longer in production, it is included for the sake of completeness. ;-)

- NCSA (`http://hoohoo.ncsa.uiuc.edu/`)—the successor to CERN and later the basis for Apache, which has largely supplanted it.

- Roxen (`http://www.roxen.com/`)—a commercial Web and FTP server. It also uses an extension to HTML called RXML (developed by Roxen) that allows pages to be modified at download time. It is available for free, or you can purchase it, along with commercial support. Source code is available, as well. Additionally, an SSL version is in progress and beta versions of it are freely available.

- WN (`http://hopf.math.nwu.edu/`)—another freeware Web server. Not as extensible as Apache, but it has some nice features for modifying pages as they are served. (Also available paired with a Gopher server under the name GN. See `http://hopf.math.nwu.edu:70/` for more information.)

- Zeus (`http://www.zeus.co.uk`)—another non-forking server (like Boa). It is commercial and somewhat pricey, but then you do get commercial support. Source code is unavailable.

SSL Servers

- Stronghold (`http://www.c2.net`)—As its alternate name suggests, this is Apache with SSL built in. It is unlike most commercial software in that it comes with source code, and thus, none of Apache's extensibility is lost. Unlike Apache, Stronghold is not the most popular commercial Web server in its class; it is the second most-popular secure server.

- Apache-SSL (`http://www.algroup.co.uk/Apache-SSL/`)—It is freeware Apache with SSL support. Since the SSL libraries that it uses were illegally exported from the United States, its use within the United States is illegal. It is essentially the same as Stronghold as far as the actual code is concerned. Both it and Stronghold support 128-bit encryption and have done so for some time.

- Roxen (`http://www.roxen.com/`)—Roxen also comes in an SSL flavor.

- Zeus (`http://www.zeus.co.uk`)—Similar to Roxen, Zeus also comes in a secure version.

15.2 Hardware Issues

One of the primary considerations, if you are using a forking server or lots of interpreted CGI, is memory. Each server child obviously takes up at least as much memory as the size of the executable. Each CGI script requires the loading of the its respective interpreter. Dynamic linking of the executables can alleviate the problem to some extent. There are four subsystems which you need to consider beyond the choice of a good personal comouter interconnect (PCI) motherboard: memory, CPU, hard disk, and network. The PCI bus has a throughput of 133 Mb/s, several times faster than even an ultra SCSI 3 adapter and is thus well equipped to handle fast peripherals.

However, there is simply no substitute for more RAM—Not swap space (your hard disk is pitifully slow compared to on-board memory.), not CPU (if you are swapping to disk, your disk is what's slowing you down), nor a faster network card. RAM is cheap; buy a lot of it.

After RAM, the next most important subsystem is either disk or CPU depending on the peculiarities of your site. If you make extensive use of CGI, SSI, or database transactions, you will probably want to put a little more CPU in your system. A note here: Don't bother with MMX CPUs. There's really no gain to be had in this situation; just get a faster CPU for the same price or put the money into RAM or hard disk.

In a situation where you are simply serving large numbers of static pages, a good fast disk is probably a good investment. Spend some money to go from a fast or ultra SCSI 2 to ultra SCSI 3. We're assuming here that you have the good sense not to use IDE (or even EIDE) drives in a server.

If you need higher network throughput and you are saturating your T1 (i.e., you have no LAN congestion issues), then you may want to look into having your server cohosted at an ISP which has T3 access to the Internet backbone and consider moving from 10 Mb/s ethernet to 100 Mb/s (fast) ethernet. A properly configured Linux Web (and/or FTP) server can saturate a fast ethernet card and thus multiple T3s.

15.3 Apache and ApacheSSL/Stronghold

Because of its popularity, rich feature set, extensibility, and power, we will concentrate on Apache, although much of the information here will apply to any Web server.

As mentioned above, Apache is freely available with source code. Apache also provides an API. These two features allow for a great deal of customization and extensibility. Additionally, Apache is HTTP 1.1 compliant. This latest revision of HTTP introduces man performance enhancements to the protocol. Unfortunately, to date, very few browsers support HTTP 1.1 and, thus, cannot take advantage of it.

Getting Started

Since Apache is freely available, a number of Linux distributions are shipped with it, RedHat and Linux Pro included. Depending on how your vendor configured your machine, you need have only a few configuration details on-hand before you begin writing HTML pages and are on your way to a Web site.

1. Where is the document root for the server? In other words, where is the directory that contains the root of the directory tree that is served when someone hits your server? It is the directory from which files are served if no path information, aside from a filename, is given, (for example, `http://www.ratatosk.org/davinci.html` versus `http://www.ratatosk.org/artists/surreal/dali.html`). This is typically something like `/home/httpd/html` or `/home/httpd/htdocs` (so the

second URL above would retrieve `/home/httpd/html/artists/sur-real/dali.html`).

2. Where are the configuration files? Typically `/etc/httpd/conf`, `/home/httpd/conf/`, `/usr/local/etc/httpd/conf`, or something similar is used for this

3. Is the server running? Depending on how the server was configured when Linux was installed, the http daemon may start automatically at boot time. You can use the `ps` command to check if httpd is running: `ps -waux | grep httpd`. If it is not, you need to invoke it as root and tell it where to find the directory containing the configuration files. For example, if your configuration directory is `/etc/httpd/conf`, you would type something like `httpd -d /etc/httpd`. If the directory containing your httpd binary is not in your path, you will need to use the absolute path to invoke it. Typically httpd lives in one of the sbin directories: `/usr/local/sbin`, `/usr/sbin`, or on rare occasions, `/sbin`.

Aside from the various modules that can be used to extend Apache at compile time, there are many items that can be specified at run time in the conf files: `httpd.conf` and `srm.conf`. These two files control parameters, such as aliases for directories, aliases for icons, images, CGI scripts/programs, virtual host directives, the document root directory, the file to be served from a directory if no other file is specified in the URL, and various access control and authentication directives.

<Directory> and .htaccess

These two tools are used to modify access of all types for directory trees. `<Directory>` directives typically reside in the `srm.conf` or `httpd.conf` files. It can also occur in the `<Virtualhost>` directive (more on this later.) The `.htaccess` file resides somewhere in a directory tree of HTML documents. In both instances, directives placed in the directories are recursively effective for all the files and subdirectories in that directory. For example, to enforce basic authorization for a directory and all its contents, you could put the following in a `.htaccess` file in that directory (say `/home/web`):

```
AuthType Basic
AuthUserFile /home/cary/etc/passwd
AuthGroupFile /dev/null
AuthName Realm of the Kazoos
```

```
<LIMIT GET POST PUT>
require valid-user
</LIMIT>
```

Or in a `<Directory>` directive:

```
<Directory /home/web>
AuthType Basic
AuthUserFile /home/cary/etc/passwd
AuthGroupFile /dev/null
AuthName Realm of the Kazoos
<LIMIT GET POST PUT>
require valid-user
</LIMIT>
</Directory>
```

The `<LIMIT>` directive tells the server what HTTP methods require a valid user, in this case GET, POST, and PUT (PUT is used for file uploading).

CGI and SSI

The Common Gateway Interface (CGI) and Server Side Includes (SSI) are the two most common ways to execute external programs. CGI is designed to both receive and send information from and to the server. SSI is more one-way; mainly it sends information. SSI can do more than simply call external programs. It can also include files, echo some simple system information such as the local time, or even execute cgi.

Perl is the preemptive language for CGI programming. This is something of a double-edged sword. On the one hand, large collections of "canned" scripts for various common CGI tasks exist. It also has very powerful features for processing strings, including a large set of regular expression atoms and operators. Since CGI frequently involves large mounts of text processing, this helps to fuel Perl's popularity. On the other hand, Perl is not the easiest language to learn, nor is its syntax particularly easy to read (there are obfuscated Perl contests!).

After Perl, there are several languages which are popular for use in CGI programs: Python, Tcl, C, and Java. Additionally there are languages which can be embedded in HTML and parsed later by a CGI program; PHP (discussed below) falls into this category. The PHP parser can also be embedded into Apache and servers based on it.

The number of books published on CGI is rather large and most cover the topic much more thoroughly than is suitable for us to do here. One criticism of most of the literature available is that it tends to focus nearly entirely on

Perl, ignoring, for the most part, C, Python and other languages. C, in particular, is very useful since, as a compiled language, CGI written in it is faster and lighter weight. Of course, development times in C are much longer.

At this point in time, all of the languages mentioned have more or less equivalent extensions/modules/libraries for dealing with the peculiarities of CGI and interfacing with everything from TCP/IP sockets, to the operating system to a database. As such, the choice of a language for CGI is largely up to you. All of the above are shipped with most Linux distributions and are available for free from their respective authors.

Web Pages for Your Users

In a situation where you have multiple users on your machine, be it at an ISP or at a publisher, some of them will likely be interested in setting up a home page for themselves.

This is not something that will typically consume a large amount of resources on your server unless you have a large number of home pages or have very popular users. Additionally, serving the static HTML poses no security concerns beyond those of running the server itself. All that aside, there will almost certainly be users who will want to use some CGI, SSI, or some other server-parsed content that will add a dynamic element to their Web pages. Now, you have a security issue.

The various solutions range from simply allowing users full access to tools like SSI and CGI (in a situation where you trust all your users) to some sort of limited SSI/CGI to completely forbidding the use of them. You can also allow or disallow the use of them on a user-by-user basis.

In a small business or possibly on a corporate LAN, you may likely choose the former route while at an ISP, where you know few of the users personally, you will likely choose one of the latter two routes.

Fortunately, Apache makes controlling access to these and other tools fairly easy via the `.htaccess` file and `<Directory>` directive.

Restricting the Use of CGI and SSI

The `<directory>` directive is your friend. It is the way you specify what can and can't be done in which directories. Couple this with the Linux user and group permissions, and you can exercise very fine control over who can do what in which areas of your Web space.

In general, unless the server is already so insecure it doesn't matter, or you can trust your users to not inadverantly or purposefully write CGI which compromises your server in some way, you will not want CGI to be executable from arbitrary directories. Of course, if the server is accessible only to you and possibly a few others, you can leave things fairly open and not have to worry about it.

Additionally, you will likely want to prohibit browsers from roaming through the file system, be it a particular user's or the root file system. In other words, if a URL points to a directory that does not contain an index file, the server will return a 404 (File not Found) error instead of displaying the directory's listing.

To make the entire file system off-limits to the server, a directive like this would be placed in the `access.conf`:

```
<Directory />
 AllowOverride None
 Order deny,allow
 Deny from all
 Options None
</Directory>
```

"Wait a sec! I want to serve Web pages!" Ahh... then you now need to tell Apache what directories it can serve pages from. A statement like this

```
<Directory /home/*/public_html>
 Order allow,deny
 Allow from all
 AllowOverrides IncludesNOEXEC
</Directory>
```

lets you serve pages from your users' public_html (this is the default directory from which files are served when a request that ends in ~username is received) directories and lets them use SSI that doesn't execute external programs or CGI scripts and

```
<Directory /home/httpd/htdocs>
Order deny,allow
Allow from all
AlowOverrides All
</Directory>
```

lets you serve pages from what is commonly the document root for the server and allows all of the restrictions to be overridden. Now you can set up CGI directories in this tree. You can do this with additional `<Directory>` directives or in an `.htaccess` file. If you choose the latter route, be sure to make the `.htaccess` file not writable by the user, unless they can be trusted not to abuse the privilege. However, if you plan to have all CGI pass by you or perhaps someone else, you may want to set up one directory that is writable by root or httpd only. In any event, to turn on CGI in a directory, assuming they can be overridden, using `.htaccess`, you need the following:

```
Options ExecCGI
```

There are many other options you can turn on and off, including the symbolic links, indexing, and multiviews. For the complete scoop on them, look at the Apache documentation.

Other Useful Modules and Directives

In Apache 1.2, a number of incredibly useful tools are available. Whole books have been written on Apache and since this is only one chapter, we're only going to touch on the more interesting and useful features. We aren't going to talk about most of the directives that appear in the configuration files since it's fairly easy to understand their syntax from the usage, and they are explained fairly well in the Apache documentation.

We've already met some of them: `.htaccess`, `<Directory>`, `Options`, `AllowOverride`, `Allow`, and `Deny`, and we've given a few examples of their usage. Now we'll discuss the other most common and useful directives.

User and Group—These set the user ID and group ID under which the server will run.

ServerRoot—This is the root of the server's directory tree. This is typically the directory where the log file, conf file, and document root subdirectories are. The locations of these can be overridden on the command line or in the configuration files.

DocumentRoot—This is the base of the document tree.

UserDir—This is the subdirectory within a user's home directory which is the root of that user's Webspace.

ServerType—This specifies the type of server (obviously), either stand-alone or proxy. Unless you are setting up a proxy server this should be stand-alone.

Port—This is the TCP/IP port at which the server will listen. Port 80 is the standard; for an HTTP request to be heard on another port, it will have to be specified in the URL like so: `http://www.wombat.net:81/`. The server must be run as root to use ports number 1023 and lower.

Listen—If you want the server to listen at an additional port, use this. It takes two arguments: the alias and the path to the directory. The path can either be relative to the ServerRoot or an absolute path.

ScriptAlias—Often, for security reasons, you will want to have the directories from which CGI programs can be executed outside of the directory tree. Or you may simply want to provide a shortcut for referencing a directory containing CGI programs.

Alias—Similar to ScriptAlias, but only non-cgi files can be served from the directory.

VirtualHost—If you want requests that come in on a different IP, server name or port to be served from a different document root, a different server name or with aliases pointing to different directories, then this is the directive for you. Any of DocumentRoot, Directory, ScriptAlias, Alias, User, Group, UserDir, or ServerName can be used as arguments inside it. A couple of examples should help to demonstrate the power of the VirtualHost directive.

A server for `http://www.dognails.com` on port 80 with its own cgi-bin and document root:

```
<VirtualHost www.dognails.com>
ServerName www.dognails.com
DocumentRoot /web/dognails/www
ScriptAlias /cgi-bin/ /web/dognails/cgi-bin/
</VirtualHost>
```

To serve all requests on port 1200 as from a separate DocumentRoot:

```
Listen 1200
<VirtualHost *:1200>
DocumentRoot /usr/local/www1200
</VirtualHost>
```

Extensions for Apache

One of the more complicated extensions with a difficult setup process, suEXEC is a wrapper which allows CGI programs to be executed under a different UID than that under which the server is running. This is often used by ISPs that let their users maintain their own CGI; this forces the script to execute as that user. This obviously strongly encourages the user to write good, secure CGI. It is also useful to allow access control similar to that allowed by the password file.

Because suEXEC can open some serious security holes, its security model imposes several additional restrictions. The target program must reside in the Apache /webspace/ and thus, the path to it cannot start with a / or have back references (..). Obviously the target user and group must be valid and their IDs must be above a minimum (typically 100 or 500), which will prohibit execution as the root user or group. The target program cannot be set uid or gid and the final, non-trivial restrictions are that the directory containing the program to be executed and the program itself only be writable by the target user and belong to the target user and the target group.

suEXEC comes in a separate C source file and accompanying header file. Before compiling suEXEC, the header file needs to be edited to reflect the particulars of your system. The following may need to be changed: HTTPD_USER, typically nobody or maybe a "web" or "www" user; LOG_EXEC, the log file for suEXEC transactions; DOC_ROOT, the root of the Apache Web space; and SAFE_PATH, the PATH environment variable for suEXEC. Then you need to compile suEXEC: gcc -o suexec suexec.c, chown it to root, set the set userID bit (chmod 4711 suexec), and copy it to its final destination.

Apache must now be recompiled to use the suEXEC wrapper. In the src/ httpd.h file you will need to add or edit a line like this:

```
#define SUEXEC_BIN "/usr/sbin/suexec"
```

to reflect where you installed the suid root suexec binary. When you start your new httpd, you should see this message:

```
Configuring Apache for use with the suexec wrapper.
```

To disable suEXEC, you can remove the binary, change its ownership from root, or unset the set UID bit.

User and Group directives in VirtualHost directives can be used to tell suEXEC the target user and group for executing CGI. Another way is for the target user to do so in HTTP requests to user directories. For example, http://thppt.org/~dweezle/somescript.cgi—somescript.cgi would then be executed as the user dweezle. If neither of these conditions exists, the script will be executed as the main User and Group.

PHP/FI

One of the most useful extensions for Apache is the PHP/FI program. PHP/ FI is actually usable as CGI, FastCGI, or compiled into Apache (linked either statically or dynamically). Which option to employ is a matter of taste and use. If you plan on using it lightly, employing it as CGI or FastCGI is fine, though for more extensive use, you will likely want to compile it into Apache, though this will raise your memory usage noticeably.

PHP/FI is a scripting language with syntax similar to Perl or C. It is embedded within HTML, set off by a variation on the comment tag: `<? >`. The code within the tag is parsed (either by the server itself or the CGI script, depending on your setup), and the output, if any, replaces the tag. This is very similar to how server side includes function. Typically, a special extension (`.phtml`) is used for PHP files to tell Apache to parse the file before sending it to the client. If you plan to use PHP in most or all of your files, you may want to tell Apache to parse all HTML files.

PHP/FI boasts many functions for connecting to and extracting information from various databases, including mSQL (1 and 2), Postgres95, MySQL (another free database server based on mSQL), Solid, Sybase, and Oracle. Additionally, it has very powerful support for Netscape cookies, file upload, and the GD library. That last is a C library for GIF creation. PHP also has additional functionality for setting arbitrary HTTP headers (besides that which sets cookies).

SSL (Secure Sockets Layer)

As mentioned above, SSL is a protocol for sending encrypted data via a network socket. This allows for some peace of mind when transmitting sensitive data over the Web. There are two implementations of Apache with SSL: Stronghold and Apache-SSL. The legality of Apache-SSL is somewhat in question for commercial use in the United States, as RSA claims the SSL libraries it uses are covered by patents owned by RSA. So for commercial uses within the United States, you will likely want to use Stronghold. In either case, full source code is available.

Since Stronghold is well documented and comes with commercial support, we'll go through the setup of Apache-SSL.

To use SSL with Apache you will need to retrieve two things: the SSLeay and the SSL patch for Apache. These will have names like `SSLeay-0.8.0.tar.gz` and `apache_1.2.0+ssl_1.8.tar.gz`, respectively. Make sure the patch you get matches the major and minor version of Apache that you are using. You will also need at least version 2.1 of patch.

SSLeay can obtained at `ftp://ftp.psy.uq.oz.au/pub/Crypto/SSL/` and Apache-SSL can found at `ftp://ftp.ox.ac.uk/pub/crypto/SSL`.

Unpack SSLeay, cd into the source directory, run `./Configure linux-elf` (or `linux-aout` if you don't have an older `a.out` system), `make`, `make test`, and finally `make install`. It should compile with some warnings but pass the make test.

Unpack Apache-SSL in the root of the Apache distribution (not in the src subdirectory). Apply the patch: `patch < SSLpatch`. If this step produces an error, it is probably because you have an older version of the patch. Get a new version from your Linux distribution's Web site or any GNU mirror. Edit `src/Configuration`, as you would normally, but you will need to change the SSL-related directives to reflect any peculiarities on your system. If you are using a fresh copy of Apache, remember to add any extras you need for other Apache modules you might be using, such as PHP.

```
./Configure
make
```

You should now have a shiny new httpsd!

If you get symbol errors, you may need to fiddle with the order of libraries in the link stage of the make as well as verify you are using the correct library paths.

The httpd.conf

This will likely seem a little bizarre to anyone used to Apache's normal run-time config file set up, but `httpd.conf` is the only config file used. `srm.conf` and `access.conf` are both empty. An example `httpd.conf` is included with the SSLpatch distribution. There are a few notes on setting up your `httpd.conf` we want to give you. These guidelines should work for Strong-hold as well, since it is so similar to Apache-SSL.

Edit the `httpd.conf` to reflect your setup and execute `httpsd`. Try connecting to the SSL server: https://your.host.com/ (note the "s" after http). If you can't, check the `error_log` and the `ssl_log` and your `conf` file. Fix any problems and restart the server with a `kill -1 /pid/`, assuming it started on the first try or just try to start it again.

Unless you want to maintain two sets of config files, you will want to run both the unsecure and secure servers on the same binary and config file. The easiest way to do this is to set up `httpd.conf` just as you would normally, except that you will need to add the contents of your `srm.conf` and `access.conf` files as well, and then use the Listen and VirtualHost directives to run the secure server on a separate port. The default port for HTTPS is 443, so you will probably want to use that. Then simply move the SSLflag on directive into the VirtualHost directive.

Start Apache-SSL and make sure you can connect to both the non-secure server (`http://your.host.com/`), and the secure one (`https://your.host.com/`).

By default, Stronghold and ApacheSSL use version 3 of the SSL protocol. On some browser/machine combinations this may cause the browsers and possibly the OS, depending on how good its protected memory is, as well. If you are having a problem with this, add this line to the base level (it can't be in a VirtualHost or any other directive) of the `httpd.conf`:

```
SSLProtocol SSLv2
```

15.4 Logging

As you might expect, Apache supports the Common Log Format (CLF). It can also write its logs in the format used by NCSA's server; this is nice if you have homegrown log analysis tools developed for NCSA httpd.

The number of tools for analyzing httpd access logs is bewildering. Many are free, but there are commercial tools out there as well, though few run on Linux. On the other hand, more of the free ones run on Linux than on Mac or Microsoft (MS) Windows machines.

Which one you choose to use is a matter of taste. We will describe a couple below, but you will likely just have to try some and see if you like them.

The log analysis tool we have found most useful is `http-analyze`. It is free and information on it can be found at `http://www.netstore.de/Supply/http-analyze/index.html`.

One particular tool deserves special note: 3Dstats. It formats its output in VRML which you can view with a VRML scene viewer like vrweb . 3Dstats's home page is `http://www.netstore.de/Supply/3Dstats/` and Vrweb's is `http://www.iicm.edu/vrweb`.

If you wish to investigate other analysis tools for your httpd logs, a Web search on http log analysis will kick up more choices than you will have time to try out.

15.5 Databases and Web Servers

With the desire for dynamic content in the presentation of large amounts of information, it is natural that databases would enter the Web equation. They are the best and fastest way (not the most space efficient, though!) to organize and retrieve data. There is support for many free and commercial databases in the popular languages used for CGI, including Python, Perl, and C.

The choice of which database to use is dependent on many factors. Among the most important is easy access via CGI or PHP if you choose to employ one of them. For a list of database servers available for Linux, see the chapter on applications.

15.6 Setting up a Killer Web Server

This section will walk you through setting up a "complete" Web server: Apache with PHP/FI compiled in and integrated support for MySQL, a freeware (for most purposes) database server. While this is not a typical setup, it is an extremely powerful one that is becoming more common.

In this setup, Apache depends on PHP which in turn will depend on MySQL. Consequently, you need to install MySQL first. It should be noted that PHP does not require any database support at all, but the idea behind this exercise is to build a web server with very fast CGI-like features tied in with a very fast database server.

MySQL

If possible, when you are anticipating large amounts of database activity, MySQL should be installed on a separate physical disk from the document root of your Web server. The MySQL source is available from the MySQL home page at `http://www.tcx.se/` as well as from mirror sites in the United States. If you prefer, you can retrieve a precompiled binary distribution. There is also an active mailing list for MySQL. Information on joining it can be found on the MySQL homepage. Documentation is available there as well.

The most recent versions of MySQL require recent versions of libc. If you don't have a new enough libc and are skittish about upgrading it, just install a binary version.

If you install a binary distribution, it will create a directory named mysql-<version> with various subdirectories for libraries, header files and data files. If you compile and install from the source, mysql subdirectores will be created in `/usr/local/lib` and `/usr/local/include`. The data folders and files will be created in `/usr/local/var`.

Note the prefix path (`/usr/local` by default), it will be needed you compile PHP and, later, Apache.

MySQL uses GNU autoconf. There are a few configuration options to be especially aware of.

`--prefix`	Installation directory prefix (/usr/local by default)
`--enable-thread-safe-client`	Make thread safe client library.

`--without-debug`	Compile without extra debugging code
`--without-server`	Only compile client library and programs
`--without-perl`	Don't build and install the Perl interface
`--enable-shared`	Build a shared client library

After the configuration finishes you can run make and then make install. If this is your first time installing MySQL, you will also need to install the grants database too. Chapter 13 has more details on installing and setting up MySQL. If you are just upgrading MySQL you need only start and restart the server.

Okay, this is the paragraph where we tell you that you need to know SQL to start using your new Web server and that this isn't a book on SQL and that you will need to either search out tutorials on the Web or buy a book on SQL. The MySQL homepage has some examples in its online documentation and a separately maintained manual, more importantly, tells what additional features MySQL has beyond standard One good SQL tutorial can be found at `http://w3.one.net/~jhoffman/sqltut.htm` and there are others to be had, as well as numerous books.

PHP

PHP/FI is the next item to compile. You will, however, need to have Apache unpacked since at the end of the compile, the PHP module and lib-php will be copied into the Apache source directory. PHP/FI's home page is at `http://php.iquest.net/`; very complete documentation, information on the PHP mailing list, the source code, and other related items can be found there.

Since you are building only the library and not the CGI version of PHP, compilation should be easy; there is no linking step, so no linking errors. All the potentially sticky linking will come when you compile and link Apache. You will need to know the mSQL install root and the location of the Apache source code. PHP, as you will notice when you run the install script (something of a misnomer since it doesn't install anything), supports a large number of databases and enhanced file upload, logging and access control. Depending on your system's resources and your Web site's style, you may want to enable some or all of these.

Obviously you will want to answer yes to MySQL support. If you have any of the other supported databases, you may want to enable them as well. PHP also supports the GD graphics library; if you wish to enable this, make sure libgd and its associated header file are in `/usr/lib` and `/usr/include` or `/usr/local/lib` and `/usr/local/include` or provide the directories in the list of additional directories to search for libraries and header files. It is fine to let PHP use the Linux system regex library and it should find the gdbm library and header that come with Linux as well. Change directories to the src directory and run make.

At the end of the make, directions for editing the Apache configuration file will be printed. You may want to copy them into a file or editor to keep them for the Apache compilation.

Apache

The Apache configuration and compilation are straightforward. Move into the source directory and edit the file "`Configuration`" and make the changes indicated at the end of the PHP make. The configuration file is loaded with various modules you can disable or enable by commenting or uncommenting the appropriate lines in the file. In general, the slimmer you can make the server, the better. Comment out what you obviously don't need. If you're not sure, leave the module in. If you anticipate having large numbers of users to authenticate, you will probably want to enable a database-based authentication scheme using (g)dbm, MySQL or mSQL. A complete list of modules and their descriptions can be found at `http://www.apache.org/`.

After you have finished editing, run the Configure script and then make. If you have linking errors, 90 percent of the time they can be solved by rearranging the list of libraries in the `LFLAGS` in the Configuration file. Most of the rest of the time it is simply a forgotten library or library path. Persevering though a little trial and error should result in a httpd binary. After testing the server a little, you will likely want to strip it to save on memory requirements.

If you still can't get your server to link, the best forums for help will likely be the PHP and/or MySQL mailing lists, unless you believe the problem to be unrelated to the addition of these packages.

Now check `httpd.conf` and `srm.conf`.

Under Linux, Apache is commonly set up as follows:

- The httpd binary lives in `/usr/sbin`.

- The logs are kept in `/var/log/http`.

- The configuration files are in `/etc/http/conf`.

- The document root is `/home/httpd/htdocs`.

All of these are alterable. Obviously you can keep the server binary wherever you choose. The configuration files location is settable on the command line and the log location and the document root are settable in the configuration files.

To tell Apache to parse .phtml files with the embedded PHP parser, add a line like this to your srm.conf:

```
AddType application/x-httpd-php .phtml
```

If you want to parse every file and end them all in .html, change .phtml to .html in the statement.

Now start up the server. With the above setup, you would enter httpd -f /etc/httpd/conf/httpd.conf -d /home/httpd. Make or edit (if it already exists) an index.html in the document root. Somewhere in the document, add a line like <? phpinfo(); ?>

The phpinfo function should spit out a few screenfuls of CGI environment variables and configuration information. If it doesn't, check to make sure you added the correct line to your srm.conf or httpd.conf to tell Apache to parse .phtml or .html files, make sure you have the right extension on your file and mod_php enabled in your Apache source Configuration file.

The PHP documentation describes how to connect to MySQL databases either locally or remotely as well as the usage of the various functions for performing queries and database and table administration.

There are other goodies you may want to consider adding to your server. If you use lots of Python or Perl CGI you can embed the interpreters for these into Apache as well. Respectively these modules are PyApache and Mod_Perl. If you wish to enhance security you can use digest authentication instead of the basic authentication. Also you can add in SSL support as mentioned earlier in this chapter. Finally there are modules for powerful URL rewriting using regex pattern matching and replacement; correcting misspelled URIs, and tracking users through the site using cookies. New modules are being added all the time and not all are shipped with the source, check the Apache web site for the most up to date list.

15.7 Streaming Audio and Video

Streaming is an alternate way to deliver content. Rather then waiting for an entire movie file to download before starting it, the data are displayed as they are sent (more or less, there is some buffering). This, of course, means that the client can start displaying the data much sooner. Additionally, it is easy to then send and output streams from streaming input (as opposed to a static file).

With the rising demand for multimedia content on the web, sooner or later (probably sooner!) you will need to be able to serve streaming audio and video from your Web server. Lucky for Linux, RealNetworks makes its RealServer for Linux.

The basic version is free and intended for personal and single-site use (i.e., ISPs do not get to use the free version). Installation is as simple as uncompressing the distribution file, running the setup script, and answering some configuration questions.

RealServer will deliver both live and on-demand (stored in a file) streams. The default port for the server is 7070.

The Plus version, which is not free and not yet available for Linux can be used by a hosting service. Additionally the Plus version has enhanced performance, a printed manual, GUI, and, as you might expect, technical and upgrade support.

The default installation directory is /usr/local/pnserver. After the installation script completes, change to the install directory and start the server:

```
# bin/pnserver server.cfg
```

You will be prompted to register the server. You can skip this step if you wish without any effect on the functionality or performance of the server. Point you Web browser at that machine you installed the server on, port 7070. You will be prompted to enter the username and password you provided during setup. This will bring up a page with links to some samples, the server status page, and links to some areas on RealNetworks' Web site.

Test the server by trying some of the sample files to be sure it's running. RealMedia files can be placed in /usr/local/pnserver/content and accessed via URLs like http://www.foo.net/ramgen/audio.rm. You can also set up aliases or subdirectories for mortal users to place their own files in.

Generating Content Files

Various encoders exist for creating real audio and video. Unfortunately, only an audio encoder exists for Linux. To encode video or audio/video, you will need an MS Win32 machine or a Macintosh.

The media encoder, rmenc, for Linux is free as well and can be used to convert .wav and .au files into RealMedia files. Additionally, if you have the OSS sound drivers, it can listen to your soundcard output and record that.

If you wish to record individual tracks from your CD-ROM, you can use cdda2wav to make .wav files and convert them using rmenc.

15.8 Summary

This chapter scratches the surface of what has become an incredibly huge and complicated subject in just a few short years. We discussed two types of servers, secure and insecure, as well as two methods of implementing them, the common forking server and the newer and less common multiplexing server.

Because of its popularity, extensibility, and power, we went into detail about Apache and its two secure derivatives: Apache-SSL, a freeware secure server of questionable legality in the United States; and Stronghold, a commercially supported and legal secure server available in and outside the United States.

We also discussed various methods for interacting with the system the server is running on: CGI and SSI, as well as PHP, a scripting language designed to be embedded into HTML and then parsed by the PHP interpreter running as CGI or FastCGI or compiled into Apache.

Setup and configuration of a server for streaming audio and video was examined. Additionally tools for creating content files were also discussed.

Lastly, we went through the compilation and setup of a non-secure Apache server with PHP compiled into it. In turn, PHP was configured with MySQL support so it can access MySQL databases locally or remotely on other machines.

X Windowing System

16

Giving a nice front end to Linux.

The X Window System (or just X if you like) is a windowing system designed to give a GUI to UNIX.

The implementation of X for Linux is XFree86, and it is almost always included in a normal Linux installation. The power behind X is that you can change just about any operation of the interface, from the size of your xterms to the way menus are presented and the contents of the menus. There's even an interface that closely resembles Windows 95.

16.1 X Concepts

The idea behind X was that you have a client/server setup. The server is really an X protocol server on the user's console. The server then talks to clients (like a window manager and applications) and puts them on the screen.

The configuration file for XFree86 is called XF86config. It can be located in any number of places including `/etc, /usr/X11/lib/X11`, or even /. Check your installation for the location. This file contains setup information for your mouse, the video card you're using, and the type of display (monitor) that you're using.

The programming for XFree86 allows you, as the user, to set your monitor and your video card to much better resolutions than you can get by default through Windows or other video graphics array (VGA) modes. The default modes (640X480, 800X600, and 1024X768) are still available, and relatively easy to set up. To get custom modes, you'll need some information about the video card (the type of card it is and dot clocks), and some information about your monitor (video bandwidth, horizontal frequency, and vertical frequency). Then you'll need to check the XFree86 documentation about how to put it all together.

16.2 Setting Up X

To set up your X System configuration with default modes, make sure your X server is installed. For normal VGA modes, this is the X_VGA file. Going from there, the Mach32 server is called XF86_Mach32, and S3 server is called XF86_S3, and so on. When you did your installation, you may have been asked for the type of video card you had. In this case, you can select the server for your particular video card. You may also want to include the regular VGA file just in case.

The xf86config program will allow you to set up some default video modes. Starting the program as root gives a few configuration screens and some text to read. Then you get into the configuration section. Select your mouse type (Microsoft, MouseSystems, Bus, etc). The preference here is to select a three-button mouse, since X will allow you to use all three buttons. If you select a two-button mouse, you'll need to hit both the left and right mouse buttons to simulate the middle button.[1]

The next few options depend on the type of mouse you selected. If you selected a three-button mouse, then you won't need to select "Emulate3Buttons." Next you'll need to enter the location of the mouse, which may be /dev/mouse. If /dev/mouse doesn't exist, enter the /dev file that has your mouse on it. Remember that COM1: under DOS is /dev/ttyS0 under Linux, and so on. A few other options may follow, including using the ALT key as the "Meta" key to generate characters not normally available on your keyboard.

---

[1] When you see "Emulate three Buttons" later on, this is what it's talking about.

Next is the monitor configuration section. This is where you need to know the horizontal sync range. There are nine predefined monitors you can choose from, and a tenth allows you to define your own range.

WARNING: Be sure that the numbers entered here are correct, because a wrong monitor and video card pair can damage your monitor, video card, or both. Don't say I didn't warn you.

Next is the vertical sync. Here you have a choice of about four monitor types, plus one to let you define your own. Once the vertical sync is set, you can enter information about your monitor. This section isn't necessary, as this allows XFree86 to use multiple monitors at the same time. You can either press enter and use the default for each, or enter a unique identifier for your monitor, along with a vendor name and model name.

Once this is completed, you set up the video card. It's important to select the correct video card because two video cards from the same vendor can have very different hardware internally. Selecting the wrong card can damage your card or monitor.

Now you get to select the type of server to run. If you selected a video card that has an accelerator chip supported by XFree86, you'll be able to select that X server.

The options are as follows.

1. The XF86_Mono server, which is a 640x480 resolution with two colors, black and white. This should work for all VGA cards. If you suspect a problem with your video card or are unsure of the type of video card you have, this may be a good starting point.

2. XF86_VGA16 server, which is also 640x480, but with 16 colors. This should also work with all VGA-compactible cards.

3. XF86_SVGA server, which provides Super VGA (SVGA) resolutions with 256 colors. This is an unaccelerated server, so most ISA SVGA cards will probably work with it.

4. Accelerated server, which is for accelerated cards. This gives more than 256 colors for most servers, and higher resolutions. These servers also utilize any of the faster chipsets in most modern video cards.

5. The server for the video card you selected earlier.

If you select 5, the best server for your card is set up for installation.

Now you must give information about your video card. First you'll probably be asked about the amount of video memory on your card. You'll get five selections from 256K to 4096K (4 Mb) and a sixth selection that allows you to enter your own amount.

Once that is completed, you'll be allowed to enter a description for your video card similar to the monitor descriptions above. You can either press enter through the entries, or type in the description, vendor, and model of your video card.

If you have an S3- or AGX-based video card, you may need to know the type of random access memory digital to analog convertor (RAMDAC) the card has. The RAMDAC is used to get high color (greater than about 32K colors) from the server. Enter the appropriate entry if you have those cards and know the RAMDAC type, or else you can just press enter.

Some video cards also have a programmable clock. Most clocks are not programmable, but if yours is (some Diamond cards and some S3 cards are), enter the type of clockchip you have. It should be found in your owner's manual, or on the card itself. If you don't have a clockchip, just press enter.

At this point, the xf86config program will attempt to find the clocks that your card supports by using the X -probeonly command. This command doesn't start X itself, but asks the video card to return what clocks it knows about. These clocks are important to determine the correct resolutions you can use.

Now you should be ready to start X. Doing this is simply getting to a command prompt and typing

```
> startx
```

This will start the X server in the lowest color depth and resolution you selected. If you configured your server to use 8-bit color (256 colors) and also for 16-bit (65K colors), just typing startx will start the X server in 8-bit mode. To start it up in 16-bit mode, use the following:

```
> startx -- -bpp 16
```

For the sake of extra memory, you may want to log out of other virtual consoles (VCs) before starting X, since you can start multiple shells (xterms) from within X. You can switch to a virtual console while in X by pressing CTRL-ALT-Fn where n is a number between 1 and 6. The first X server usually uses virtual console 7. You can see what VC is being used when X starts up, or by going through the virtual consoles.

Once you enter the startx command, you should see some text fly off the screen. The screen will change to a graphic screen and a mouse cursor. The look here can change based on a few things.

16.3 xdm

The xdm program is a graphical login window, instead of the regular text-based login and password prompt most UNIX users are familiar with. It's better for use with newer users or in a lab environment, since the user doesn't have to issue any commands to start X running. You can automatically have xdm start on boot by changing the default runlevel to 5 and rebooting.

16.4 Using the X Window Managers

The way that X looks is determined by two things: the contents of the window and the window manager. The windows merely interact with the X server and there is no real way of moving the windows around the screen, or resizing the windows. This is where the window manager comes in. The window manager places a border around the window and can provide maximize (full-screen) or minimize (iconize) buttons. The window manager also allows you to resize, move, or kill windows. The window manager also provides for menus and the general "look and feel" of the X display.

There are a few different window managers available, such as twm, fvwm, olwm, and the commercially available mwm. Each window manager has its own look, and mwm even has its own header files and libraries to use some extra functions not present in the other window managers. The openlook window manager also has its own extra libraries and interface. The two remaining window managers, twm and fvwm, have their specific window borders and default menu options.

```
[twm.tif, fvwm.tif, mwm.tif and fwvm95.tif]
```

Even though the windows look different, they perform many of the same functions. One advantage that fvwm has over twm is that fvwm provides for virtual desktops. That is, you can have more than one main window (also called the root window) available to you at one time. This lets you have a neater X desktop, or it can let you open more windows and be able to see all of them.

MWM

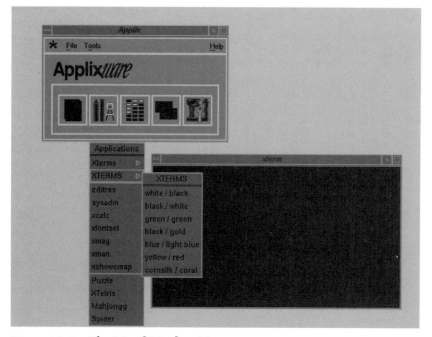

Figure 16–1   The Motif Window Manager

Motif is really a group of widgets that make for a common look and feel for programs. The Motif Window Manager (MWM) is one of the programs behind the Common Desktop Environment (CDE) which is trying to give a standard interface to all UNIX workstations. The downside to Motif is that it's commercial. The upside is that you don't need to purchase Motif to use programs that were built using it. Programs compiled using Motif libraries can be copied freely.

FVWM

The Feeble (Fine?—no one knows what the F stands for anymore) Virtual Window Manager (FVWM) is one of the most popular window managers around. The program itself is relatively small; it comes with a lot of features from virtual windows to menu buttons. You can also set it up so specific programs start only on a certain virtual window.

FVWM2-95

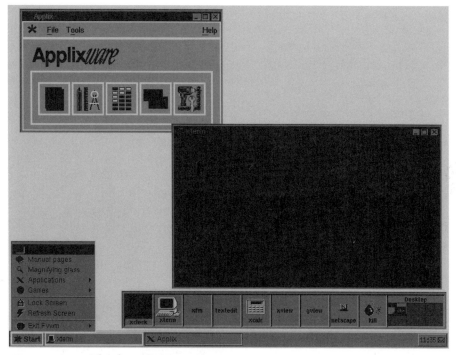

Figure 16–2   The fvwm2-95 program

The fvwm2-95 program is an extension of FVWM which has a Windows 95 look and feel. However, the interface is much more configurable. You have the advantages of the task bar and start menu, but you get additional features such as "focus follows mouse" where the current window is wherever the mouse is. You also get the advantage of configuring all the mouse buttons however you like. This is the most popular window manager for those coming from the windows environment since it's so familiar.

The nice advantage, though, is that fvwm2-95 doesn't crash.

The .fvwm2rc (or .fvwm2rc95) file contains startup information for FVWM. Many of the commands are similar between fvwm2 and fvwm2-95. Since for our purposes the two window managers are rather similar, we'll use .fvwmrc to talk about both the .fvwm2rc and .fvwm2rc95 files.

Focus

There are three ways to determine which window has the "focus," that is, what window will be controlled by the keyboard. The first method is the one you're most familiar with—click in the window to make it the active window. This is called "Click to Focus" and it is turned on in the .fvwmrc file with the following:

```
Style "*" ClickToFocus
```

The other two methods, Mouse Focus and Sloppy Focus, are very similar. Mouse Focus means that wherever the mouse pointer is has the control. Sloppy Focus is the same as Mouse Focus, with the exception that if the mouse pointer leaves the window but does not enter another window (for example, goes to the root window), the window you were just in remains focused. You can turn on this focus method with either of these options:

```
Style "*" MouseFocus
Style "*" SloppyFocus
```

Menus

Besides the regular start menu that has about the same configurability as the Windows 95 start menu, there are also menus available if you left-click on the root window. These menus are also defined in the .fvwmrc file. The menus are pretty much self-documenting. The "AddToMenu" line adds a menu definition called "Quit-Verify" that has a title of "Really Quit Fvwm?"

The next lines define the items in that menu. The + at the beginning of the line means it's part of the menu, followed by the text in the menu. You can include an icon in this if you enclose the icon name in %. The last part of the menu line is the actual command. The "Restart" in this menu means to quit fvwm and then start the named program. This allows you to quit fvwm and start another window manager. If a menu option has no text and has an action of "Nop," then it will create a separator in the menu. Replacing the "Restart" with "Exec" will start the new program without quitting fvwm—but note it's not a good idea to start multiple window managers.

```
#
# This menu is invoked as a sub-menu—it allows you to quit,
# restart, or switch to another WM.
#
AddToMenu "Quit-Verify" "Really Quit Fvwm?" Title
+ "Restart%mini-turn.xpm%"    Restart fvwm95-2
+ "" Nop
```

```
+ "Start twm"                Restart /usr/X11R6/bin/twm
+ "Start MWM"                Restart /usr/X11R6/bin/mwm
+ "Start olvwm%mini-olwm.xpm%" Restart /usr/openwin/bin/olvwm
+ "Start olwm%mini-olwm.xpm%" Restart /usr/openwin/bin/olwm
+ ""                         Nop
+ "Yes, Really Quit%mini-exclam.xpm%" Quit
+ "No, Don't Quit%mini-cross.xpm%" Nop
```

Modules

One of the reasons that everyone likes fvwm2 so much (besides the configurability, cheap price, number of people who have configuration files, look and feel of Windows 95, etc.) is the fact that many functions of fvwm are in modules that don't always have to be loaded in memory. This allows one configuration to have a very bare-bones setup, while another setup may have all the bells and whistles (literally).

Modules get started either in the .fvwmrc file or can be started from the menu. Here's some of the major modules you'll see in fvwm2:

pager—Sets up a virtual desktop, allowing you to have multiple desktops to work in. fvwm can also be configured to start specific programs in specific virtual desktops for easier use.

task bar—This is one of the critical parts of fvwm2-95. The task bar acts very much like the task bar of Windows 95, giving a list of running programs, the current time, status of any incoming E-mail, and the ever-popular start menu.

buttons—If you look above the task bar in the fvwm2-95 window, you'll see a series of buttons, a clock, and the desktop (the pager module). This is the button module, and it cannot only create buttons to start programs (Netscape, xterm, etc.) but it can also have the output of some programs running inside it. The clock and the FVWM pager are two examples of this. Some users have CD players, system load programs, and other programs running within the buttons. As with most FVWM functions, the style, size, contents, and location of the buttons can be set from within the .fvwmrc file.

audio—Yes, if you choose, you can have FVWM make noises when you do things within FVWM (opening windows, starting FVWM, stopping FVWM, etc.).

auto—This module allows you to automatically "raise" (bring to the front) a window after a certain amount of time. The window must have the focus for the allotted time before the window gets raised.

KDE

In case you ever wanted the functionality that Windows 98 is supposed to have without all the excess Microsoft baggage, there's KDE. The beta we're using to write this section (Beta3) seems to be rather stable and is a magnificent environment for first-time users. Like Windows 98, many of the functions of the desktop are integrated, with drag and drop capabilities, and there is a heavy dependence on browsers. KDE comes with its own HTML browser that, while not as full featured as something like Netscape, does the job quite well. The only drawback is that for applications to take full advantage of this, they have to be written to work with KDE. However, there are a number of applications already written in KDE from CD players to editors to games. More are being written and should quickly have enough components to equal what Windows 98 took three years to develop. Another downside is that some of the applications expect you to be connected to the Internet. For example, the CD player (kscd) will talk to the CDDB database at cddb.cddb.com to get information about the CD you're playing. If you're not connected to the Internet, this feature is somewhat wasted. However, if you have a dial up connection, you can get the CD information and then save it locally so you'll have it next time.

The file manager (called KFM) allows for seamless use of FTP, HTTP, tar and GZIP files. As files or Web pages are selected, they get opened and displayed (or an appropriate application that can handle the file is started). KDE is similar to CDE in that there is an application and virtual window manager on the bottom of the screen. This can be configured to autohide, much like the Windows95 taskbar. Each window in KDE has a thumbtack attached to it to make that window "sticky" and show that window in each virtual screen. This makes it handy for clocks or other applications to always be seen. KDE also remembers what applications you were running last time and starts them up the next time you start KDE. Much of the configuration, from virtual windows, autohiding, and background, autoraise of windows, and so on, can be done in KDE itself all without restarting the window manager. Unlike many other window managers, KDE does not require you to edit configuration files.

For the large numbers of applications and amount of configurability that KDE gives, it's well worth the drive space, especially if you have fans of Windows 95 who don't like the normal X interface. Their web page is `http://www.kde.org` and figure 16–3 shows a screen shot of KDE in action.

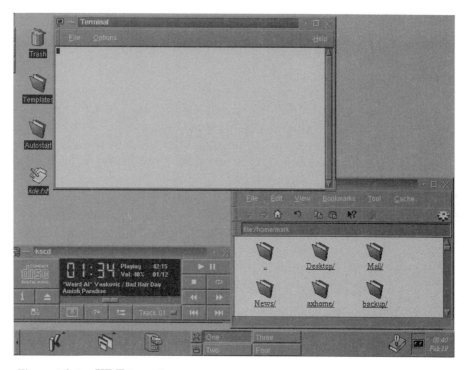

Figure 16–3   KDE in action

16.5 User Programs

The default X setup has a bunch of user programs, including shells, utilities, and a couple of games. These programs all have a few default options that you can set when you first start them. I'll show this by introducing the xterm, which is the X terminal emulator. This is almost the same as logging into the shell. The big difference here is that the .login file is not read, but the .cshrc is, instead.

Here are a few of the common options you can use with almost all X programs:

```
-display <host>:<display>
```

Send the display (not just the output) to the named host and display number. In most cases, the display can be 0.0 which means the first X server and the first display on that X server. The program still gets executed on the remote CPU, but the window gets displayed elsewhere. This setting will override the DISPLAY environment variable if it's set. If the DISPLAY variable is set and the -display option is not used, the window will automatically be displayed on the host and display set in DISPLAY.

```
-bg <color>
```

Sets the color of the background of the window. Color can either be a name of a color ("grey" or "blue") or as collections of RGB (red, green, blue) values in hex. The syntax for this is `rgb:h/h/h` where h is a hex number relating to the amount of red (in the first slot), green (in the second slot), and blue (in the third slot) to make a particular color. The hex number can be one to four characters long, depending on the number of colors your X server supports. For example, `rgb:0/0/0` is black, while `rgb:ffff/0/0` is red. A list of colors that have names is available in the `/usrX11/lib/X11/rgb.txt` file. Each entry has the RGB values in decimal (0 to 255) and a name, which can be used instead of the `rgb:h/h/h` entry.

```
-fg <color>
```

sets the color of the foreground.

```
-fn <font>
```

specifies the default font to use in the window. You can get lists of the available fonts using the xfontsel or xlsfonts programs.

```
-geometry <WIDTH>x<HEIGHT>+<XOFF>+<YOFF>
```

Sets the size and position of the window. For an xterm, this is in terms of characters, so a geometry of

```
> xterm -geometry 80x25
```

would create a window that is 80 characters wide and 25 lines long. The XOFF and YOFF set where the upper-left-hand corner of the window should be placed. In the case of positive XOFF or YOFF, the offset is from the left or top sides, respectively. For negative XOFF or YOFF, the offset is from the right or bottom sides, respectively. Here's some example screen placements:

```
+0+0    Upper-left-hand corner
-0+0    Upper-right-hand corner
-0-0    Lower-right-hand corner
+0-0    Lower-left-hand corner
```

Note that you can enter either a geometry or an offset, but you can't enter only XOFF or width by itself. Both the geometry and the offset have to be entered as a pair. That is, you can't enter

```
> xterm -geometry 80
```

or

```
> xterm -geometry +0
```

but the following will work:

```
> xterm -geometry 80x25
```

or

```
> xterm -geometry +0+0
```

There's one other way to specify default settings for X programs, and this is through the .Xdefaults file. Anything you can set through the command line can be stored in the .Xdefaults file so when you start the program, you don't need to give all the options. These options are known as resources.

16.6 X RESOURCES

An X resource can consist of four item types:

```
program.widget[.widget..].resource: value
```

where:

program: Program name

widget: One or more levels of widgets, which are sub-portions of the window. A widget can be a button, menu, scrollbar, option list, and so on.

resource: The "least common denominator" of the widgets. The resource may be used by more than one program. For example "geometry" is used by all X programs and is a resource.

value: What the resource gets set to. Can be a number, boolean (true or false), color, or some other value. It depends on the resource.

Any text from a ! to the end of the line is commented out.

To get from the most-specific widget (program) to the least-specific widget (resource) the widgets must be combined. These combinations can be specified by either a period or a star. A period indicates a tight binding and a star (or asterisk) represents a loose binding.

In a loose binding, the link between two widgets does not have to be direct, and it acts almost like a regular expression in grep. That is, you can have an entry such as

```
*geometry: 80x25
```

This would say that all geometry settings would be 80x25. While this is good for text-based programs, a graphical application with a setting of 80x25 pixels would be rather small indeed. If you have a particular program, you can then become more specific. That is, if you want all programs that use the vt100 widget to have a geometry of 80x25, you can make the setting like this:

```
*vt100.geometry: 80x25
```

And you can get even more specific. Say that you want your terminal emulators to have a size of 80x25, and you want your Seyon[2] emulator to have a size of 80x40. Then you would have two settings of

```
xterm.vt100.geometry: 80x25
Seyon.vt100.geometry: 80x40
```

Here you have tight bindings. The Seyon program uses the vt100 widget, which then sets the geometry. Using a loose binding for Seyon,

```
Seyon*geometry: 80x40
```

This would cause all of the windows that Seyon creates to be 80x40. Since Seyon creates a few graphical-based windows, this would bring us back having graphical windows that are 80 pixels by 40 pixels.

Note that you can replace tight bindings with loose bindings. The following two entries have identical effects:

```
Seyon.vt100.geometry: 80x40
Seyon*vt100*geometry: 80x40
```

Here are a few sample entries that apply to the xterm:

```
xterm*scrollBar: true !    Turn on the scroll bar on the left side
```

---

[2] Seyon is a terminal emulator.

```
xterm*geometry: 80x25 !   Set the size to 80x25
xterm*background: gray68 ! Gray background
xterm*foreground: black !  Black characters
```

16.7 X APPLICATIONS

Along with xterm and Seyon, there are a number of other client programs that you can run. Almost all X programs use the -display, -geometry, -background commands plus some extra options. Note that while these options override the settings in the .Xdefaults file, it is really up to the window manager to make the settings. These options (and the settings in .Xdefaults) are really suggestions to the window manager. The window manager often allows the requests, but there may be a case where the window manager does its own thing.

-fg <color> or -foreground <color>—foreground color

-fn <font> or -font <font>—Default font

-iconic—start the program as an icon

-title <text>—give a window a title

Available X applications:

xmh—E-mail handler

bitmap—bitmap editor

xman—X interface to the man program

xclock—digital or analog clock

xcalc—calculator

xkill—kill a window

xwd—dump a window image to a file

There are also other X applications not part of the X project that are sometimes installed with Linux:

seyon—communication program

xsysinfo—system information (CPU idle, memory free, and so on.)

xpaint—paint program

ghostview—view PostScript files

As Linux's popularity has grown so has the number of "non-server" applications. These range from the frivolous to so-called personal productivity applications usually associated with Windows or Macintosh desktops.

Most of the applications we have discussed so far have been server oriented or programming languages. The few exceptions have been office suites, word processors, and spreadsheets.

Here we want to talk about some of the "fun" software for Linux. These range from pure eye candy to the semi-useful to various games. Some of these were developed under Linux; others have been developed elsewhere, some even predate Linux.

Eye Candy

Xsnow

A silly little program. It creates snow on your X desktop which accumulates on your window tops. Periodically a sleigh pulled by reindeer flies across the screen and it blizzards. Run it around Christmas. Figure 16–4 shows a screenshot of Xsnow and gets in the holiday mood!

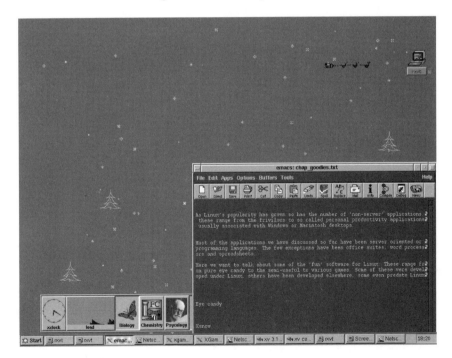

Figure 16–4   Xsnow

Semi-Useful

Workman

Sure, a basic CD audio player comes with almost every OS these days, but why be satisfied with just play, pause, stop, and skip? Workman is a very full-featured CD player. It sports play lists, a CD database, balance control, playmodes, just about everything you would expect. Many Workman users make their CD databases available for download. Figure 16–5 shows the main Workman interface that you use to control the CD player. Figure 16–6 shows the track and CD information screen used to input tracks, playlists, and so on.

As a result of its SunOS heritage, Workman requires the Xview libraries to run. If you want to compile it yourself, you will need the header files as well. Luckily these are freely available.

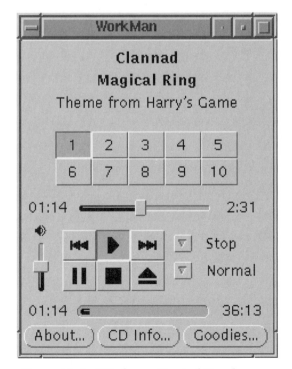

Figure 16–5   Workman Control Panel

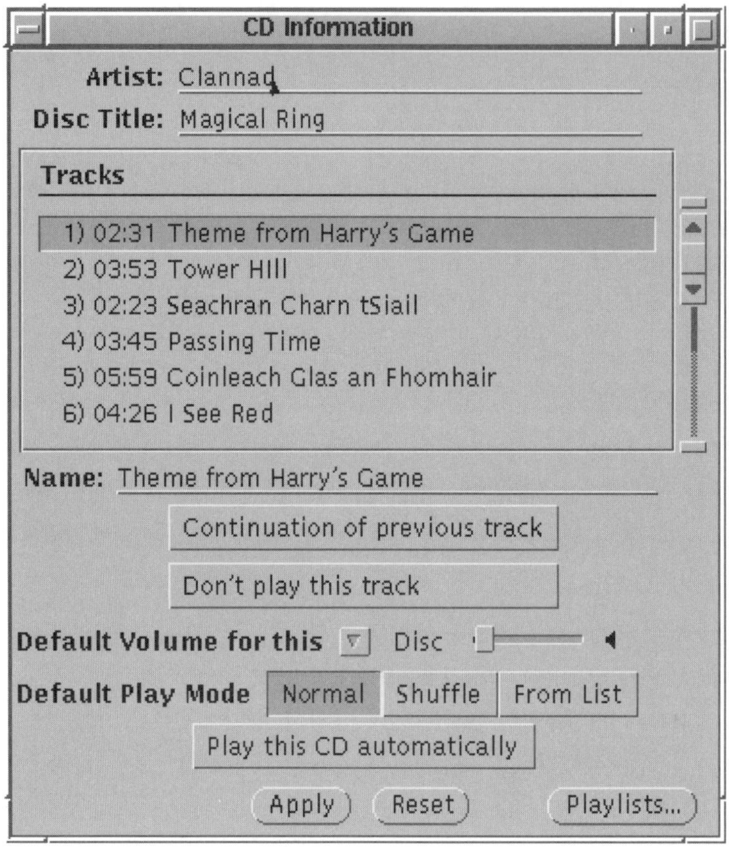

Figure 16–6   Track and CD Information

Xcthugha

Xcthugha is another CD player. Compared to the interfaces of Workman and Xmcd, it is pretty thin. However, Xcthugha's forte is not its interface; it's what else it does with the music. It creates a visual representation of the sound stream.

Depending on the music and the individual, it induces anything from mesmerization to motion sickness. It can be run in an X or full-screen VGA mode. Under X it can run in a window, the root window or as a screen saver. Finally, it can be used in a client/server mode.

Figures 16–7, 16–8, and 16–9 show Xcthugha, its control panel, and the CD controls (reached by typing F1, c).

Cthugha
Where is the music?

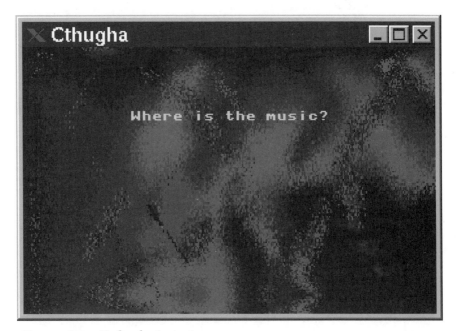

Figure 16–7 Xcthugha in Action

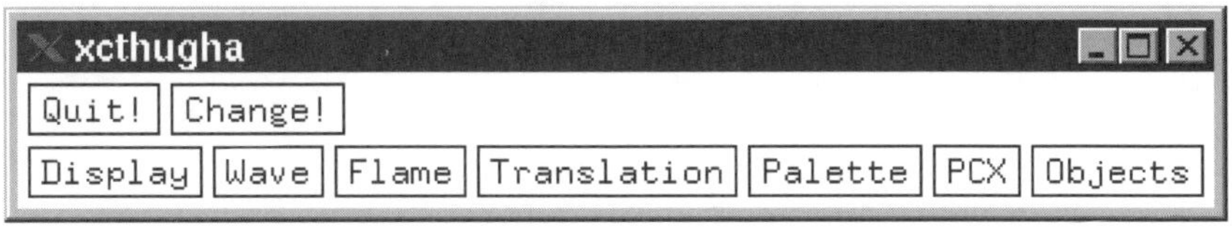

xcthugha
Quit!
Change!
Display
Wave
Flame
Translation
Palette
PCX
Objects

Figure 16–8 Xcthugha Control Panel

Figure 16–9   Xcthugha Status Information

MpegTV player

MpegTV is a real-time, software-only (i.e., no hardware acceleration) real-time player for MPEG-1 video and audio layer 1 or 2 streams. The stream can be file or network based. It supports mono or stereo audio and video depths from 8 to 32 bits. Finally, under Linux only, it can play video CDs.

xanim

If you ever wanted to watch AVI or MOV files on your Linux machine, then xanim is for you. It brings up a window that shows the movies along with a control panel to fast forward, rewind, and so on. There are a number of CDs on the market with movies or episodes of the Three Stooges that you can get for under $20 that are in AVI format and work perfectly with xanim.

SoundStudio

As its name implies, this is a well-featured application for recording, mixing, and editing sound. It is commercial software, but the Linux pricing is very low. Also, it uses Motif, so be sure to get the statically linked version if you don't have Motif (as of this writing, it would not run with Lesstif, a free Motif clone). The main window of SoundStudio is shown in Figure 16–10.

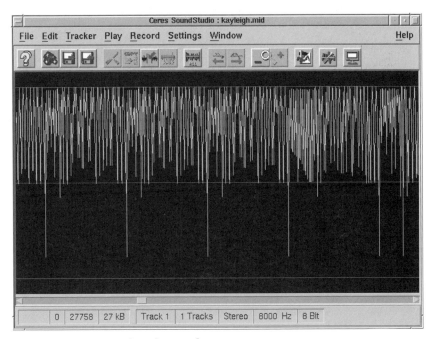

Figure 16–10   SoundStudio window

RealPlayer

RealNetworks makes a free version of their integrated RealAudio and RealVideo player for Linux. With RealPlayer you can listen to and/or view streaming audio/video served from RealNetworks' streaming audio and visual server.

The Plus version, which can record and features enhanced performance and preset buttons (like a car radio) is not available for Linux yet.

RealPlayer can run as a standalone application or as a plugin for Netscape. The plugin version will not play video in an 8-bit color display although the standalone will.

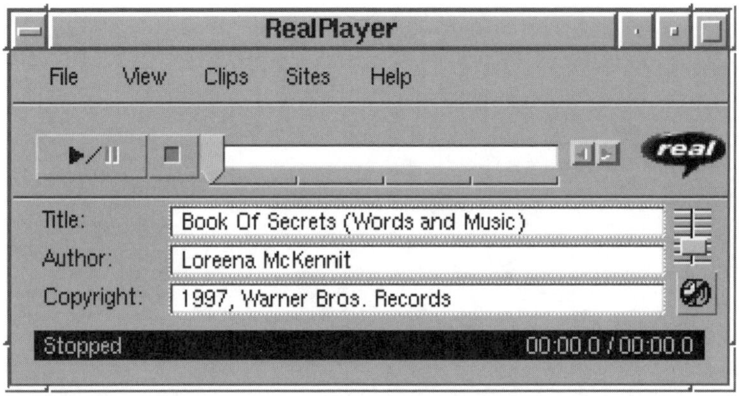

Figure 16–11   RealPlayer Control Panel

16.8 Amusements and Games

xpat

For those of you who want just a simple game, xpat may be for you. It's a collection of solitaire games (including the classic "solitaire" and "freecell" games that are popular on other operating systems).

Quake/Quake II

It's not hard to ignore these rather popular games (and their predecessor—Doom and Doom II). Quake and Quake II are available for Linux and provide all the same features that are in the Windows version. Linux provides three display types for playing: X11, SVGAlib, and 3Dfx. The X11 interface brings Quake up in a window and allows you to play with other applications up at the same time. The SVGAlib allows for a full-screen play but requires root access and exclusive use of the screen and keyboard. The 3Dfx version (GLquake) uses the Mesa GL library and a 3Dfx-based 3D card to provide superior texture mapping and graphics. The Mesa library and 3Dfx can also be used with VRML applications to make very high-quality graphics. Check the Id software home page (www.idsoftware.com) for more information about Linux Quake.

16.9 Using Remote Displays

The biggest advantage of X over Macintosh, Windows 95, and even the standard Windows NT is that X can send the output of a program to another X server. That is, I can be running the program in New York, with the display in my office in Massachusetts. Or, programs can run across an office, allowing you to practically control a Linux machine from anywhere.

Three things are required for the remote displays to work. First, there has to be a TCP/IP connection between the two machines. This can be Ethernet, PPP, ATM, and the like. Next, the X server (where you'll be watching the program) has to know that a client wants to send a display. This can be done with the xhost program. Running xhost + will allow connections to your X server from anywhere. Running xhost +*host* adds *host* to the list of machines that can access your display. You can deny access using xhost -*host*. Note that by default, only the local machine has access to your display. Every other machine that wants to send a window to your display must be given access. The third item is the client program needs to know where to send the display. This can be done using the -display *display* or by setting the DISPLAY environment variable. I prefer setting the DISPLAY variable myself.

Displays are set with two items: the host to display on and the X server running on that host to display to. The server itself is broken into two parts: the server number and display number. Since X can handle multiple monitors at the same time, you will need to specify the host, X server, and monitor to send the client program to.

Fortunately for most Linux installations, this is easy. The X server and monitor always begin counting at 0, making the first X server 0.0. Tie this in with the host name (let's call it wayga) and you get a setup shown in Figure 16–12

```
setenv DISPLAY wayga:0.0
```

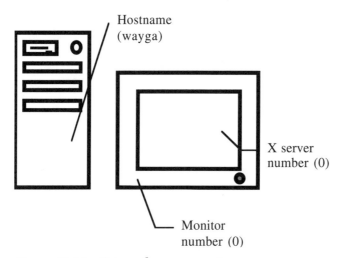

Figure 16–12 Xview of your computer.

16.10 Commercial X Products

A number of commercial products related to X11 are available. Here we try to give you a fairly complete list and a short description of each. Few of these packages are available for architectures other than the x86, though Alpha and Sparc versions are beginning to crop up.

Xservers

AcceleratedX

AcceleratedX is a high-performance replacement for the Xservers that come with XFree86. It is produced by XiGraphics (`http://www.xinside.com/`).

AcceleratedX supports hundreds of video cards, considerably more than XFree86 alone does. Additionally, it supports more monitors and often supports higher resolutions than XFree86. Typically it will also squeeze better performance out of your video card and monitor.

However, this increase in performance comes at a cost, AcceleratedX will also consume more system resources than Xfree86.

XiGraphics also makes a multiheaded Xserver, allowing you to run X on up to three monitors simultaneously. Metro-X has support for up to four displays built in.

Metro-X

Metro-X is another commercial Xserver. It also boasts support for more cards and monitors than XFree86, though not as many as AcceleratedX. Its performance is not as good as AcceleratedX's either. It does, however, cost less and consume fewer resources.

X Libraries

In addition to the many additional freeware or shareware X libraries and toolkits, there are a couple of commercial toolkits for X.

Motif

Motif was developed by the Open Software Foundation. Its specification is freely available, which has allowed the LessTif project to work on a free clone of Motif.

Motif is popular because it provides a number of widgets that allow for the building of complex and powerful, but aesthetically pleasing GUIs. It is somewhat resource-intensive, but most developers find it a fair trade.

Both XiGraphics and Metrolink offer an OSF-certified Motif library. Metrolink offers versions 1.2.4 and 2.0.1, the latter for both x86 and Alpha architectures. XiGraphics offers version 2.0 for the x86 only. Additionally, Redhat (`http://www.redhat.com/`) ships Motif 2.0.1 for the x86, Alpha, and Sparc.

OpenGL

OpenGL is a three-dimensional graphics library developed by SGI. It quickly became a standard part of nearly every 3D developer's toolkit.

Metrolink offers its OpenGL package for Linux/x86.

CDE

The Common Desktop Environment (CDE) is an effort by several commercial UNIX vendors to make a common X/Motif-based environment for use on all X desktops, thus providing a common look and feel regardless of which platform you are using.

16.11 Summary

Versions of CDE are available from XiGraphics and RedHat. X is pretty much a standard for graphics display on Linux and UNIX. It can be configured however you want, providing the control and interface that suits you best, instead of having to change the way you work to suit the operating system. The applications that are available for X rival those of Windows95, and more are being written every day.

Securing Linux 17

It may not seem easy, but it has to be done.

With most of the machines in the world connected via the Internet, security is a big concern whether you have hundreds of machines or one dial-up machine.

No system can be completely secure from outside attacks. Anyone determined enough has a good chance of cracking[1] into your system. The best thing you can do is to prepare yourself and your machine and make it as hard as possible and also be able to detect when you're being cracked.

17.1 Physical Security

The first part of keeping the system secure is making sure the hardware cannot be tampered with. Part of the C2 security specification for computer sys-

---

[1]Contrary to popular belief, people who break into systems are called "crackers" and not "hackers."

tems says that the computer must not be physically accessible to anyone without access. That is, it can't be on the network and must be in a locked room to begin with. Chapter 2 has a good list of instructions to keep a typical PC reasonably secure from outside attacks. To quickly sum up:

- Lock the BIOS and set the BIOS to boot only from the C drive.
- Don't use LILO or at least make it boot directly into Linux.
- Don't have DOS or any other OS on the machine.
- Lock the PC case.

You should also have people on hand to assist with problems and prevent anyone from having the chance to take a computer apart.

17.2 Software Security

This section is just a bit larger than the hardware security section, and for good reason. With TCP/IP having over 65,000 ports available for connecting to a single machine, this gives anywhere up to 65,000 and beyond possible ways for a cracker to enter your system.

Monitoring Software

Programs like COPS and TripWire allow you to routinely monitor your system to detect possible holes or to detect some forms of break-ins. You should probably get both programs and use them routinely. A program like SATAN will monitor an entire network and report on possible holes. Since many crackers probably have a copy of this, it is probably best to beat them to the punch and run it on your own network before they do.

Preventing Root Logins

The first way that crackers cause real trouble on your system is by getting root privileges. There are a few ways to do that, and I'll list some of them here, along with suggestions on preventing such things from happening.

First, **change the root password often**! This way, even if a cracker does get the password, it won't be valid for too long. Also keep an eye on your /etc/securetty file. This file lists the locations from which root can log in directly. To get root power from any other location, you must first have a valid user account; then use the su command to become root. Root can only log in at the console by default (tty1 through tty8).

Another item that should be done is modifying the su program so only members of the wheel group can su to root. This is a big problem with the Linux su program, in our opinion. The wheel group was designed to be the only group of users that can su into the root account. This limits the number of accounts that can be cracked to get into root. However, the GNU people think this is a bit authoritarian and have their su program designed to allow anyone to su to root, assuming they have the password. Other operating systems, such as SunOS and Solaris, require a user to be in the wheel group before being allowed to su to root.

Secure Shell (SSH)

You should also start using programs that encrypt passwords as they go over the network. The SSH[2] (secure shell) program is excellent for this, as it not only encrypts the password, but also the entire connection. As TCP/IP works now, all data are sent over the network in cleartext (i.e., not encrypted). Anyone who has a network sniffer on any machine on the network, or on any network between you and your destination, can read the password you type in. Bad stuff. The SSH program encrypts all this, plus does some host checking to verify the host you're connecting from and the host you're connecting to. You should be using this program both within your LAN and when connecting to other sites. Commercial versions of SSH for Windows and other platforms are available, allowing all the clients on the network to have secure connections.

The SSH program is designed to be a replacement for the "r" commands (`rlogin`, `rsh`, `rcp`) and can install itself so it replaces those commands. If your users have `.rhosts` files set up, SSH will still use those files. Users will not have to change their configuration much, but their connections will be more secure.

Setting up SSH requires that you run SSH on the machines you will be talking between. Let's call the client (your personal machine) foo, and the server (where you want to connect, do some administrative work, etc.) bar.

---

[2]Due to export restrictions and various patents, SSH can't be on the CD-ROM. Go look at the big Web search engines for SSH. Read the licensing carefully to make sure you're not breaking any patents or U.S. or local laws in using, compiling, or having the software.

Bar will run the SSHd (the SSH daemon) which gets started from either the inetd or on bootup in daemon mode. If you have a lot of users with SSHd, it might be better to run in daemon mode as SSHd is always ready to make a connection.

The "configure" command sets the stage for compiling and then "make" compiles it. There are few other things you need to do for a typical installation.

The SSHd program runs on the server (bar) and should be started by root on startup. The client machine (foo) then issues an SSH command similar to rlogin. The command to connect would then look something like this:

```
ssh -l mark bar
```

If the bar host is not known to foo, you'll get prompted if you want to add it to your list of known hosts. Add the host, and you'll be able to give your password to login.

The global configuration files are located in /etc. These files are /etc/sshd_config for server configuration and /etc/ssh_config for SSH configuration. The options for these files are listed in the man pages for SSH and SSHd.

New hosts can be added to SSH in a global method using the make-SSH-known-hosts which finds all hosts in a domain that run SSH and gets their public keys. Users can add their own hosts by copying the contents of the /etc/ssh_host_key.pub into $HOME/.ssh/known_hosts. The public keys can be sent to any host—it doesn't matter if they're transferred in an insecure manner.

Users can create their own RSA keys using the SSH-keygen command, which creates a public/private key pair. If regular password authentication is not used, the RSA key generated by SSH-keygen is used. The public key (located in $HOME/.ssh/identity.pub) should be added to the $HOME/.ssh/authorized_keys of all the machines you want to log into.

tcpd

The tcpd program can not only cut off your site from a bad site but can also specify what sites can come in. This is a kind of "poor man's packet filter," but it works pretty well for a small installation. The tcpd program matches up an incoming IP address with a table. If the IP address is listed in the "hosts.allow" file, the connection is allowed. If it is listed in the "hosts.deny" file, connection is refused. If the IP address matched neither, then access is granted. You can set up the hosts.deny file to deny access to everyone and then put fully trusted hosts into the hosts.allow file. The tcpd program works only with programs that are typically started with the inetd program. This includes telnet, finger, ftp, talk, and a few other programs. You can customize so no one can telnet in, but anyone can finger the machine (for example). It also allows for RFC 931 lookups, which can report on what user is on the remote machine using the identd program.

In setting up tcpd for allowing or disallowing connections, the access control is the same. In fact, the man pages for hosts.allow and hosts.deny is the same page. The way to set up an access control is by following this pattern:

```
daemon_list : client_list [ : shell_command ]
```

The daemon list is the name of the program that is running (telnetd, ftpd, and so on). The client list can be any of the following:

- Strings beginning with a . are assumed to be part of a domain (.wayga.net would be any host in the wayga.net domain).
- Strings ending with a . are assumed to be an IP address net or subnet (128.55.213. would be all the machines that start with that IP address).
- A string starting with @ is assumed to be an NIS netgroup (@hosts would be all the hosts defined in the NIS netgroup).
- n.n.n.n/m.m.m.m is a net and mask pair. This gives a bit finer control over the above for matching IP addresses.

There are also a few special keywords:

- ALL—This matches everything.
- LOCAL—All hosts that do not have a dot (.) in the hostname, since local hosts do not typically use the FQDN.
- UNKNOWN—A user whose name is not known (RFC 931 checking) or a host whose name or IP is unknown.
- KNOWN—Reverse of unknown—a user whose name is known, and both the name and address are known.
- PARANOID—Any host whose reverse DNS does not match the host name it's using. Sites with multiple domains may run into this if the reverse DNS and hosts are not synced.

The access control also accepts the word EXCEPT to give something like the following:

```
192.55.242. EXCEPT PARANOID
```

which would match all IP addresses from the 192.55.242. net except ones whose reverse DNS does not match what the host says it is.

The shell command is optional and is sent to `/bin/sh` for processing. This should be a secure script that sets its PATH and other environment variables.

In order to have a completely closed off system (from the perspective of tcpd) start with this in your `/etc/hosts.deny`:

```
ALL:ALL
```

This will deny access for all tcpd services to all hosts. Next, you can start opening the system up by adding to the `/etc/hosts.allow` file:

```
ALL: LOCAL
```

which now allows all local machines to have access to all tcpd services.

As you add more services (POP, IMAP, tftp), you can add tcpd support as you install the service. In the `/etc/inetd.conf` file, make your line look like the following:

```
telnet  stream  tcp     nowait  root    /usr/sbin/tcpd  in.telnetd
```

The location where the command is typically run gives tcpd instead, with an argument of the program you want to run in the end (telnetd in this case).

Other programs not started by inetd (such as sendmail and httpd) have their own host-based access mechanisms built into the program. Just be sure that as you compile your list of bad hosts (or good hosts), you include them in all your programs that interact with TCP/IP.

17.3 Denial of Service Attacks

Denial of service deals with the fact that a user may be doing valid things (such as pinging your host or sending E-mail) but doing it in a way that prevents you from getting things done. For example, a ping takes up at least 64 bytes and sends one at least once a second. If a malicious cracker were to send pings that were 2K in size, it would flood a 28.8K modem link, making it not usable for downloading data, receiving E-mail, browsing the Web, or anything else. The entire link is taken up responding to pings. Linux has some protection against this, but any system is susceptible to this. Another similar attack involves sending SYN packets to a host. The machine then opens a connection, waiting for more data. As more SYN packets come in, more connections open up, until eventually the machine crashes or is made unusable. Linux also has some protections against this attack, but since SYN and ping are both in the standard (and heavily used), there is not a whole lot that can be done.

Another type of attack involves sending so much E-mail that it floods the mail partition. Linux usually stores its E-mail in /var/spool, which is usually part of the root partition (/). The /tmp directory is also part of the root partition. Should you get so much E-mail that root fills up, then /tmp can't store any temporary data. This can then cause crashes of various programs, such as vi, that depend on having access to /tmp. This can potentially also cause a kernel crash. The moral here is twofold: Make /tmp a mounted directory, and make /var a mounted directory as well. Also have frequent monitoring of the mail files to make sure that the partition isn't filling up quickly. Some users may need to be told to clean out their E-mail every few weeks. My E-mail typically swells to about Four Mb per month. I then save the entire month to a file in my home directory and compress it to save space. 4MB per month times 30 users is a 120 Mb /var partition, plus other files such as log files that go in /var.

17.4 Network Security

For a small office setting, it's probably best to have a single host that will interact with the outside world (Web, FTP, Sendmail, etc). Protect the rest of the network using a packet filter, or a firewall package like Firewall Toolkit (FWTK). Disallow all telnet and finger. Monitor the anonymous FTP and WWW logs for break ins. You can disable FTP users by creating a file called / etc/ftpusers. Any user that is listed in there has no ability to FTP in. List all your users in this file, including root. For users who travel a lot (salespeople or engineers working from home), either establish a dial-up connection, or use very trusted hosts for connections. For users that require only E-mail, you can have that E-mail forwarded[3] to an external account. This way, your external users don't have to try getting into your system. Also be aware of who is on vacation or other leave, and make sure they're not logged in.

This gives a bit of balance to the security and convenience issue. Internal employees can go out to the rest of the Internet without using proxies. Proxies can get on everyone's nerves (including yours) as they have the ability to

---

[3]Check Chapter 7 for the use of E-mail forwarding.

log HTTP, FTP, and telnet traffic. This lacks the security of the next method, but this is one of the downsides to this kind of setup.

For a larger office setting with a lot of travel, invest the time in getting programs like S/KEY and SSH set up. Also have a full firewall set up, where you have two to three trusted hosts doing the work for the Web, FTP, and E-mail (see Figure 17–1).

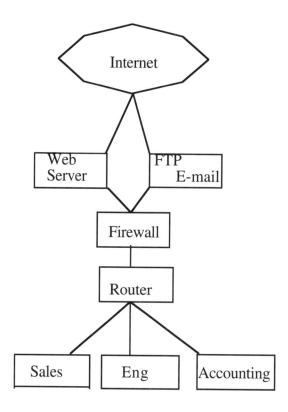

Figure 17–1   Secure environment using a firewall.

All the traffic that goes in or out of the router first passes through the firewall. Anyone wanting to use the Web, download data using FTP or telnet to a remote host must use a proxy, or first connect to the firewall and then perform a connection. The Web and FTP servers are almost entirely cut off from the internal network by the firewall. The firewall forwards only E-mail from the E-mail host—other E-mail is not accepted (or you can have the firewall accept E-mail). Programs like tripwire run on all hosts that have direct access to the internet. One of the benefits of a program like tripwire is that it can monitor certain files (/etc/password, for example) and know when these files change. If a file is changed, it sends an alert that a potential crack is in progress.

Any remote users trying to get into the system have to log into the trusted host (the firewall) first. The firewall is the only machine that has access to both the outside world and the internal network. Once a user is verified by the firewall, they can then get access to the internal network, receive E-mail, make connections to hosts, and so on.

Larger sites are left as an exercise to the reader, but you may want to get some books on computer and network security to assist you.

PGP

One of the earliest implementations of freeware cryptography is in the PGP (Pretty Good Privacy). Due to export controls, munitions laws, and various patents, we can't include this on the CD-ROM. There are legal ways to download this software in the United States and many other countries. Be sure you're not breaking any domestic, international, patent, or local laws by using this software. Some countries have severe restrictions on encryption. The main basis behind PGP is to allow personal security in sending E-mail. The E-mail can either be authenticated as originating from you (to prevent spoof E-mail) or completely encrypted for opening by only another person, or both. The PGP program creates two keys: one private that must be guarded by you at all times, and a public key, which the recipient of your E-mail must be able to read in order to authenticate your E-mail.

Building PGP on Linux is not an easy thing, given that Linux has changed since the last release of PGP.[4] Patches that allow PGP to compile cleanly under Linux are available. You can find PGP by searching the major Web search engines.

To compile PGP for Linux, grab the pgp-patcher.tar.gz file. Put the pgp262s.tar.gz and the pgp-patcher.tar.gz files in the same directory (make a /usr/src/pgp or $HOME/pgp for this). Now, run the following commands:

```
tar -zxvf pgp-patcher.tar.gz
cd pgp-patcher
installer
```

---

[4]Version 2.6.2 of PGP was released in 1994.

This will unpack the PGP sources, patch them to work with Linux, compile them, and install the binaries in `$HOME/pgp`. If you choose to have the binaries installed somewhere else, replace the "installer" with "patch-only." This will unpack the archives and patch the files to install. You can then edit the Makefile and have the sources installed somewhere else if you choose.

Once PGP is installed, you have to generate a public/private key pair. The `pgp -kg` command will allow you to generate this. Note that you'll probably want to have multiple E-mail addresses verify the same key (for example, if you have a home E-mail address, one for work, one for the Linux User Group, and maybe an alumni account from school). PGP can handle this, and you need to generate only one key one time. The `pgp -ke` command will allow you to edit (and add, delete, etc.) the names associated with your secret key once you have it generated. When asked for your ID, put in your full name, followed by your E-mail address. My primary PGP ID looks something like this:

```
Mark F. Komarinski <markk@auratek.com>
```

Next you're asked for your passphrase. This phrase can be as long as you like, but be sure that you don't forget it, and no one else gets hold of it. Next you'll be prompted to type in gibberish on the keyboard to generate random numbers to use with your key. A few minutes later, your PGP key is stored in `$HOME/pgp`. Next you'll have to generate your public key for others to read and authenticate what you send. The `pgp -kx` will extract your public key in binary format. If you want the key to be in ASCII format, suitable for displaying on a Web page or using in finger information, add the `a` option to the mix, which stands for ASCII.

Many mailers today have access to using PGP. Readers like mutt have much of it built in, and readers like pine have patches to allow you to use PGP. Others have the E-mail piped to PGP for verification. In order to sign a message yourself, use the `pgp -sta <textfile>` command. Anyone with your public key will then be able to verify that you wrote the contents. You can verify an incoming message by just piping the file to pgp, or using pgp `<textfile>`. If you have the public key of the sender, you'll get a message saying that the message is valid, or it is not valid. If you don't have the public key, then no verification can take place. Find the public key and add it to your "keyring" by using the `pgp -ka <file>` command. The `<file>` contains the ASCII or binary version of a person's public key ring.

PGP does even more than this, including encrypting a message with multiple recipients and revoking keys listed in its documentation. Be sure to read the `pgpdoc1.txt` and `pgpdoc2.txt`. `pgp -h` will give a listing of available commands as well.

17.5 Summary

Even the best of sites can get cracked with a small security hole. With your Linux servers physically secure and secure on you network, you will make it harder to get cracked.

Kernel **18** Administration

Managing the state-of-the-art Linux kernel.

The kernel is the heart and soul of your operating system. It manages the memory, the CPU, and disks; every piece of hardware in your system needs it to function. The Linux kernel is one of the most flexible and customizable in existence, and managing it is fairly straightforward but can be tricky at times.

18.1 Customizing Your Kernel

In virtually every flavor of UNIX it is possible to configure the kernel to some extent. Usually this is done by specifying a set of external, loadable modules to insert into the kernel at boot time. With Linux you can do this and much more. In addition to being able to insert code modules manually at boot up, Linux can also load modules on demand and later unload them.

On top of all that, you can, since the code for the Linux kernels is freely available, compile your own custom kernel. This includes specifying which drivers and features you wish to compile directly into the kernel and which you wish to leave as loadable modules.

The Linux developers have worked hard to make this as painless as possible, so this flexibility has not cost as much ease of use as you might expect. The kernel has two menu-driven configuration options: one X-based and the other screen-based. Additionally, there is the simple line-based, linear configuration.

18.2 Which Kernel?

If you are familiar with Linux, you probably already know that at any given time there are two current kernel versions: a production version and a developmental version. The developmental (sometimes called experimental) kernels typically have experimental and sometimes buggy or unstable features, though it should be noted that a truly buggy release of either a production or developmental kernel will be fixed very quickly with a new release.

Production kernels always have an even minor release number, while development kernels are odd minor releases. The minor release number is the second of the three numbers that make up the kernel version number. For example, 1.3.88 is a development kernel, but 2.0.30 is a production kernel. The next minor revision up from a production kernel is developed in parallel with the production kernel (e.g., 1.2 and 1.3 were developed concurrently just as 2.0 and 2.1 are being developed concurrently now).

In general, unless you need a feature available only in a developmental kernel, it's usually best to stick with a recent production kernel. With the incredible flurry of version 1.3 releases (over a hundred!), the 2.0 kernel has a huge set of options to choose from and supports a wide range of hardware.

18.3 Getting Ready

There are a few things you will need or want to have handy while you are rolling out a new kernel. First, the manuals for your peripherals and your motherboard. You will at least need to know the model number of your various peripherals and, in some cases, some hardware settings like Interrupt Request Lines (IRQs) and memory addresses.

You will also want to make a copy of your existing kernel and set up LILO, so you are able to boot in case your new kernel has something wrong with it or simply won't boot.

Also, you will want to have a bootable floppy (which you should have already) in case things really go awry. If you need to make a boot floppy, see the chapter on boot up and shutdown. Also, if you are a little paranoid, you might want to back up your root partition as well.

18.4 Adding Kernels to LILO

As mentioned above, it is good practice to keep an old, reliable kernel around that you can boot up in a pinch. LILO, the LInux LOader, is a utility that allows you to choose which kernel to boot at startup. With LILO you can also boot 386BSD, DOS, Windows 95, UNIXware, and a few others.

LILO uses a configuration file, `lilo.conf`, located in `/etc`. Here is an example of one:

```
#
# LILO config file: /etc/lilo.conf
#
boot=/dev/sda1
map=/boot/map
install=/boot/boot.b
verbose=2
prompt
timeout=100
message=/boot/message
image=/vmlinuz
        label=1
        root=/dev/sda1
        initrd=/boot/initrd
        read-only
image=/boot/vmlinuz2
        label=12
        root=/dev/sda1
        initrd=/boot/initrd.old
        read-only
image=/vmlinuz.old
        label=old
        root=/dev/sda1
        initrd=/boot/initrd.old
        read-only
```

The first line simply tells LILO what partition contains the boot sector, or if a device is specified (i.e., /dev/sda instead of /dev/sda1) which device contains the master boot record. Next the map file is specified (/boot/map is the default); it tells LILO where all the files are that it needs to boot an OS. Third is the boot loader. It is loaded into the BIOS and subsequently loads the selected kernel. Next is the verbosity level—higher is more verbose. The "prompt" entry tells LILO to present a prompt to allow you to choose which kernel to boot. The "timeout" is how long it will wait in tenths of a second before booting the default kernel. If no timeout line is present, LILO will wait indefinitely. In either case, simply hitting return at the prompt boots the default kernel. The next line specifies the message file which contains text that will be displayed before the LILO prompt is presented and the kernel is loaded.

The next three sections tell LILO about the specific kernels you want to be able to boot. As expected, the first entry is the default one. In this case (as is typical), it points to where the kernel is installed by default: /vmlinuz. The "label" sub-entry is the text that is given at the LILO: prompt to boot this kernel, "1" in this case. The "root" line specifies just that, the partition containing the root directory for the OS or kernel. "Initrd" tells LILO what file to load as the initial ramdisk, and "read-only" tells it to mount the root partition read-only, so that fsck can be run at boot time. (fsck cannot be run in batch mode on a partition that is mounted read-write.)

The subsequent entries specify additional Linux kernels, each with their own, unique label but otherwise the same as the first. A good portion of the time, this is all you will need to know about LILO, especially if you bought your Linux system already configured. However, you may also still want to use DOS and MS Windows or Windows 95 (for games, word processing etc.). Adding entries into your /etc/lilo.conf for other OSes is fairly straightforward. Here is an example of an entry to boot MS DOS from a second SCSI drive:

```
other=/dev/sdb1
      label = dos
      table = /dev/sdb
      loader = /boot/chain.b
```

There are two new parameters here: "table" and "loader." The first specifies the location of the partition table for the foreign OS and the second what chain loader to use to boot up the OS's kernel.

The most important thing to remember with regard to LILO is to run /sbin/lilo after changing anything to do with LILO (editing any of the files associated with it, updating a kernel with an existing lilo.conf entry, and so forth). Failure to do so could potentially prevent your machine from booting.

18.5 Modules or Compiled In?

One thing to note here is that not all drivers behave the same as a module does when compiled into the kernel. This can range from slight differences in functionality to its simply not working at all.

The choice of when to make a particular feature available as a module or to compile it is usually fairly straightforward. In general, if it is infrequently used and performs as needed as a module, you should compile it as a module. This often includes things like floppy disk drivers (in this day of networking, how often do you really use the thing anyhow?), drivers for other filesystem types (Cary uses his DOS `fs` driver about as often as he uses his floppy disk), CD-ROM drivers, drivers for sound cards, or networking drivers on a machine that uses dial-in PPP for its access.

If the feature is used frequently or continually, then there really isn't much point in compiling it as a module since it will be loaded all the time anyhow. This includes items such as your hard disk controller or SCSI controller, network drivers on a machine permanently networked, AppleTalk drivers on a fileserver for your Mac network, and so forth.

In cases where functionality between the compiled version and the module version differs, it is usually noted in the help pop-up for that option and in any related HOWTOs.

It should be noted that these are for the most part just guidelines. Ultimately you need compile in your kernel only what you need to boot your machine.

18.6 Dive On In!

Let's go through and outline how you might roll a kernel for a networked Linux machine you're using as your desktop machine and a file server for a network of Windows and Mac machines. You also have a sound card (they're cheap and you have a hundred CDs at home you could also be listening to at work). The machine has a SCSI controller with a CD-ROM and hard drives attached to it.

First, make sure you have the kernel sources installed. Even if you do, you may decide you want to get a more recent version. The default location is in `/usr/src/linux`. `linux` may be a link to `linux-x.y.z`, where `x.y.z` is a kernel revision. Once you make your way into `/usr/src/linux`, type "`make xconfig`" (assuming you are in X, highly recommended), this will do some preliminary work and then bring up a window with buttons that take you to various sections of the kernel configuration.

As you may have guessed, the first time through it's best to start at the top and go through all the menus.

To the right of each button is a help button that gives a small amount of information on the driver and some hints to help you decide if you want to enable it or not.

Configuring the Kernel

If you are in X, run "`make xconfig`" from `/usr/src/linux`. If you are using a character terminal, run "`make menuconfig`." If you are using a character terminal with poor emulation, you are stuck running "`make config`."

When you `make` with the `xconfig` option, a nice GUI pops up as seen in Figure 18-1.

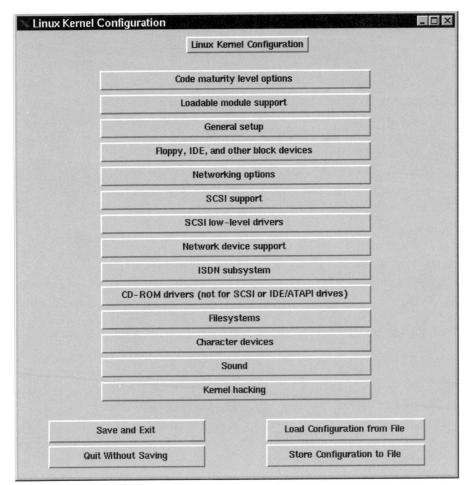

Figure 18–1   Kernel X-based configuration tool.

Once you go into a submenu, you can get help on the various options there. See Figures 18-2 and 18-3 for examples.

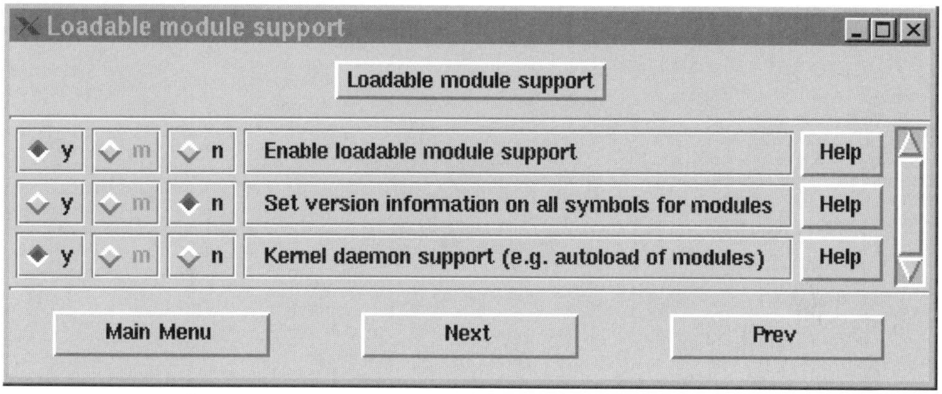

Figure 18–2   Submenu pop-up.

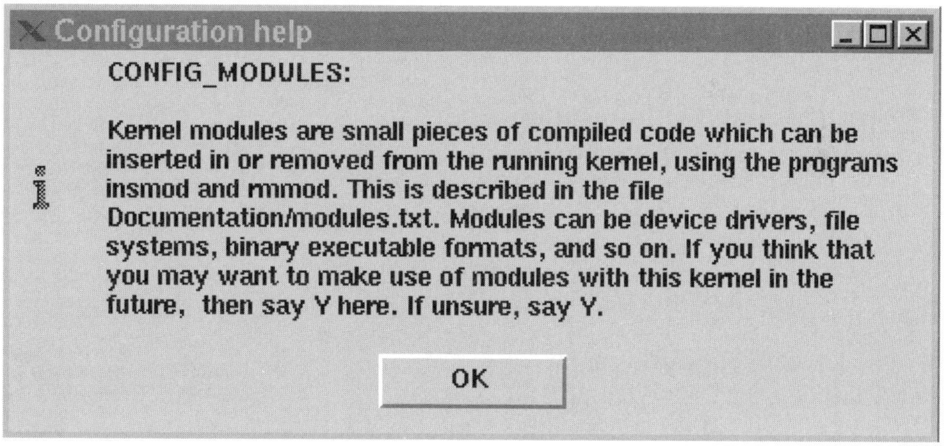

Figure 18–3   Submenu help pop-up.

Now, you are ready to start configuring your new kernel.

Code Maturity Options

Answering yes to the one option here will not change the kernel. It will simply give you options later on for various experimental or incomplete drivers. Say yes. It doesn't hurt anything. You can always say no to any experimental drivers you are offered.

Some experimental modules available in the current 2.0 kernels include PCI bridge optimization, IP proxy support, IP multicast routing, ethernet bridging, frame relay support, Amiga FS support, and support for numerous pieces of less common hardware.

Loadable Module Support

As you might guess, we highly recommend that you enable the use of loadable modules and kernel daemon support. The kernel daemon, `kerneld`, is the program that manages the loading and unloading of modules. It is available separately from the kernel distribution.

General Setup

You will definitely want to enable networking support, System V IPC, and support for ELF binaries. You should also enable `a.out`, probably as a module since all newer Linux distributions are ELF-based. You should also compile the kernel in ELF format if you have a newer distribution.

If you plan on using the machine for Java development, enable Java binary support. It's fine to go with a module here unless you want to be able to run applets from the command line as well. If you do, you will need to compile the module into the kernel.

Set the processor type appropriately unless you have an old version of GCC for some reason. In that case you will have to say 386 or 486.

Floppy, IDE, and Other Block Devices

Enable floppy disk support, probably as a module unless you use the floppy drive a lot. Leave out (E)IDE support if you are sure you don't need it (i.e., you have only SCSI hard drives and CD-ROMs).

The various chipset support and bug fixes can be left off unless you have an older motherboard, particularly one that uses Intel's Neptune chipset.

Networking Options

The one option you will definitely want to enable here is TCP/IP networking. Enable it.

Most of the rest of the IP and network-related options you will not need unless your machine is acting as a TCP/IP router/gateway. You might need to enable multicasting if you are going to be accessing the MBONE (the Multicast Backbone which sits on top of the Internet).

Further down you find the support for other networking protocols: IPX, AppleTalk, and AX.25. Enable these as you need them. If your machine is going to be a server using one of these protocols, you might as well compile it in the kernel. It will likely end up being loaded nearly all of the time anyhow.

SCSI Support

Assuming we have beaten the dead horse enough, you will need at least SCSI support and SCSI disk support. Probably you will need SCSI tape and CD-ROM support as well. If you have other SCSI devices, like a scanner, you will also need to enable generic SCSI support. Unless you have a device with multiple logical unit numbers, you should say no to the option for probing all logical unit numbers (LUNs). An example of such a device is a CD jukebox.

If you are having problems with your SCSI bus, you may want to enable verbose error reporting to help track the errors.

SCSI Low-Level Drivers

Enable the driver(s) for your SCSI adapters. If you are using a Zip or Jaz drive on the controller that came with it, you will need to enable its driver. See the chapter on peripherals for more information.

If you are using a zip drive on the parallel port, you will need to enable support for it here. This type of drive contains a parallel-to-SCSI converter that essentially turns the port into a SCSI host.

Network Device Support

Enable network device support (duh). After that, enable other options as you need them. In most cases it should be clear. Further down in this pop-up is the list of ethernet cards. Once again, the correct choice should be obvious, assuming you know what kind of card you have.

ISDN Subsystem

Enable this if you need it. You will likely have to contact your service provider to find out if they support synchronous PPP and compression. Enable the driver for your ISDN adapter as well. Enable the remaining options as needed.

CD-ROM Drivers (Not for SCSI or IDE/ATAPI Drives)

If your CD-ROM is attached to your IDE controller, its own controller, or your sound card, answer yes to the first option and then enable the proper driver.

Filesystems

If your machine is used for shell access, you may want to enable quota support. Quota support will also work with AppleTalk users since they are "real" users and have /etc/passwd entries. Depending on how Samba or IPX is set up, it may be useful to enable quota for use with their users as well.

Leave mandatory lock support off unless you know you need it and have newer AppleTalk, NFS, and/or Samba daemons.

Enable the second extended filesystem support. This is Linux's native filesystem type. It will likely be safe to leave Minix, first extended fs, and xiafs off as they are older and not used in newer Linux systems.

It will likely be useful to enable the DOS-and Windows- related filesystem types since these machines are so ubiquitous. Enable them as modules unless you use them frequently.

Enable /proc. It's needed by several programs. You really shouldn't even be given the option to turn it off.

You will know whether or not you need the rest of the options; enable them as necessary. In particular you will want to include CD-ROM (ISO9660) filesystem support.

If you have a very heterogeneous LAN, you may want to enable virtually all of these for use with removable media (floppy, Zip or Jaz drives).

Character Devices

You will almost always want to enable serial support, for your mouse if nothing else. Even if you use a bus mouse and have nothing on any serial port, at least compile it as a module. There are so many devices that use the serial port, it is inevitable that you will need it sooner or later.

You will also need to enable parallel port support if you have a printer or parallel port Zip drive. Additionally, you will need this driver if you are using parallel line internet protocol (PLIP).

If you have a multiport serial board, enable support for it here.

Various tape drives that attach to parallel or serial ports have their driver support controlled from here as well.

If you are running on a laptop, consider enabling support for the BIOS-level power management. This is probably the only situation where you will want this enabled.

The watchdog timer may be useful if you want your machine to automatically reboot upon a lockup. The software level support is not 100 percent reliable as a lockup could easily lockup the software, as well. There is also a driver for hardware watchdog boards which are much more robust and can monitor other things such as temperature.

Sound

If you use the console of the machine and have a sound card, you will want to enable support for it here. You will definitely need the manual for your sound card as there are a number of hardware parameters you need to compile into the kernel.

There are a large number of combinations of hardware and parameters—too many to try to cover here. If you are careful and keep your card's manual handy, you should not have any serious trouble getting your card fully supported (at least as far as the current drivers will allow) under Linux. Some manuals can be a little sparse, and you may have to fiddle with the settings to get your card working.

Kernel Hacking

Unless you are hacking the kernel, say no here.

Compile the Kernel and Modules

To properly build the kernel, issue the following commands:

```
# make depend
<lots of output here>
# make clean
<lots of output here>
# make
<several bucketloads of output here>
```

Now, if you want to install the compressed kernel in the root partition, type

```
# make zlilo
<output ending in...>
tools/build bootsect setup compressed/vmlinux.out CURRENT > zImage
Root device is (8, 1)
Boot sector 512 bytes.
Setup is 4348 bytes.
System is 368 kB
sync
if [ -f /vmlinuz ]; then mv /vmlinuz /vmlinuz.old; fi
if [ -f /System.map ]; then mv /System.map /System.old; fi
cat zImage > /vmlinuz
cp /usr/src/linux/System.map /
if [ -x /sbin/lilo ]; then /sbin/lilo; else /etc/lilo/install; fi
Added 1 *
Added 12
Added 13
make[1]: Leaving directory `/usr/src/linux-2.0.29/arch/i386/boot'
```

This last command installs the kernel and reruns lilo to update the boot map. If you want to install it on a floppy instead, run make zImage (instead of zlilo) and then copy the image to a high-density floppy.

```
# cp /usr/src/linux/arch/i386/boot/zImage /dev/fd0
```

Reboot your machine with your new kernel:

```
# /sbin/reboot
```

If the new kernel doesn't boot, you can reboot again (using the familiar CONTROL-ALT-DELETE key sequence) and at the LILO: prompt tell it which other kernel to boot. As you can see from the above output, there are three kernels installed. If you typed "12" at the LILO: prompt, the kernel whose label is "12" in /etc/lilo.conf will be booted. Now check your hardware and its settings against your configuration (just run `make xconfig` and it will load your last configuration into the GUI).

18.7 Summary

Hopefully we've managed to take some of the intimidation out of the process of compiling your own kernel. On the other hand, we also want to be sure that you take a few simple precautions in case you make a kernel that won't boot up on your system.

If you are interested in the inner workings of the kernel, you can consult various HOWTOs, in particular the Kernel Hacking HOWTO for Linux-specific information or any of a number of books on general OS theory and design.

For more detailed information on booting and LILO, see the chapter on booting and shutdown.

System 19 Monitoring

Using syslog to keep an eye on your system.

Monitor your Linux machine from the console or remotely using the syslog program.

The syslog program monitors kernel and user events and routes the messages based on what you want to do. These events can be minor things, such as root logging in, or can be serious, such as a hard drive failure, kernel panic, or reboot.

The syslogd program gets started up at boot time and uses the `/etc/syslogd.conf` file to know what to do. Here's the default file for RedHat 4.1:

```
# Log all kernel messages to the console.
# Logging much else clutters up the screen.
#kern.*                                          /dev/console

# Log anything (except mail) of level info or higher.
# Don't log private authentication messages!
*.info;mail.none;authpriv.none                   /var/log/messages
```

```
# The authpriv file has restricted access.
authpriv.*                                  /var/log/secure

# Log all the mail messages in one place.
mail.*                                      /var/log/maillog

# Everybody gets emergency messages, plus log them on another
# machine.
*.emerg                                                *

# Save mail and news errors of level err and higher in a
# special file.
uucp,news.crit                             /var/log/spooler
```

Any line with a # in front of it is ignored and is a comment. Each line is an entry and consists of two fields. The first field lists the events to monitor. The second field lists what to do once that event has occurred.

Each event is in two parts, separated by a period. The first part is the facility, or type of program generating the event. The second part is the priority or severity of the event, ranging from debug to emerg.

There are twenty facilities available:

- auth
- auth-priv
- cron
- daemon
- kern
- lpr
- mail
- mark
- news
- syslog
- user
- uucp
- local0 through local7

There are eight priorities available:

- debug
- info

- notice

- warning

- err

- crit

- alert

- emerg

19.1 Facilities and Priorities

The facility/priority combination you list will then report all the messages that get sent to syslog for that priority and higher. A priority of degug will report all messages, and a priority of none will report no messages.

Replacing either the facility or priority with an * will report for all facilities or all priorities, depending on where you put the * (before or after the period). You can combine multiple facilities to one priority by separating them with a comma.

The syslog that Linux uses has a few extensions to it that are not in the original BSD version of syslog. Putting a = sign in front of a priority says to report only this priority in a list. Putting a ! in front of a priority says to ignore that priority and all higher priorities. Combining the two (!=) would ignore only that priority.

The man pages for the particular programs you want to monitor will usually list what facilities the program uses. You'll note that there are eight user-defined facilities you can use in your programs or other scripts.

19.2 Actions

The second field lists where the message should be sent. This can be a file (if the destination starts with a /), a remote host (if the destination starts with an @), all logged-in users (if the destination is a *), or a specific user (if it starts with none of the above three characters). The file destination can also be a tty file, such as /dev/console, which will send the message to the Linux console.

You can also use the | character to pipe the message to an external command or a fifo.

Using the remote host logging can centralize a group of computers to log all their messages to one machine. However, if there was a severe enough problem (the ethernet card goes bad, kernel panic, etc.), the message for this may not get sent to the remote host. Of course, the same thing can be said for logging to the hard drive should the drive or its controller go bad.

19.3 Logging Procedures

How you log depends on what you want to log. For an initial setup, you should probably start by logging just about everything. For programs like pppd, this will greatly increase the amount of debugging information you have. As the system becomes stable and it is working correctly, still continue debugging but change the priority to something like warn or err to keep out regular debugging information. You may also choose to have different facilities for different files. For example, send all E-mail logs to /var/log/maillog, and bad logins to /var/log/authlog. This can make it easier to separate problems if they arrive. Bad login problems? Check the authentication log. The downside to this is that some logs maybe intertwined. For example, a bad login may be a result of someone's cracking in sendmail. If you don't examine the mail log, you may not realize what's going on.

19.4 Summary

One of the keys of having a long uptime is knowing everything that is going on in the system. By monitoring your machine carefully, you can catch potential problems or breakins as they occur, and fix the problem before it gets out of hand.

Backing Up 20
Your Data

When all else fails . . . restore from backup!

Keeping good backups is frequently the only way to recover from many accidents, disasters, or break-ins. Linux has a number of methods for archiving your data, ranging from tools like tar or cpio that come with Linux to feature-rich, sophisticated commercial packages.

There are a number of ways to keep backups, ranging from simply taring your entire file system to a tape to using dump and a well-designed backup schedule to running a high-end commercial backup and restore program.

Of course, you also have a variety of backup media to choose from: floppies (if you are truly desperate), tape drives (from old nine tracks up to DAT), write once, read many (WORM) drives, magneto-optical floppies (written magnetically, read optically), and Zip and Jaz drives. Of these, only the newer tape options and JAZ drives have gigabyte capacity and only exabyte and DAT can handle more than a couple of gigabytes. Unfortunately, tapes are in many ways the most cumbersome to work with because of their sequential access nature.

With the new proposed standards for CD-ROM- (and thus WORM-) based filesystems this media will soon sport multiple gigabyte capacity. Though they will still be write-once, the easier access (random instead of sequential) will likely make them popular once their price drops into the affordable range. In actuality, the technology for this has existed for some time, but the popularity of the current standard has kept it from being replaced. But the need to store large amounts of data reliably has grown tremendously in recent years, and CD-ROMs are a big win over tape in both ease of access and longevity (decades versus years).

The rest of this chapter assumes you have some form of large capacity media on which to backup your data, though many of the guidelines are useful regardless of the media being used or its capacity.

In general, you will want to run your backup during times of low activity for two reasons. One, it's not a good idea to have lots of files open or changing while the backup is running. Some programs will lock a file and the backup will, at best, be able to skip it or, at worst, the backup will exit or crash. Second, backing up your system will tend to consume a lot of system resources, and if your server is fairly loaded already, it will likely be bogged down considerably if you try to run the backup during "normal" business hours (whatever those might be).

20.1 tar and mt

tar, as you may know, stands for Tape ARchive. Before the more recent versions of GNU, tar was not really suitable for use as a backup tool. It had no way of performing incremental backups and properly handling files with holes (so-called sparse files).

At the base level, you can create a cron job that will compress and archive all of your filesystems and network volumes to a tape drive every night or every few nights. There are a couple of drawbacks to this method.

Typically only a small fraction of the filesystem changes over the course of even a week. Making a copy of the whole filesystem every other night is overkill. It would be better if incremental backups could be made.

It's very possible that you could have more stuff to backup than you have capacity on your particular combination of tape and drive. In this case you would have to break up the backup and change tapes at some point to complete the backup. Once again, incremental backups would alleviate this.

If your backup, or sections thereof, is small enough, you may want to put more than one on a single tape and you may need some way to access a particular archive at some later point. You could use tar's append feature but then the ability to maintain different versions is lost. When the archive is unpacked, the appended files will overwrite ones with the same names which were extracted earlier.

Since tapes are not randomly accessible, special care needs to be taken when writing multiple archives to a single tape. To move around on a tape you will likely use mt. It can move along the tape from archive to archive as well as rewind or fast-forward. It takes at least two arguments: the tape device and the movement to take. Movements can be relative to the current position or absolute (using the beginning of the tape as the reference point). It's obviously safer to use absolute movements, though if you are in a hurry, a relative movement is quicker.

Now, we have beaten up on tar quite a bit, so let's point out a few things that tar is good at doing.

tar can archive files that aren't currently needed or take a snapshot of a project. If one of your users has some data they still need but aren't going to be using for a while, take advantage of this to tar the data to a tape and remove them from the server. Also, you may need to keep snapshots of projects but not necessarily need to keep them on-line.

As mentioned earlier, tar is commonly used to create packages or distributions of documentation, source code, or precompiled software.

Finally, tar can be used to transfer directory trees around in your filesystem. Its many command-line options let you control preservation of permissions, modification dates, and the following of symbolic links. This allows you to re-create a directory tree on another partition with more control than cp -a. An example illustrates this nicely:

```
# (cd /home ; tar cf - caryc) | tar xf -
```

This will re-create the directory /home/caryc as a subdirectory in the directory where you invoke the command. It will preserve the permissions and ownership of the files and re-create (but not follow) symbolic links (assuming the links are not stale).

In general, it is not a good idea to follow symbolic links unless you know where all the links in the tree are pointing. If a link points back down to a directory that is within the archive, you will start recursively re-creating the directory tree within the subdirectory and very quickly eat up a large amount of disk space.

20.2 cpio

In many ways cpio is similar to tar. It supports more formats (including the format used by tar) and can also deal with archives from machines with different byte orders. It does not have an equivalent to the `--update` option. Like tar, cpio can write or read to network devices as well as local ones. Finally, cpio can be used in pass-through mode to copy directory trees.

The choice between using cpio or tar to perform backups is largely a matter of preference.

20.3 dump and restore

dump is probably the best free alternative for performing backups. It makes a fairly low-level copy of the filesystem. Because of this, any type of file (including sockets and block and character devices) can be archived and files which have empty blocks in them are properly saved. Additionally it can perform incremental backups and archives can span multiple tapes. One final nicety is that dump has no limit on the length of file- or pathnames.

Incremental backups are controlled by assigning a dump level to a particular backup. Dump levels range from 0 to 9, and when a dump of a certain level N is performed, all files that have changed since the last dump of level N-1 or lower are sent to the tape. As you might guess, a level zero dump dumps the entire filesystem.

dump requires you to know the length and density of the media being used for the backup. In the case of devices using data compression, there is a virtual length associated with the device, which is simply the compression ratio times the actual tape length. It's usually best to be conservative here; the compression ratio is really an average; not all files compress equally. If you over-estimate the amount of compression, dump will try to write after the tape has run out and the dump will be ruined.

dump is one of the lowest-level methods for backing up your system, but it is also one of the least fault-tolerant. Unless you understand it and your backup device very well, you may want to choose another method of backing up your system.

20.4 Commercial Backup Products

BRU

The Backup and Restore Utility (BRU) is strongly based on tar but adds many more features. It runs a daemon which manages the backup schedule. It comes in two versions, the more expensive of which supports backing up NFS disks; the less expensive works only on local disks.

BRU also comes with a menu-driven interface in both X and ASCII. The concept of backup levels is supported, and backup targets can be any character device.

Other features include the following:

- Keeps track of the number of uses of a tape to help you decide when to throw out older tapes.

- Contains powerful features for recovering data from corrupt archives.

- Has support for NIS (Network Information Services, a networked system for `passwd`, `group`, and `host` files and much more).

- Has support for SMB (Samba) and Netware volumes.

- Archives can span more than one backup device.

BRU is available for Linux on the x86, Alpha, and PowerPC. Se e `http://www.estinc.com/` for more information.

PerfectBACKUP+

PerfectBACKUP+ is widely acclaimed as the fastest backup and restore program. Previously sold as FASTBACK PLUS for UNIX, it began life as the UNIX version of DOS FASTBACK PLUS. It comes with menu-driven ASCII and Motif interfaces, networking support, compression, verification and recovery, and scheduling and it is compatible with both tar and cpio. It will also backup a variety of network drives, including NFS, Windows, Netware, and WindowsNT.

Other features include

- Compression.

- Network backup devices.

- Multiple backup devices—when one is full, it will move to the next device in the list.
- Locking files during backup to allow safer backups in multiuser mode.
- Support for all file types, including sockets, pipes, and so forth.

More information on PerfectBACKUP + is available from `http://home.xl.ca/perfectBackup/`.

BACKUP/9000

Though this is available only in beta for Linux as of this writing, it has one feature that prompted us to include it. It is designed to work with Oracle to allow live, safe backups of Oracle's tablespaces. If you are running Oracle (for SCO using the IBSC emulation, there is no native Linux version), you will undoubtedly find this feature of great use. Beyond this, Backup/9000 supports what you would expect of a commercial backup and restore program:

- Nice user interface.
- Scheduling tool.
- Support for local and network backups
- Uses tar or cpio format
- Encryption
- Parallel backups to multiple local and/or network tape drives
- Backup of raw partitions and FIFO streams in addition to normal files
- Multiple backups on one tape

20.5 Backup Strategies

How often you make what kind of backup depends on several factors, including

- The capacity and speed of your backup device, particularly important for unattended backup.
- How active your file systems are. What percentage of files are changing per day or week? Most likely, this will vary from partition to partition.
- Whether or not you can make live backups.

- If you can't make live backups, how much downtime is acceptable and when is it least inconvenient.

In general, if more than a few percent of a particular filesystem is changing daily, you should perform incremental backups every day or two, a lower-level backup weekly, and a full backup monthly. Lower activity levels mean you can space this out more, though there's really no excuse for not performing a full backup once a month.

Buy lots of whatever your backup media is; it's cheaper than having to pay the office for a day of doing work a second time.

For very active systems which more or less cannot be taken off-line except at 3 A.M. on a Sunday, you should get a commercial backup utility that will perform safe, live backups at least during low traffic periods. You will then hopefully be able to perform unattended incremental backups late at night, possibly full backups if you can fit the whole system on one tape.

The more complicated databases are typically problematic when it comes to live backups. Usually, your backup utility cannot make a proper snapshot from the database's point of view. Fortunately most databases can create a snapshot of themselves, and that can be placed in your archive. Failing this, the database will have to be taken off-line before being backed up.

You will probably want to keep some backups off-site in case of a big disaster (flood, UFO crashing into your office, dinosaur rampage, etc.). You may have to buy a new system, but at least you'll have what is likely hundreds, if not thousands, of man-hours of work saved.

20.6 RAID and Disk Mirroring

These are other techniques for protecting the integrity of your data. RAID stands for Redundant Array of Inexpensive Disks. It is a fairly new concept, having been introduced in 1987 at the University of California, Berkeley.

The basic idea behind RAID is that by using multiple small disks (as opposed to few large disks) and possibly some additional "parity" data, you will be able to reconstruct data lost when one of the disks fails instead of losing a few gigabytes (albeit temporarily, assuming that you have a backup).

There are several different levels of RAID, cleverly numbered from 0 to 5. Their features are given in the following table. Only levels 1, 4, and 5 are available for Linux, and only in software (as opposed to a hardware level implementation).

0Data striping—This doesn't actually provide any protection against data loss but does enhance performance. Requires a controller that supports synchronized disks; none are available for Linux.

1Disk mirroring—A second set of disks are used to provide a complete copy of your data. An expensive option, since you need twice as many disks.

2Level 0 with a check disk for storing error correction information. Poor performance has made this option unpopular.

3Level 0 with a separate disk for byte-level parity information to help reconstruct lost data. If the parity disk is lost, you lose all data integrity. Synchronized disks help boost performance despite the bottleneck of the single parity disk.

4Level 3 with block level parity information stored on a separate disk. Better read performance but worse write performance than level 3. Since synchronized disks aren't used, it can be implemented in software.

5Level 4 but with the parity information spread over the disks as well. Higher performance since a separate parity disk is no longer a potential bottleneck. Write performance is still not as good as for level 3.

To implement RAID on your Linux box, you need a kernel patch available from `http://www.linuxhq.com/patch/20-p0632.html` and a 2.0.30 kernel. The patch is still in beta and supports RAID levels 1, 4, and 5.

Separately available, `raidtools-0.3` can be used to create or repair a set of RAID disks.

20.7 Summary

A variety of backup and restore tools were discussed, ranging from simple ones that ship with every Linux distribution to commercial ones with enhanced functionality and interfaces.

In general, for sites where short amounts of down time is acceptable, the built-in tools are fine. For 'hot' backups, you will probably have to resort to commercial means.

Talking to Your Peripherals 21

It's not all disk drives and video cards!

As anyone knows, there are many more resources to be shared, served, and managed than applications and disk volumes (though we will cover adding disks, too). Scanners, modems, printers, tape drives, and Zip and Jaz drives can all be made available to other machines on your LAN.

Printer setup and sharing are covered in a separate chapter, because other than disk sharing, the printer is the most frequently shared resource.

One problem that frequently plagues PCs with many peripherals is IRQs or interrupt conflicts. There are a number of ways to deal with these which will be discussed at the end of this chapter.

21.1 Scanners

Most scanners can be purchased in either SCSI or parallel port form. Currently Linux supports only scanners connected via a SCSI adapter. The

canonical way to talk to a scanner under Linux is via an adaptation of the xv
program known as xvscan. Xvscan is a commercial program that is available
for $50 from tummy.com Ltd. (`http://www.tummy.com/xvscan/`).

Typically SCSI scanners will come with their own, low-grade SCSI card.
Unless you're running out of SCSI IDs, it is not going to be worth your while
to attempt to get Linux to talk to the scanner through this controller, assuming a Linux driver even exists for it.

Your kernel will need to have the generic SCSI driver compiled in it or as a
module. Next you will need to check and possibly set the SCSI ID of the scanner if it conflicts with existing devices on your controller. The device corresponding to the scanner will then be `/dev/sg[a-f]`. Here "a" would be a
SCSI ID of 0; "b" would be 2; and so on up to "f" which would have an ID of 6.

xvscan communicates with the scanner via `/dev/scanjet`, so you will
have to either create a link to the device or a copy of it. Also, if you want mortal users to be able to access the scanner, you will need to modify the permissions of the device file.

Assuming your scanner's SCSI ID is 3, its device entry is

```
crw-rw-rw-   1 root    sys            21,   3 Aug 28 00:12 /dev/sgd
```

To set up a copy of the device accessible to users in the scanner group,
issue the following commands as root:

```
# mknod /dev/scanjet c 21 3
# chgrp scanner /dev/scanjet
# chmod 660 /dev/scanjet
# ls -l /dev/scanjet
crw-rw----   1 root    scanner    21,   3 Aug 28 00:15  /dev/scanjet
```

21.2 Modems

There are a number of reasons you might want to attach a modem to your
machine:

- Faxing—incoming and outgoing
- Backup (or primary!) network connection
- Dial-up for remote access

If you have an external modem, the only issue you have to worry about is
having the serial port driver available. If you have an internal modem, which
adds its own serial port to your machine, you may run into IRQ problems.

Additionally, if the modem has a non-standard chipset, Linux may not recognize it.

In all likelihood you will have to do nothing to get Linux to talk to your modem. The one thing needed (serial port support) is almost always present in the kernel, usually for the mouse.

If you have an external modem attached, it will attach to one of the onboard serial ports and should have no problems with IRQ conflicts. If you are installing it internally and do have an IRQ conflict, there are a couple of ways of resolving it.

1. If you aren't using both of your built-in serial ports, disable one of them in the BIOS. The serial port on the modem card in some cases will simply become the lowest number serial port it can and then use the IRQs for that port. Otherwise you may have to set the serial port with jumpers on the card. Consult the documentation that came with your modem.

2. You can use setserial to assign the serial port on the card a different IRQ. If your built-in serial ports are both in use and you add an internal modem, it will present itself to the system as the third serial port. To change the IRQ it uses

```
% setserial /dev/cua2 irq 5
```

This will assign the third serial port. A number of other options can be set with setserial. Consult the man page for more information.

21.3 Tape Drives

There is a rather large and bewildering selection of tape drives. If you need to back up large amounts of data in a reasonable amount of time, however, you can eliminate ones using the parallel port as they have lower throughputs. IDE and EIDE tape drives also exist, and at least in the case of EIDE, the throughput is comparable.

Assuming you decide to use a SCSI tape drive, you will need to enable SCSI tape support in your kernel. As in installing any SCSI device, check to make sure you have chosen a unique ID for your tape drive before installing it.

Device files for tape drives contain the letters "st." If your tape is SCSI ID 6, it will have two device files: st6 and nst6. The first is used if the device is rewinding and the second if it is not. Most tape drives are non-rewinding so you will need to refer to them as /dev/nst$n$, where n is the device number.

21.4 UPS

Until the last few years, few people thought of un-interruptible power supplies as peripherals for the reason that the computer and the UPS didn't exchange information or take action based on the state of one or the other. Now though, this is not the case. A few years ago Uniterruptible Power Supplies (UPSs) with serial ports started appearing, along with snazzy GUI front ends to allow the battery and power level to be monitored and for actions to be set up based on the conditions reported. However, only commercial OSes are supported. Some manufacturers have published the language used to communicate with their UPS, allowing others to write their own programs for interacting with it.

There are two ways UPSs can be categorized: by how they perform their function of providing uninterrupted power, and by the level of interaction they have with the computer to which they are attached. The first has three types: stand-by, in-line, and line interactive.

The first simply sits and waits for the power to drop below a certain level and then, usually in a matter of milliseconds, switches to providing power via its batteries. The second actually filters all power through itself. It thus can condition the power that it puts out and kick in during brownouts. This method also provides about half again the wear and tear on the batteries, obviously shortening their lifetime.

There are several programs, most of them with some sort of GUI for talking to your UPS. Most of them are also somewhat feature-poor when compared to their Microsoft Windows-based counterparts. To date, Best is the only vendor that supplies control software which can be compiled for use under Linux. Because of their popularity, a strong effort has been made to provide good controller software for use with them. Most of the other tools are fairly generic and can talk to UPSs only in dumb mode.

> `checkups.tar`—Straight from Best's Web sites, this package will control their UPSs in dumb and a more advanced mode (not really a full "smart" mode). It includes the source code which you will need to compile. In the less dumb mode, the following alarms can be detected: High Ambient Temperature, Near Low Battery, Low AC Out, or User Test Alarm. You can also tell checkups to start a shutdown when it detects that it has a particular amount of power left.

> powerd-2.0—This is not the same powerd shipped with the System V init package. It differs in that it can be run in a master or slave mode, allow-

ing you to manage the shutdown of other machines on the same UPS or LAN from a single, master machine. Also, powerd-2 uses a config file whereas the stock powerd required you to edit the code and recompile it when changing the configuration.

Enhanced_APC_UPSD-v1.4—Support for America Power Conversion (APC) UPSs in both smart mode and dumb mode.

apcd-0.5—Another APC controller. Includes support for master and slave machines. The machine designated as the "master" will signal the other machines to shut down during a power outage or low battery condition.

smupsd—A third program for APC UPSs. Supports APC UPSs in "Very Smart" mode. Uses a Java-awt based tool for monitoring the UPS.

genpower-1.0.1 —A more generic UPS package. It comes with sample configurations for UPSs from Tripp and APC. Probably the best documented package mentioned thus far.

More documentation (thin though it is in some cases) comes with each package.

21.5 Adding a New Hard Drive

It is likely that at some point you will want to add additional disk space to your machine. Installing a new hard drive is a fairly painless procedure. In this section, we're assuming you are using a SCSI host adapter. Also, you presumably have SCSI, SCSI disk, and support for your SCSI controller already available, possibly set up by the vendor that sold you the machine.

This being the case, adding another hard drive is as simple as checking the new drive to ensure that it has a unique SCSI ID, installing it in the CPU case or an external case, and rebooting. Typically the SCSI ID is set by a set of jumpers. Where on the disk they are and how to set them should be explained in the manual that came with the disk.

Once you have the hard drive installed you will need to create some Linux partitions on it. Start by running fdisk.

```
# fdisk /dev/sda
```

The number of cylinders for this disk is set to 1030.
This is larger than 1024, and may cause problems with

1. software that runs at boot time (e.g., LILO)

2. booting and partitioning software from other OSes (e.g., DOS FDISK, OS/2 FDISK)

```
Command (m for help): p
Disk /dev/sdb: 64 heads, 32 sectors, 1030 cylinders
Units = cylinders of 2048 * 512 bytes

Device Boot    Begin    Start    End    Blocks    Id  System
/dev/sda1          1        1    100    102384     6  DOS 16-bit >=32
```

When you first get the drive, there can be any number of strange, possibly nonsensical, partitions on it. Just delete them with the "d" command in fdisk so you can start with a clean slate.

To add a new partition, use the "n" command:

```
Command (m for help): n
Command action
   e   extended
   p   primary partition (1-4)
p
Partition number (1-4): 1
First cylinder (1-100): 1
Last cylinder or +size or +sizeM or +sizeK ([1]-100): +50M

Command (m for help): p

Disk /dev/sdb: 64 heads, 32 sectors, 100 cylinders
Units = cylinders of 2048 * 512 bytes

Device Boot    Begin    Start    End    Blocks    Id  System
/dev/sdb1          1        1     51    52208     83  Linux native

Command (m for help): n
Command action
   e   extended
   p   primary partition (1-4)
p
Partition number (1-4): 2
First cylinder (1-100): 52
Last cylinder or +size or +sizeM or +sizeK ([52]-100): 100

Command (m for help):
```

By default, partitions are created as Linux native (extended 2) filesystems. If you need to change the fs type, for example to add a swap partition instead, use the "t" command:

```
Command (m for help): t
Partition number (1-4): 1
Hex code (type L to list codes): 82
Changed system type of partition 1 to 82 (Linux swap)
```

Contrary to conventional wisdom, performance-wise it is better to have few large partitions as opposed to many small partitions, though your system's needs should probably play the largest role in determining how you partition your disk.

After you've set up your partition or partitions, you need to run `mke2fs` on them to actually create the filesystems:

```
# mke2fs /dev/sdb2
```

Now you can mount it:

```
# mount /dev/sdb2 /tmp2
```

You will likely want to add an entry to `/etc/fstab` to automatically mount your new partitions at boot:

```
# device  mountpoint  filesystemtype  options  dump  fsckorder
/dev/sdb2   /tmp2         ext2          defaults  1       2
```

See the man page for fstab for details on all the options available.

If you have difficulties getting your system to recognize your new disk, booting the system at all with the drive in, or other SCSI problems, here are a few things to check:

- Does it have power? (Hey, check the easy things first!)
- Are all the cables attached firmly?
- SCSI buses must be linear; if you have external devices, make sure you are using only one of the internal connections on your card. Wide SCSI cards in particular will often have a narrow and a wide connection for internal use.
- Does the device have a unique ID on the bus? Remember that controller has an ID as well, typically 7 but 6 is not unheard of.
- Make sure your new disk isn't terminating the bus. If your bus was fine before, its termination should work with the new drive in place.
- If you are using a cable that came with a disk and have a another cable you know is good, try the drive on the good cable. If it works, the new cable is very likely bad.

21.6 Zip and Jaz drives

Hard drives which supported removable media almost became popular about
a decade ago but then faded. Recently, however, Iomega has resurrected
them in the form of its Jaz and Zip drives.

Other companies have begun making comparable products, but none are
currently supported under Linux.

Zip drives have capacities of 100 Mb and Jaz drives 1 Gb. Because of their
relatively large sizes, they are much better suited for use as backup media
than floppy drives. Additionally, both have considerably better performance
than floppy drives. In the case of Jaz drives, the performance is comparable
to a SCSI-I hard drive. A Zip drive has a seek time a few times longer than
and a transfer rate about one-fourth that of a Jaz drive.

Installing a Zip drive

The external SCSI Zip drive is shipped with its own controller based on
Adaptec's AHA1520, which Linux supports. Optionally, you can connect it to
your existing controller. The parallel port version actually comes with a parallel to SCSI adapter which will make the Zip drive appear as if it is a SCSI
device.

If you have the parallel port version of a Zip drive, you will need to enable
support for it in the kernel either compiled or as a module. If you have an
older kernel (pre 1.3.74) you will have to get the driver from `http://`
`gear.torque.net/pup/ppa.c` and compile it as a module. If you have only
one parallel port and have other devices you want to attach to it, it is possible
to daisy-chain them. However, Linux will not allow more than one driver to
be active on the port. The solution is to compile all the various drivers (Zip,
lp, PLIP, etc.) as modules and then load and unload them as needed.

If you have the SCSI version, you need only to support SCSI, SCSI disks,
and your controller. Thus, if you plan to use the drive on an already existing
controller, you don't need to do anything besides attach the drive to your system. If you have the internal version and have other internal SCSI devices on
the same controller, make sure bus termination is disabled or you will likely
be unable to talk to some SCSI devices after you reboot.

One final note. The Zip drive's SCSI ID can be set only to 5 or 6. This
could potentially conflict with other devices on the SCSI bus, so you may
need to do a little rearranging.

Installing a Jaz drive

Since the recently available parallel port version of the Jaz drive is not yet supported in Linux, you will obviously have to use the SCSI version. As with the SCSI Zip drive you will need only support for SCSI disks (and SCSI obviously) and the controller itself.

The drive is shipped with its own controller. There are two versions in use. One is based on the Adaptec AHA78xx series. This series of controllers is supported by the AHA2940 driver. The other is based on the Advanced Systems family of controllers which is also supported under Linux. As before, you may instead choose to place the drive on an existing controller. Jaz drives may be assigned any SCSI ID between 0 and 6.

Caveats

It is generally difficult or impossible to have two identical SCSI controllers in the same system because various settings frequently conflict. If you already have a controller of the type that your Zip or Jaz drive uses, you should probably consider just putting the device on the existing controller. This will also help conserve system resources like IRQs, which frequently can be in short supply.

Using the Drive

After you reboot, you may need to check the boot information to get the device that corresponds to the drive. You can retrieve boot output with the `dmesg` command. Find the section where your Zip or Jaz drive is detected and scan down a few lines to locate the device reported for your drive.

Once you know the device, you can mount a disk in the drive. Typically the disk shipped with the drive has a filesystem on its fourth partition. Unless you need compatibility with the OS that supports the `fs` type, you will likely want to format the drive with the Linux native `ext2fs`. (See the section on installing a new hard drive for instructions on formatting a disk.)

Now edit `/etc/fstab` and insert a line like this:

```
/dev/sde1/jazext2  noauto 0 0
```

The `noauto` option tells Linux not to mount the device automatically. This is typical for an entry of a device with removable media.

Using serial ports may seem a bit strange in the UNIX world, but there is a somewhat logical way of looking at it.

First, there are two device files for each serial port. One is /dev/ttySx and the other is /dev/cuax where x is the serial port number. To understand the what you'll read in the next few paragraphs, you first have to know a bit about how serial port work.

21.7 Quick Guide to Serial Ports

You're probably familiar with how serial ports need speed (BPS), bit size, parity, and stop bit settings. That's on the software side. On the hardware side, things are a bit more complicated. The typical serial port has about eight pins associated with it:

Pin	Signal	Meaning
1	DCD	Carrier Detect
2	Rx	Receive Data (Data come in this line)
3	Tx	Transmit Data (Data go out this line)
4	DTR	Data Terminal Ready
5	GND	Signal Ground
6	DSR	Data Set Ready
7	RTS	Ready to Send (1/2 of out of band flow control)
8	CTS	Clear to Send (1/2 of out of band flow control)
9	RI	Ring Indicator (Not used)

The above is the pinout for a standard 9-pin PC serial connection. When a device like a terminal is connected to the serial port, you need a special pin connection called a null-modem cable. In short, pins 2 and 3 are crossed (leading Tx to Rx and vice versa) and the RTS/CTS lines are crossed. When connecting to a modem, a "straight through" connection is sufficient.

Now, what does this have to do with /dev/cua and /dev/ttyS? Pin 1 is DCD, or Carrier Detect. When a modem makes a connection with another modem, this signal is active, or becomes "high." This tells the computer that someone has connected to this modem and is probably waiting for a login prompt. So the program that controls the serial ports (getty in this case) has to wait for

CD to become high before issuing a login prompt to the serial port. Otherwise, getty is sending the modem a login prompt, which will make the modem a bit confused if no one is connected to the modem. To make things easier, the only way a /dev/ttyS device will successfully open is if the DCD pin is high. So programs like getty will try to open the port and then just wait until someone dials in and makes a modem connection.

State of CD on Dialing Modem(/dev/cua)	State of CD on Dialed modem (/dev/term)	Event
Low	Low	Kermit gets started
Low	Low	Kermit dials remote modem
Low	High	Remote modem answers and negotiates speed
Low	High	Connection made, login prompt

Now this leads the question: How do you dial out with a modem? The /dev/cua device files ignore the state of DCD and will let you connect if it's high or low. So, if you wanted to dial out using kermit or minicom, you connect to a /dev/cua device instead of a /dev/term.

Lock Files

In order to prevent confusion about who actually is using the port (since you could theoretically have a /dev/term and /dev/cua file that points to the same serial port open at the same time) there are lock files. These lock files tell other programs that try to open a port that the port is already in use. This prevents someone from opening a connection to a modem if someone else is already dialed into that same modem. The problem with this, of course, is that each program that wants to use a lock file has to use the same location. For most, this is /var/lock, but could be in /var/spool/lock or other locations. You can usually configure where the lock files go. The other problem with lock files is when they don't correctly clean up, which happens when a program crashes before it finishes running. Then you have lock files for programs that are no longer running, preventing other programs from using the device.

Flow Control

In order for the DTE and DCE to know when to stop transmitting, there are two main methods of stopping communication temporarily. First is software (or in-band) flow control. This is sending a ^Q in the stream of data. Once the remote side sees this character, it stops sending data until it sees a ^S. The problem with this is that it breaks down at high speed. At anything above 9600bps, too much data may come down the line between the time that the receiving side sends the ^Q, and the sending side processes that character and stops transmitting data. This can cause data loss. The advantage of in-band flow control is that only three wires are needed: Tx, Rx, and GND.

The other method is using hardware (or out of band) flow control. In this setup, two pins (RTS and CTS) are used outside the data stream to start and stop the flow of data. Since that is all these signals are used for, processing a "stop" in out of band flow control is much quicker than for in band, and is recommended for all speeds greater than 9600 bps.

UARTS

A UART is the chip inside your PC that actually handles the RS-232 communication. Most chips in newer PCs are either 16550- or 16550-based (meaning they will emulate the 16550 chip). Earlier PCs has 8250s and 16450. These earlier chips would not handle speeds greater than about 38400bps, which is inadequate for today's high-speed modems with compression. These earlier chips had only a 1-byte buffer, meaning that each time a character came in the serial port, a CPU interrupt was generated. For 9600 bps rats, this means 9600 interrupts per second. Each of these CPU interrupts prevents the CPU from doing something else. The 16550A chips have a 16-byte buffer, which means that at 9600 bps, there were fewer than 1000 interrupts per second.[1] This left the CPU a net gain of 8600 interrupts per second to devote to other things, such as running programs. When speeds reach 38400 bps, the difference is even greater. Most of the "dumb" serial boards use 16450 or 16550 chips to do their processing, while "smart" serial cards use anything from an Intel 80186 to Cirrus Logic CD-2400 chip to provide greater speeds and extra functionality, like multiple serial ports per IRQ.

---

[1]When you have a fairly large buffer, you have a point (high-water mark) where the buffer is close to being full and should be emptied. Thus, you may not always have 16 bytes in the buffer when an interrupt occurs.

Types of Modems

One question that is asked frequently is: "What kind of modem should I get?" There's a choice between getting an external or internal modem for your PC. The internal modems are a bit cheaper and have their own UARTs built in, which prevents data loss at high speeds. External modems don't take up a precious ISA slot in your machine (assuming your machine even has an ISA slot) and give you pretty lights to look at when downloading Web pages and FTP files. The best kind of modem you can get for Linux is an external modem, especially if you have a good 16550-based serial card[2] for the following reasons:

1. You get the pretty lights to show that everything is working. With internal modems, you have to rely on other software to get modem states, and so on.

2. You won't accidentally buy a "WinModem." These modems actually require a lot of CPU time and are not supported by Linux.

3. If you need to move modems, it's pretty easy to do.

4. You can put in as many modems as you have serial ports, which is probably more than the number of ISA slots you have

5. Works with all versions of Linux, be it Linux on Sun, Linux on Alpha, Linux on PPC, or Linux on i386. RS-232 is a cross-platform standard.

Baud and BPS

To start this section, there is no such thing as a 28,000-baud modem that works with plain old telephone lines. If there were, we'd have some really fast modems out there. Up until the age of 2400 bps modems, baud and BPS were synonymous. A baud is defined as the number of changes in a signal per second. To get to higher-speed modems, more bits were encoded in each baud. Thus, a 9600 bps modem has 4 bits per baud, and a 14400 bps modem has 6 bits per baud. On top of this, compression of the actual data is used to increase the throughput, making some 28.8 kbps modems send data at up to 115.2 kbps.

---

[2]Linux will report what kind of UART is in your machine. You can also look at the motherboard, and you may find the chip.

21.8 Summary

We've tried to discuss a reasonably large list of hardware here, but there is no way for us to cover all of the hardware available for Linux. Similarly, there are dozens of ways each piece of hardware can be problematic. We discussed how to troubleshoot the most common stumbling blocks, but less common, more esoteric ones certainly exist.

The best places for information on how to deal with problematic hardware are the HOWTOs, the manuals for the hardware, and the manufacturer. Also, some hardware types have their own news groups or mailing lists. These are likely to be the best places to ask for help on particularly difficult problems.

Linux Distributions and Upgrading Your System

22

Linux for every platform!

Linux has been or is being ported to virtually every popular hardware platform. The x86 architecture pioneered by Intel remains the most popular platform, mainly by virtue of its low cost.

22.1 Supported and Work-In-Progress Architectures

As of this writing, the following architectures are supported for Linux:

- DEC Alpha—`http://www.azstarnet.com/~axplinux/`
- Sun Sparc 4m, 4c—`http://www.geog.ubc.ca/s_linux.html`
- SGI MIPS—`http://www.linux.sgi.com/`
- Other MIPs—`http://www.village.org/villagers/imp/linux-mips-faq.html`

- Motorola 68K—`http://www.clark.net/pub/lawrencc/linux/index.html` for Motorola MVME, Atari, and Amiga 68Ks or `http://www.maclinux.org/index.html` for Apple 68Ks

- PowerPC—Depending on your exact platform, neither, one, or both of mkLinux (`http://www.mklinux.apple.com`) or Linux/PPC (`http://www.linuxppc.org/`)

- x86 (AMD, Cyrix and Intel)—`http://www.linux.org/` or any of hundreds of other sites

Not all of these ports are as far along as others. As you probably know, the Linux/x86 is the most mature. The SPARC, Alpha, mkLinux, and PPC versions are nearly as mature; they are all self-hosting and multiuser with stable XFree86 ports.

The non-Apple 68K port has recently been declared stable by its development team. Amiga and Atari users may want to check it out.

The SGI/Linux project is also multiuser and self-hosting on SGI's Indy platform but lacks a stable port of Xfree86. If you do not plan on using the console a lot, you may want to investigate it for use as a server.

22.2 Commercial Linux Distributions

Linux is free and protected under the GNU Public License, meaning that anyone can take it, modify it, and sell it as long as they make the source code available for free. For most of us, the convenience of having distribution media and some installation support is worth $50 to $100.

Since the first CD-ROM releases of Linux, a number of commercial Linux distributors have sprung up. We'll try to at least mention all of them and go into some detail on RedHat, Workgroup Solutions, Slackware and Caldera. The focus will be on the x86 versions of these but much of what is in this chapter will apply to most Linux ports.

Probably around 90 percent of the software that comes with any of the distributions is the same: the modulo software version. They all include a recent Linux kernel; XFree 86; compilers for C, C++, Fortran, Smalltalk, and Pascal; interpreters for Perl, Python; Tcl/Tk; many extra widget sets for X: Athena, Xview; Apache; various shells: bash, tcsh, zsh, ash, ksh; editors: pico, emacs, vi; numerous X window managers: fvwm, fvwm2, olvwm, twm; all the standard UNIX command-line utilities, usually GNU versions of them; various desktop applications ranging from CD players to drawing tools; and text processing/layout applications such as nroff, troff, TeX, and LaTeX.

It is fair to say that Linux comes with the majority of third party freeware that typically gets installed on a commercial UNIX machine. Linux and other UNIX users want and use these tools, and Linux obligingly comes with most of them. Those that don't come with it can frequently be found precompiled for Linux, or else they compile easily on it (one of the virtues of being POSIX compliant).

Caldera

Caldera's OpenLinux actually comes in several different flavors, ranging from a "lite" version up to a deluxe version. OpenLinux at all levels is aimed at commercial users as opposed to single endusers. They provide excellent support and an impressive array of desktop applications.

The four "flavors" of OpenLinux are

- Lite: A free, evaluation version aimed at companies that wish to sell it or bundle it with other products.
- Base: A low-cost version with an integrated desktop, client and server applications for Internet and LAN connectivity.
- Standard: The base version with Netscape Communication Corp's Fast-Track Web server, which includes client support for Novell NetWare Network Directory Services.
- Deluxe: The standard with full NDS client and server support.

Caldera provides excellent support, as you would expect from a company that wants to provide a serious platform for business use. They have said that they are willing to "take it on the chin" in their support of OpenLinux.

Caldera also offers a rich desktop environment and a set of desktop applications for it. Caldera Desktop, also known as Looking Glass, is a full-featured application launcher and workspace. It has features such as drag and drop and application launching by double-clicking on a datafile produced by that application (Mac users especially are familiar with this, as are Win95 users), as well as a full-featured file manager.

Most of Looking Glass's options are GUI configurable but some are not there yet, so it is not the user interface (UI) panacea that the Linux world needs to really compete on the desktop market, but it is an excellent start. Most hard-core users of X will likely still choose their favorite X window manager or common desktop environment (CDE) over it, but for people who are uncomfortable at the thought of editing a `.fvwm2rc` file and want some of the features of the MacOS finder or the Windows Explorer, it is a welcome product.

Caldera also sells a port of Wabi for Linux and resells a number of X-based desktop applications, including StarOffice, WordPerfect for UNIX, Z-Mail and various commercial X servers and Motif versions.

They also make and support OpenDOS, a freeware version of DOS, and Netscape's FastTrack Web server.

RedHat's Package Manager (RPM) software package system is employed by Caldera and includes glint, the GUI interface to RPM. See the section on RedHat for more information about RPM.

RedHat

RedHat Software produced the first "commercial" release of Linux. It is commercial in the sense that they offer installation support, and it is possible to purchase more extended support plans. It quickly became the most popular Linux distribution and still holds this honor today.

Part of what made this distribution so popular is its installation program. It is straightforward and easy to use and does a fair amount of hardware detection during the installation process. Recent versions of RedHat include Metro-X, a commercial X server that takes the place of the XFree86 server (but not XFree86 itself). See the chapter on X for more information on XFree86 and commercial X servers.

RedHat's other big selling point is the RedHat Package Manager or RPM. It is both a program for installing, upgrading, or uninstalling software and a format for software packages. Solaris users will find it similar to pkgadd, but with additional features. The RPM program checks dependencies and verifies that the proper package and version are installed. If a dependency is not fulfilled, rpm reports what RPM file needs to be installed and exits. The RPM program also has various querying options for querying package files and searching for which RPMs contain what programs. RPM has support for two kinds of packages: precompiled and source code. If you prefer to examine the source and build it on your own machine, or there are machine-specific options for a package, it will be distributed as a source-code package. On installing the package, the source code is compiled and installed.

There is also a GUI front end for RPM written in Python/tkinter called glint. Glint will first query the installed packages and if you have your RedHat distribution CD in the CD-ROM drive and mounted on `/mnt/cdrom`, glint will also query it and determine which packages on it have not been installed.

All in all, glint is an incredibly handy tool for helping a system administrator manage much of the software on a Linux server. RedHat also sports another tool for system administrators.

Control-panel is a Tcl/Tix application. It is really a sort of meta-application; it launches all the other handy sysadmin tools that RedHat includes in its distribution. There are graphical tools for managing nearly every other aspect of the system: users/groups, local and network printers, network interfaces, time/date, the kernel daemon and modules, local and NFS file systems and a few others.

RedHat is the only commercial distributor selling versions of Linux for more than one architecture. Versions are available for Sparc- and Alpha-based systems.

WGS

Work Group Solutions (WGS) releases a "more fully debugged, more stable, more professional and more comprehensive version of Linux" called Linux Pro. It makes more of an effort to be stable rather than be on the bleeding edge. It also comes with a demo version of WGS's FlagShip, a database server.

WGS's product is aimed more at business and industry. They sell subscriptions on an annual basis as well as maintenance contracts. Even though the regular Linux Pro install does not use the latest and greatest software, the distribution comes with supplemental CDs containing more up-to-date versions.

Linux Pro is currently based on RedHat and, as a result, includes the tools that come with RedHat. Because of its focus on stability, Linux Pro typically lags behind RedHat by as much as one major release.

If stability is of paramount importance of you, then Linux Pro is probably the distribution you will want to use. Beware, however, that you may need to upgrade certain parts of the system, usually the kernel or system libraries, to use newer versions of third party software.

Slackware

The Slackware distribution is the oldest existing Linux distribution and also the one with the largest amount of extra (non-necessary) software. This distribution is typically the most up-to-date and least well supported.

Slackware doesn't possess a formal mechanism for upgrading individual applications, libraries or packages, so you can either upgrade the whole system when a new distribution comes out or upgrade the various pieces as is necessary or possible. Slackware uses a rudimentary packaging system that does not have the features of a more advanced system such as RedHat's RPM. However, if you're the kind of person who doesn't care about packaging formats and prefer compiling from original source, Slackware would be great for you.

Linux on Sparc

We had the opportunity to install RedHat on a Sparc SLC for testing. The SLC is a low-end machine, probably slower than a 286. The system we used had 16 Mb of RAM and a 200 Mb hard drive. The surprising thing about the installation was that it was almost exactly the same as doing an install for Linux on Intel, even installing the hard drives as */dev/sda* and */dev/sdb* as you see in the Intel counterpart. After booting, virtual consoles were available, and all the commands were the same. The differences come in that the boot loader is called SILO (Sparc Linux Loader), but provides the same capabilities as LILO. Also, the configurations for XFree86 are a lot more limited, since Sparc has only a few graphics cards available, and the SLC has only a black-and-white display. At the time of this writing, Linux isn't completely working on the Ultra architecture, but the kernel does boot and a few small programs are working. The sun4c and sun4m architectures work just fine with S/Linux.

22.3 Updating Your System

We've talked a little about upgrading, mainly in the context of what distributions use which methods of installing, removing, and upgrading various software packages. We have not talked about upgrading more critical parts of your system, such as the kernel, libc, or the ld library. Or, perhaps less critical (as least as far as the machine booting, maybe not to your business or job!) programs like your Web server, database server, and compilers or interpreters. This last group of programs can be very problematic, especially when changing major revisions, but even between minor revision or patch levels/beta releases.

Even upgrading a simple library, if improperly done, can result in no one being able to log in or the system failing to boot. The point here is not to scare you into never upgrading, but to make you paranoid enough to make backups and boot disks and keep the last version of whatever you are upgrading around just in case. These backups will save you later on.

Upgrading Your Distribution and Kernel

Kernel customization has its own chapter so we're not going to go into it here. There are a few notes that bear mentioning/repeating here about installing a new kernel.

In general, unless you need the features, it is better to stay with a production versus a developmental kernel. Linux always develops two kernels simultaneously. Those with an even minor revision number are "production" kernels and are more stable and more thoroughly debugged. The next minor revision up is the experimental kernel. As updated or new code is introduced, it is refined in the experimental sequence of kernels and then, once it is stable enough, introduced into the production kernels.

Despite all this, it is still possible to enable experimental features in the production kernels. Most of the features that are available this way are there by popular demand. These include things like transparent proxy support, multicast routing, frame relay, and support for less common hardware and file systems.

All of the commercial distributions install a production kernel by default, typically a fairly recent one, though rarely the most recent. This means that when you upgrade your distribution you will almost always upgrade the kernel. When a newer kernel is installed, it may be a large kernel (putting as many drivers as possible directly into the kernel) or it installs a number of loadable modules (not all of which you'll need). After upgrading your distribution, it's usually best to recompile the kernel to suit your particular needs. As the production kernel revisions advance, features from the development kernels are incorporated. If a feature you need or would like to use makes it into the production kernel and your distribution isn't available with a kernel that includes it, it is fairly simple to upgrade the kernel only; see the chapter on kernel administration.

There are two things you should be shot for not doing when upgrading or modifying your kernel:

1. Making a boot disk.

2. Making a copy of your current, working kernel, and editing `/etc/lilo.conf` so you can boot it if your new kernel fails.

If you installed Linux on the machine yourself, you should have a boot disk from the installation process. Otherwise whoever did the installation for you likely has given you or sent with your system a boot disk. If you don't have one, see the chapter on Linux boot and shutdown for instructions on making a boot disk.

When you upgrade your entire distribution, you will definitely want to back up at least the / (root) and /usr file systems, and probably your whole machine, as well. It doesn't happen often, but it is possible for a critical library or program not to upgrade properly, crippling your machine. You should probably also back up your /etc directory and /home directories.

The upgrading process for RedHat Linux and distributions based on it is usually an across-the-board upgrading of all the RPM files. Thus it is possible to perform essentially the same operations gradually by FTPing the RPM files from their FTP sites or a mirror as desired or needed.

22.4 Summary

As Linux has moved further into the commercial and public eye, the need for easy upgrading has grown and been answered. Most distributions allow you to upgrade easily from previous versions with only an hour or two of down time.

With package management tools, it is also straightforward to upgrade specific programs or groups of programs. Of course it is always possible to simply obtain the source code and upgrade various programs "manually."

Connecting to 23
the Internet

*A case study in connecting a small
business to the Internet.*

This chapter covers three items many small companies
face—how to connect to the Internet with minimal cost, how
to allow everyone in the company to use it, and how to protect it from crackers.

23.1 Overview

Firewalls are mainly designed to prevent unwanted activity on a network, so
the basic function is to block connections from one network to another. In
most applications, this would be from the Internet to your local network, and
vice versa.

The are thousands of different firewall methodologies, but we will narrow
our discussion in this chapter to ipfwadm. Let's assume that the local network is
Ethernet with less than 254 machines, and connections to the Internet are
made via a modem. The end result will be a network that will have a non-per-

manent connection to the Internet, but the users on the network will not have to dial a modem or remember to disconnect when finished. What they will see is a momentary pause (between 15–60 seconds, depending on your modem and ISP) upon initial connection to an outside machine. Over a 33.6 Kbps modem, three or four people actively using a Web browser at once works quite adequately (assuming non-graphic intensive pages, with the users randomly clicking on links. The idea is that most of the time, two people will not concurrently need the full bandwidth). Using an ISDN line will obviously make things faster, but most Linux users will have a 28.8 or 33.6 modem.

23.2 Software Versions

The configurations in this chapter use Linux kernel 2.0.30, PPP 2.2.0f, diald 0.16, and ipfwadm 2.3.0. If you are not planning to do IP masquerading, but still use diald, then kernel 1.2.X (X > 0), and PPP version 2.2.0x should work fine. Diald is constantly undergoing changes, and from the version released over a year ago (0.14) to the current version, many improvements and enhancements have been made.

Links to the current version of the kernel, PPP, and ipfwadm can be found at `http://www.linuxhq.com/`.

Web Pages:
```
Diald     http://www.dna.lth.se/~erics/diald.html
ipfwadm   http://www.xos.nl/
```

23.3 Networking

The local network should be a private network and should not advertise its IP addresses beyond the firewall. RFC #1597 (Address Allocation for Private Internets) specifies the address blocks which are reserved for internal use only. While not necessary, using these blocks of addresses is suggested. You can alternatively use a class of addresses assigned to you by the InterNIC, but if any mistakes happen, and one of your local networks IPs ends up outside the firewall, it will be ignored by the rest of the world as an invalid IP if it belongs to one of the following address blocks:

```
ADDRESS RANGE                           TYPE              # of machines
10.0.0.0 -> 10.255.255.255              single class A    1 x 16777214
172.16.0.0 -> 172.31.25.25516          class B           16 x 65534
192.168.0.0 -> 192.168.255.255          class C           255 x 254
```

For a small site, a good choice of an address block(s) to use would be one of the available class C networks, allowing 254 machines on your network. For this chapter, we will use the class C network of 192.168.1.0. There are two reserved IPs in the 192.168.1.0 block: 192.168.1.0, which represents the network itself, and 192.168.1.255, which is the broadcast address for the network. Another address to set aside would be 192.168.1.1. This is commonly the gateway machine, and, in our case, the firewall. This is not necessary; just a good rule of thumb.

In `/etc/sysconfig/network/` you will find a file named `ifcfg-eth0` that should look like

```
#!/bin/sh
#>>>Device type: ethernet

#>>>Variable declarations:
DEVICE=eth0
IPADDR=192.168.1.1
NETMASK=255.255.255.0
NETWORK=192.168.1.0
BROADCAST=192.168.1.255
GATEWAY=none
ONBOOT=yes
#>>>End variable declarations
```

After the network is configured, reboot the machine and perform the following test:

The output from **netstat -nr**, should read:

```
Kernel routing table
Destination     Gateway     Genmask         Flags Metric Ref Use Iface
192.168.1.0     0.0.0.0     255.255.255.0   U     0      0   28  eth0
127.0.0.0       0.0.0.0     255.0.0.0       U     0      0   14  lo
```

The output from **ifconfig**, should read:

```
lo        Link encap:Local Loopback
          inet addr:127.0.0.1  Bcast:127.255.255.255  Mask:255.0.0.0
          UP BROADCAST LOOPBACK RUNNING  MTU:2000  Metric:1
          RX packets:0 errors:0 dropped:0 overruns:0
          TX packets:42 errors:0 dropped:0 overruns:0

eth0      Link encap:10Mbps Ethernet  HWaddr 02:60:8C:49:05:57
          inet addr:192.168.1.1  Bcast:192.168.1.255  Mask:255.255.255.0
          UP BROADCAST RUNNING MULTICAST  MTU:1500  Metric:1
          RX packets:0 errors:0 dropped:0 overruns:0
          TX packets:26 errors:0 dropped:0 overruns:0
          Interrupt:5 Base address:0x300
```

Try to ping:
localhost: `ping 127.0.0.1`
local IP: `ping 192.168.1.1`
other IP on the network

If you cannot ping 127.0.0.1 or 192.168.1.1, recheck your configuration files. If none of the machines of your local network respond, then check the cabling from this machine to the rest of the network. If you cannot ping some of the machines on the local network, chances are there is a problem with them, and not with the firewall machine.

NAMESERVICES

Before continuing to the PPP section, two other files should be checked

```
/etc/resolv.conf
order   hosts,bind
search localdns_server, ispname.net
nameserver <IPForNameserver1>
nameserver <IPForNameserver2>


/etc/hosts
127.0.0.1          localhost
192.168.1.1        gateway.localether.net
192.168.1.2        bob.localether.net
192.168.1.5        ralph.localether.net
```

I suggest keeping the local hosts table simple—only the names of the machines on your local Ethernet. While it is true that adding the names of some commonly used machines to the local hosts file will save a little time when looking up names, it can lead to problems if you have a machine in the hosts file that has changed its IP address.

23.4 PPP

PPP connectivity is fairly easy, since there are few configuration files to deal with. There are only two main programs to use for PPP: pppd, the daemon itself, and the connection script. Distributed with it, and commonly used, is a program known as chat. It is a program solely designed to do a "wait for this string, and then send this string" application. Another well-known program is expect, but its flexibility and features are overkill for our application. The default configuration files distributed with PPP will work fine but are not suggested to be used because they are security holes. I suggest doing the following.

There are three main script/configuration files for use with PPP. They are */usr/local/bin/ppp-on*, */usr/local/bin/ppp-off*, and */etc/ppp/ppp-chatfile*. For security reasons, ppp-chatfile should be owned by root and file permissions set to 0600. This file will contain passwords and UIDs. Also, pppd and chat should bet SUID (chmod +s) to allow them to read the ppp-chatfile.

There are also security problems with this method. A fully secure method would be to use a C wrapper program that calls ppp-on and ppp-off. Both of these scripts should then be set with the permissions 0700 and pppd and chat should have the permissions set to 0100. The ppp-on script should check the ownership and file type of the ppp-chatfile and make sure the lock directory is owned and only writable by root. This will ensure that a PPP session can only be started with the flags set in the ppp-chatfile and that no non-root user can create his/her own config file to dial out.

`/usr/local/bin/ppp-on` should read

```
#!/bin/sh
#       ppp-on
#
#       Set up a PPP link

LOCKDIR=/var/lock
DEVICE=modem
OUR_IP_ADDR=111.222.333.444
REMOTE_IP=555.666.777.888
NETMASK=255.255.255.0
CONNECT_SCRIPT="/usr/sbin/chat -v -f /etc/ppp/ppp-chatfile"

if [ -f $LOCKDIR/LCK..$DEVICE ]
then
    echo "PPP device is locked"
    exit 1
fi

/usr/sbin/fix-cua $DEVICE

/bin/stty 19200 -tostop

/usr/sbin/pppd asyncmap 0 lock netmask $NETMASK defaultroute modem
   crtscts    \    $OUR_IP_ADDR:$REMOTE_IP    /dev/$DEVICE    connect
  "$CONNECT_SCRIPT"
```

For most applications, only the "OUR_IP_ADDR" will have to change. If you have a static IP, place it here; otherwise change it to 0.0.0.0 to obtain a dynamic IP. Note that some ISPs will provide you with your static IP number, even if you leave this as 0.0.0.0. Also, the "-v" option, included in "CONNECT_SCRIPT" for debugging purposes, maybe removed. The "-v" flag will log the conversations that it had with your ISP to /var/log/messages. You may also have to set "REMOTE_IP," sometimes referred to as the gateway. Some ISPs will automatically supply it during PPP negotiation.

```
/usr/local/bin/ppp-off
#!/bin/sh

DEVICE=ppp0

#
# If the ppp0 pid file is present then the program is running. Stop it.
if [ -r /var/run/$DEVICE.pid ]; then
    kill -INT `cat /var/run/$DEVICE.pid`
#
# If unsuccessful, ensure that the pid file is removed.
#
    if [ ! "$?" = "0" ]; then
        echo "removing stale $DEVICE pid file."
        rm -f /var/run/$DEVICE.pid
        exit 1
    fi
#
# Success. Terminate with proper status.
#
    echo "$DEVICE link terminated"
    exit 0
fi
#
# The link is not active
#
echo "$DEVICE link is not active"
exit 1

/etc/ppp/ppp-chatfile
ABORT'    \nBUSY\r'
ABORT'    \nNO ANSWER\r'
''        ATZ
OK        ATDT5551212
CONNECT       ''
login:        <your account>
password: <your password>
```

This is the bare minimum for your chat script, and obviously you will need to change the phone number, UID, and password. You may also want to add another line after the "ATZ" that changes specific modem registers to suit

your application. I normally like to have the S11 register set at its lowest setting. This can be done by adding the following line, just before the telephone
number in the chatfile.

```
OK      ATS11=55
```

After PPP is configured, start the daemon with ***ppp-on***, and perform the
following test:

The output from `netstat -nr`, **should read:**
```
Kernel routing table
Destination Gateway         Genmask         Flags Metric Ref Use Iface
555.666.777.8880.0.0.0      255.255.255.255 UH    0      0   0   ppp0
192.168.1.0 0.0.0.0         255.255.255.0   U     0      0   28  eth0
127.0.0.0   0.0.0.          255.0.0.0       U     0      0   14  lo
0.0.0.0     555.666.777.888 0.0.0.0         UG    0      0       ppp0
```

The output from `ifconfig`, **should read:**
```
lo        Link encap:Local Loopback
          inet addr:127.0.0.1  Bcast:127.255.255.255  Mask:255.0.0.0
          UP BROADCAST LOOPBACK RUNNING  MTU:2000  Metric:1
          RX packets:0 errors:0 dropped:0 overruns:0
          TX packets:42 errors:0 dropped:0 overruns:0

ppp0      Link encap:Point-Point Protocol
          inet addr:111.222.333.444  P-t-P:555.666.777.888
          Mask:255.255.255.0
          UP POINTOPOINT RUNNING  MTU:552  Metric:1
          RX packets:0 errors:0 dropped:0 overruns:0
          TX packets:0 errors:0 dropped:0 overruns:0

eth0      Link encap:10Mbps Ethernet  HWaddr 02:60:8C:49:05:57
          inet addr:192.168.1.1  Bcast:192.168.1.255
    Mask:255.255.255.0
          UP BROADCAST RUNNING MULTICAST  MTU:1500  Metric:1
          RX packets:0 errors:0 dropped:0 overruns:0
          TX packets:26 errors:0 dropped:0 overruns:0
          Interrupt:5 Base address:0x300
```

Try to ping:
localhost: `ping 127.0.0.1`
your ISP: `ping ispname.net`
other IPs on the network

Another good test now would be to use a Web browser and try to pull up
your favorite Web page, or telnet to a shell account provided by your ISP.

After testing the link, execute ***ppp-off***. After this, attempting to telnet to a
remote host should come back with an error stating "host not found."

Diald

Diald, written by Eric Schenk, is available from `http://www.dna.lth.se/ ~erics/diald.html`. Diald is a utility used to automatically connect your machine via a modem or ISDN to your ISP when external data is requested. It will also automatically disconnect you when the connection has been idle for a specified period of time. If your PPP connection dies for some reason, diald will automatically try to reconnect. If you have a static IP and you are in the middle of downloading the latest Linux kernel, this feature can be a real stress reliever. Ever downloaded 10 M over a 28.8 and had the modem die on the last 5 percent?

Diald's only system requirements are that the kernel be compiled with SLIP enabled, and that whatever connect protocol you are using is configured and working correctly (PPP in these examples). Diald uses SLIP to monitor the network traffic and if a non-local IP is requested, diald tells the modem to dial out and connect to your ISP.

Installation is as simple as obtaining the source code, unpacking it, performing a "make depend," followed by "make," and then "make install" as root. In the three versions I have installed on two different machines, I have never had an error message. After installing the latest version (at the time of writing, it was version 0.16), there are three files that you will need to check. The first is `/usr/lib/diald/diald.defs`. This file is a list of internal filter rules for diald and does not usually need to be touched. If you need to make any changes, refer to the diald man pages on the format of this file.

The second file to examine is `/usr/lib/standard.filters`. You may wish to copy this file to a different location and name. I suggest `/etc/ diald.conf`. While leaving it in /usr/lib should work, I have had some problems that were solved by moving it to `/etc/diald.conf`, the location of the config from previous versions of diald. This file is a list of services from `/etc/ services`, and how many seconds that service will get of "up-time." This doesn't mean that if you are telnetting somewhere diald will automatically kick you off while your typing. What it does mean is after so many seconds of idle time, diald will shut the modem link down. The default file is very well documented and easy to understand.

The third and last file is a script to start diald. I suggest starting it from `rc.local` by adding the line "`/etc/rc.d/rd.diald`" to the end of your /etc/ rc.d/rc.local file. You may even just add the lines to your rc.local file, but it is more convenient to keep things separate so it can be run as a stand-alone program. Notice that we are using the same chat file used in the PPP section, but we are not using the `ppp-on` program.

```
/etc/rc.d/rc.diald
#!/bin/sh
echo -n "Starting auto-dialer: "
/usr/sbin/diald /dev/modem accounting-log "/var/log/diald" -m ppp
   defaultroute modem \ crtscts local 111.222.333.444 remote 0.0.0.0
   connect "/usr/sbin/chat -f /etc/ppp/ppp-chatfile"\ fifo "/etc/
   diald.fifo"
echo "diald"
```

At least the local option, and maybe the remote option, will have to be changed. If you have a dynamic IP (thus setting local to 0.0.0.0), this may cause some difficulties when telnetting to a machine on your local network. A static IP is highly recommended when using diald, or the IP masquerading in the following section. Also, if you know the remote IP, I would suggest setting it.

The FIFO argument is optional. The FIFO allows diald to communicate with a few programs that come with the diald distribution for monitoring the diald activity. If you notice that your connect is slow, or if ifconfig reports that there are lots of errors on the PPP link, you may wish to remove the FIFO option.

The accounting-log argument is also optional. This writes information about call duration to a file. It is useful if you wish to find out exactly how long your modem has been active.

After customizing this file, you may either reboot, or just execute the file by hand. Depending on how recent your /etc/services file is, diald may complain about unknown services. A common one I've seen is tcp.www. If you receive one of these errors, there are two solutions. One solution is to comment out the offending line in /etc/diald.conf and let the catchall line at the bottom of /etc/diald.conf give that service up-time. The other solution is to update your /etc/services file to contain the appropriate information. Ideally, you should update /etc/services; this will give you greater control over diald, as it will allow you to narrow down modem usage.

If you check the output from netstat and ifconfig without diald making the connection to your ISP, you should see

The output from `netstat -nr`, should read:

```
Kernel routing table
Destination     Gateway    Genmask           Flags Metric Ref Use  Iface
0.0.0.0         0.0.0.0    255.255.255.255   UH       1    0   0    sl0
192.168.1.0     0.0.0.0    255.255.255.0     U        0    0   0    eth0
127.0.0.0       0.0.0.0    255.0.0.0         U        0    0   1    lo
0.0.0.0         0.0.0.0    0.0.0.0           U        1    0   0    sl0
```

The output from `ifconfig`, should read:

```
lo    Link encap:Local Loopback
      inet addr:127.0.0.1  Bcast:127.255.255.255  Mask:255.0.0.0
      UP BROADCAST LOOPBACK RUNNING  MTU:3584  Metric:1
      RX packets:12 errors:0 dropped:0 overruns:0
      TX packets:12 errors:0 dropped:0 overruns:0

eth0  Link encap:10Mbps Ethernet  HWaddr 02:60:8C:49:05:57
      inet addr:192.168.1.1  Bcast:192.168.1.255  Mask:255.255.255.0
      UP BROADCAST RUNNING MULTICAST  MTU:1500  Metric:1
      RX packets:0 errors:0 dropped:0 overruns:0
      TX packets:0 errors:0 dropped:0 overruns:0
      Interrupt:5 Base address:0x300

sl0   Link encap:Serial Line IP
      inet addr:111.222.333.444 P-t-P:555.666.777.888 Mask:255.255.255.0
      UP POINTOPOINT RUNNING  MTU:1500  Metric:1
      RX packets:0 errors:0 dropped:0 overruns:0
      TX packets:2 errors:0 dropped:0 overruns:0
```

If you check the output from netstat and ifconfig with diald making the connection to your ISP, you should see (which can be done as simple as telnet <ispname>)

The output from `netstat -nr`, should read:

```
Kernel routing table
Destination      Gateway     Genmask         Flags Metric Ref Use Iface
0.0.0.0          0.0.0.0     255.255.255.255 UH    0      0   0   ppp0
0.0.0.0          0.0.0.0     255.255.255.255 UH    1      0   0   sl0
555.666.777.888  0.0.0.0     255.255.255.255 UH    0      0   0   ppp0
192.168.1.0      0.0.0.0     255.255.255.0   U     0      0   0   eth0
127.0.0.0        0.0.0.0     255.0.0.0       U     0      0   1   lo
0.0.0.0          0.0.0.0     0.0.0.0         U     0      0   0   ppp0
0.0.0.0          0.0.0.0     0.0.0.0         U     1      0   2   sl0
```

The output from `ifconfig`, should read:

```
lo    Link encap:Local Loopback
      inet addr:127.0.0.1  Bcast:127.255.255.255  Mask:255.0.0.0
      UP BROADCAST LOOPBACK RUNNING  MTU:3584  Metric:1
      RX packets:12 errors:0 dropped:0 overruns:0
      TX packets:12 errors:0 dropped:0 overruns:0

eth0  Link encap:10Mbps Ethernet  HWaddr 02:60:8C:49:05:57
      inet addr:192.168.1.1  Bcast:192.168.1.255  Mask:255.255.255.0
      UP BROADCAST RUNNING MULTICAST  MTU:1500  Metric:1
      RX packets:0 errors:0 dropped:0 overruns:0
      TX packets:0 errors:0 dropped:0 overruns:0
      Interrupt:5 Base address:0x300
```

```
sl0      Link encap:Serial Line IP
         inet addr:111.222.333.444 P-t-P:555.666.777.888
         Mask:255.255.255.0
         UP POINTOPOINT RUNNING  MTU:1500  Metric:1
         RX packets:0 errors:0 dropped:0 overruns:0
         TX packets:2 errors:0 dropped:0 overruns:0

ppp0     Link encap:Point-Point Protocol
         inet addr:111.222.333.444 P-t-P:555.666.777.888
         Mask:255.255.255.0
         UP POINTOPOINT RUNNING  MTU:1500  Metric:1
         RX packets:5 errors:0 dropped:0 overruns:0
         TX packets:5 errors:0 dropped:0 overruns:0
```

23.5 IP MASQUERADING

Most of the options suggested in this chapter haven't needed any specific version of the kernel. In order to do IP masquerading, it will require at least version 2.0 of the Linux kernel along with version 2.3.0 of **ipfwadm**. Actually, the kernel supports IP masquerading in the 1.2.x kernels, but ipfwadm didn't support it at that time.

Also, please note that currently all forms of network traffic are not supported. Common forms of traffic, such as mail (POP and SMTP), telnet, ftp, Web (HTTP), news (NNTP), ping, and many more are supported.

The simplest form of IP masquerading firewall is two simple lines:

```
ipfwadm -F -p deny
ipfwadm -F -a masquerade -S 192.168.1.0/24 -D 0.0.0.0/0
```

These are known as "F"orward rules. The first line sets up a default policy (-p) to "deny" all connections unless specifically stated. You can also do a default policy of "accept," but this would defeat the purpose of the firewall. The second line appends (-a) a masquerade (m) policy from the source (-S) of 192.168.1.0/24. This is our local Ethernet network, with a net mask of 255.255.255.0 The 24 means that the first 24 bits of a 32-bit IP are set, thus a netmask of 255.255.255.0. The destination of 0.0.0.0/0, pretty much represents everything else in the world.

If we wanted only a few machines on the local network to have access to the Internet via the Linux box, the second line could be replaced with

```
ipfwadm -F -a m -S <local machine IP>/32 -D 0.0.0.0/0
```

Just replace the `<local machine IP>` with the IP of a particular machine. This line can occur as many times as needed once for each machine that you want to allow to masquerade its IP. Keep in mind that we could also do this by manipulating the netmask instead of making an entry on a per machine basis. The per machine basis is easier to understand to the naked sys-admin eye, but a netmask is easier on your CPU.

So far, all that's been set up is a simple masquerading firewall using Forwarding rules. There are three other styles of rules: "I"ncoming, "O"utgoing, and "A"ccounting.

Incoming rules are generally the fastest of the rule types.

Outgoing rules have a big advantage over Incoming and Forwarding rules, but they are slower in comparison of Incoming and Forwarding rules. Outgoing rules can block traffic from any machine on your network, while the others cannot block traffic from the firewall itself. If you want to block traffic to a particular site, but your firewall machine itself is not secured from the individuals in question, they then could access a particular site by going to the firewall machine before going to the particular site.

Accounting rules do little other than allow you to monitor network traffic. The current version of ipfwadm will only allow you to measure traffic between two points. If you truly wish to monitor traffic, I suggest monitoring *all* of the network traffic, and then the network traffic between the firewall and individual machines. This will give a percentage of the traffic that one person, or machine, has created on your network.

If you wish to block traffic to a particular site from your network, one approach could be

```
ipfwadm -F -a reject -W ppp0 -S 192.168.1.0/24 -D forbidden.site.com/32
```

The general format for all rules is the following. Please note that there are more options, including inserting rules, and logging than those mentioned here. This is just a brief overview of what is available

1. Flush the old rules to clear any previous erroneous rules.
   - **ipfwadm -[FIOA] -f**

   The "-f" means to flush all rules

2. Set up a default policy of deny.
   - **ipfwadm -[FIO] -p deny**

   The "-p" means policy standard values are accept (default) and deny.

   Note: This does not apply to Accounting rules.

3. Set up the rules themselves, keeping in mind the rules are processed in order and do not continue after the first match.

- **ipfwadm -[FIOA] -a** *<accept | deny | reject | masquerade>* [**-V interface IP | -W interface name**] **-S** *<source IP>* **-D** *<destination IP>*

The -a option is to append a rule to the rule list and should be followed by a policy. Valid policies are accept, deny, reject, and masquerade.

Note: This does not apply to Accounting rules.

The -V and -W options are optional. They specify on which interface a packet will be transmitted or received for this rule. If not specified, it is assumed that the packet will be accepted on all interfaces. Either the -V (IP number) or the -W (interface name) can be used, but not both

-S and -D refer to the Source and Destination of a packet, respectively. Source and Destination IPs can be the dotted quad number or hostnames. I suggest using IPs as it will not require a name lookup.

The following pages include descriptions of a simple masquerading firewall, with some minor protection from intruders. If more in-depth information is required, read the ipfwadm man pages and perhaps one of the many books dedicated to firewalls. Most books will not discuss ipfwadm specifically but will give theories that can be applied to your Linux box.

Below is a sample /etc/rc.d/rc.firewall. As with diald, you should call it from rc.local upon boot time.

```
#!/bin/sh

PATH=/sbin:/bin:/usr/sbin:/usr/bin

#
# /etc/rc.d/rc.firewall, define the firewall configuration,
# invoked from rc.local.
#

PATH=/sbin:/bin:/usr/sbin:/usr/bin
MY_ETH0=192.168.1.1
MY_NET=192.168.1.0
MY_STATIC=111.222.333.444

# Forwarding rules
# first flush any old rules from memory
ipfwadm -F -f
# then set a default policy to deny everything
ipfwadm -F -p deny
```

```
# lastly, we want to masquerade the IPs from MY_NET (eth0) to
# the ppp0 interface (but we may need to stop at the sl0
# interface if diald needs to start the ppp connection first!)
ipfwadm -F -a masquerade -W ppp0 -S $MY_NET/24 -D 0.0.0.0/0
ipfwadm -F -a masquerade -W sl0 -S $MY_NET/24 -D 0.0.0.0/0
# Incoming rules
# first, flush all old rules from memory
ipfwadm -I -f
#then set a default policy to deny everything
ipfwadm -I -p deny

# packets coming in from my local network (can only be eth0) to any-
  where else are allowed
ipfwadm -I -a accept -W eth0  -S $MY_NET/24 -D 0.0.0.0/0

# but packets pretending to be my local network that come from
# the outside are denied
ipfwadm -I -a deny -W ppp0 -S $MY_NET/24 -D 0.0.0.0/0 -o

# packets going to the firewall, from a remote network is valid
# (i.e. if we are using the firewall machine for mail, or someone
# VALIDLY telnetting into the firewall)
ipfwadm -I -a accept -W ppp0 -S 0.0.0.0/0 -D $MY_STATIC/32

# We may also want to use localhost for testing, so make it valid
ipfwadm -I -a accept -V 127.0.0.1 -S 0.0.0.0/0 -D 0.0.0.0/0

# Outgoing rules (basically the reverse of the Incoming rules)
# as usual, flush all old rules
ipfwadm -O -f
# and setup a default policy of deny
ipfwadm -O -p deny

ipfwadm -O -a accept -W eth0 -S 0.0.0.0/0 -D $MY_NET/24

# deny someone trying to fake the masquerade
ipfwadm -O -a deny -W ppp0 -S 0.0.0.0/0 -D $MY_NET/24
ipfwadm -O -a deny -W ppp0 -S $MY_NET/24 -D 0.0.0.0/0
ipfwadm -O -a deny -W ppp0 -S 0.0.0.0/0 -D $MY_NET/24

# all other outgoing data from the firewall is valid, and
# remember, we need to make it valid for sl0, just incase
# diald hasn't enabled ppp0 yet.
ipfwadm -O -a accept -W ppp0 -S $MY_STATIC/32 -D 0.0.0.0/0
ipfwadm -O -a accept -W sl0 -S $MY_STATIC/32 -D 0.0.0.0/0

# and.... yeah.... localhost is still valid
ipfwadm -O -a accept -V 127.0.0.1 -S 0.0.0.0/0 -D 0.0.0.0/0

echo "done"
```

Following is a sample /etc/rc.d/rcFirewallAccounting script. This should be kept separate so that you can restart it and monitor different machines without disturbing the rest of the firewall. There is also a way to set all accounting rules to 0 bytes of traffic, but this way allows you to easily add and delete machines from the accounting list. Once more, this can be started from rc.local. This script expects a file named /etc/FirewallAcctList to exist and contains a list of the machines you wish to monitor.

To monitor the traffic, a cron job can be created to view the output of the firewall accounting and via mail.

```
#!/bin/sh

PATH=/sbin:/bin:/usr/sbin:/usr/bin

#
# /etc/rc.d/rc.firewall, define the firewall configuration,
# invoked from rc.local.
#

PATH=/sbin:/bin:/usr/sbin:/usr/bin
MY_ETH0=192.168.1.1
MY_NET=192.168.1.0
MY_STATIC=111.222.333.444

echo -n "Starting firewall accounting rules: "

# Kill the old rules
ipfwadm -A -f
# These are the system rules!!  They log all traffic as a
# reference point
ipfwadm -A in -i -S $MY_NET/24 -D 0.0.0.0/0
ipfwadm -A out -i -S 0.0.0.0/0 -D $MY_NET/24

ipfwadm -A in -i -S $MY_NET/24 -D $MY_ETH0/32
ipfwadm -A out -i -S $MY_ETH0/32 -D $MY_NET/24

#These are to log traffic to individual machines named
#in FirewallAcctList.... its just a list of machine names or
#IPs
for i in `cat /etc/FirewallAcctList`; do
        echo -n $i" "
        ipfwadm -A in -i -S $i/32 -D 0.0.0.0/0
        ipfwadm -A out -i -S 0.0.0.0/0 -D $i/32
        ipfwadm -A in -i -S $i/32 -D $MY_ETH0/32
        ipfwadm -A out -i -S $MY_ETH0/32 -D $i/32
        done
echo   "done"
```

23.6 Summary

When connecting a LAN to the internet in a secure way there are three items to consider. First, the selection of a private (i.e. non-routable) network. Second, connecting your firewall machine to the LAN and the Internet; in this example via an on-demand dial up line using PPP. Last, allowing certain machines on your LAN access to the Internet and possibly disallowing access from various external machines or networks.

Appendix  A

Here is a list of the URLs we referenced in the book. These URLs contain information about the programs used in these chapters.

Chapter 5. Networking

Netatalk: http://www.umich.edu/~rsug/netatalk/ (general),
　　　　　http://thehamptons.com/anders/netatalk/ (Linux netatalk)
Printing: http://www.giub.unibe.ch/~eugster/appleprint.html
BIND: ftp://ftp.isc.org/isc/bind

Chapter 7. E-mail

IMAP: http://www.imap.org
Sendmail home page: http://www.sendmail.org/
Qmail: http://www.qmail.org

Chapter 8. Internet Agencies

InterNIC: http://www.internic.net/
US top level domain, ISI: http://www.isi.edu/
http://www.isi.edu/div7/iana/domain-names.html
CERT: http://www.cert.org/

Chapter 9. Samba

Samba: http://lake.canberra.edu.au/pub/samba/samba.html
Microsoft: http://www.microsoft.com/

Chapter 10. Netnews

INN patches: http://thereisnocabal.news.erols.com/patches/
    ext2_no_atime.diff
INN: http://www.isc.org/inn.html
http://www.oceanwave.com/technical-resources/unix-admin/news.html
http://www.cis.ohio-state.edu/~barr/INN.html
http://thereisnocabal.news.erols.com/patches/

Chapter 11. FTP

WU-ftpd: ftp://wuarchive.wustl.edu/packages/wuarchive-ftpd/
Virtual FTP patches for wu-ftp: http://www.westnet.com/providers/
    multi-wu-ftpd.txt
XFTP: http://www.llnl.gov/liv_comp/xftp.html

Chapter 12. Desktop Applications

Applix, Inc.: http://www.applix.com/
Star Division: http://www.stardivision.com/
Corel WordPerfect 7: http://www.corel.com/
The Software Development Corporation: http://www.sdcorp.com/
Corel Office for Java: http://www.corel.com/javastrat/index.htm
NExS, X Engineering Software Systems: http://www.xess.com/
TeX, Latex, CTAN: http://www.tex.ac.uk/
GIMP (GNU Image Manipulation Program):
    http://www.XCF.Berkeley.EDU/~gimp/

Mapedit, Boutell.Com, Inc: http://www.boutell.com/mapedit/
Mathematica, Wolfram Research: http://www.wolfram.com/
Executor, ARDI: http://www.ardi.com/
Wabi: http://www.caldera.com/doc/wabi/wabi.html
WINE: http://www.qbc.clic.net/~krynos/wine_en.html
Acrobat Reader, Adobe: http://www.adobe.com
LessTif: http://www.lesstif.org/

Chapter 13. Databases

MySQL: http://www.tcx.se/
mSQL: http://hughes.com.au/
Xforms: http://bragg.phys.uwm.edu/xforms
Solid: http://www.solidtech.com/
Empress: http://www.empress.com/
Texpress, KE Software: http://www.kesoftware.com/
Essentia, Intersoft: http:/www.inter-soft.com/
Sybase: http://www.sybase.com/
Oracle: http://www.oracle.com

Chapter 14. Programming Languages

C, GCC: http://www.fsf.org/software/gcc/gcc.html
C++, G++: http://www.accu.org/
Perl: http://www.perl.com/
Python: http://www.python.com/
Lisp: http://www.cs.cmu.edu/Groups/AI/html/cltl/cltl2.html
Scheme: http://www-swiss.ai.mit.edu/scheme-home.html
Java: http://www.blackdown.org/
Tcl/Tk: http://www.sunlabs.com/research/tcl/
FORTRAN: http://www.fortran.com/fortran/
Basic: http://www.Uni-Mainz.DE/~ihm/basic.html
Pascal: http://sun01.brain.uni-freiburg.de/~klaus/pascal/fpk-pas/
Cobol: http://www.cobol.org/
Smalltalk: http://st-www.cs.uiuc.edu/
Icon: http://www.cs.arizona.edu/icon/www/index.html
Rexx: http://www.rexxla.org/
Eiffel: http://www.eiffel.com/
Sather: http://www.icsi.berkeley.edu/~sather/

Chapter 15. Web Serving

Apache: http://www.apache.org
Boa: http://www.boa.org/
W3C (CERN) httpd: http://www.w3.org/pub/WWW/Daemon/
NCSA httpd: http://hoohoo.ncsa.uiuc.edu/
Roxen: http://www.roxen.com/
WN: http://hopf.math.nwu.edu/
Zeus: http://www.zeus.co.uk/
Stronghold: http://www.c2.net/
Apache-SSL: http://www.algroup.co.uk/Apache-SSL/
mSQL: http://hughes.com.au/
SQL tutorial: http://w3.one.net/~jhoffman/sqltut.htm
PHP/FI http://php.iquest.net/

Chapter 16. X

XiGraphics: http://www.xinside.com/
RedHat: http://www.redhat.com/
AcceleratedX, XiGraphics: http://www.xinside.com/
Metro-X, Metrolink: http://www.metrolink.com/

Chapter 20. Backups

BRU: http://www.estinc.com/
PerfectBackup+: http://home.xl.ca/perfectBackup/
RAID patches: http://www.linuxhq.com/patch/20-p0632.html

Chapter 21. Peripherals

Xvscan: http://www.tummy.com/xvscan/
Zip drive kernel driver: http://gear.torque.net/pup/ppa.c

Chapter 22. Distributions

DEC Alpha: http://www.azstarnet.com/~axplinux/
Sun Sparc 4m, 4c: http://www.geog.ubc.ca/s_linux.html
SGI MIPS: http://www.linux.sgi.com/
Other MIPS: http://www.village.org/villagers/imp/linux-mips-faq.html

Motorola 68K (Motorola MVME, Atari and Amiga 68Ks): http://
   www.clark.net/pub/lawrencc/linux/index.html
Apple 68Ks: http://www.maclinux.org/index.html
PowerPC: mkLinux: http://www.mklinux.apple.com/
   Linux/PPC (http://www.linuxppc.org/
x86 (AMD, Cyrix and Intel): http://www.linux.org/ or any of hundreds of
   other sites.
RedHat: http://www.redhat.com/
Caldera: http://www.caldera.com/
Workgroup Solutions: http://www.wgs.com/

Chapter 23. Connecting to the Internet

Linux Headquarters: http://www.linuxhq.org/

Chapter Other Resources

Linux: http://www.linux.org/
Yahoo Search: http://www.yahoo.com/

Appendix   B

Documentation from Caldera

B.1   Introduction to OpenLinux

Welcome to Caldera OpenLinux™, a complete multitasking, multi-user operating system for your organization. With OpenLinux, you get the power and reliability of a UNIX® operating system from a personal computer.

If you're new to OpenLinux, you should read this chapter to learn about Caldera's product line and user rights. This chapter explains these topics:

- OpenLinux product line
- Getting information
- A word about copyrights

B.2   OpenLinux Product Line

The Caldera OpenLinux product line is a multitasking, multi-user operating system that gives you the power and reliability of UNIX® on a personal computer. OpenLinux is Caldera's distribution of Linux technology. It includes the complete Linux operating system and this release includes the 2.0.29 kernel.

Caldera provides a four-tier product line to meet users' needs. The product line includes

- OpenLinux Lite. This product only includes Caldera's distribution of the Linux operating system.
- OpenLinux Base. This product provides new Linux and UNIX users with a complete Linux operating system, including commercial components such as Netscape Navigator, CRiSPLiTE, and a graphical desktop.
- OpenLinux Standard. This provides Internet and intranet solutions, giving you full authoring, publishing, and browsing capabilities. (See "Components Included in Standard" for more.)
- OpenLinux Deluxe. This product provides complete solutions for the workgroup and small office environments that need to utilize all systems.

Caldera added "Open" to its product line (for example, OpenLinux) to emphasize that the operating source code is open, so you can see exactly how the operating system works. That way, you can configure your system to operate as efficiently as possible.

Components Included in Standard

In addition to Caldera's easy installation, what makes Caldera's OpenLinux technology unique among Linux distributions is its many other commercial components. These commercial components give your system the power and functionality you expect to run a business. Here's a listing of some of the components that accompany OpenLinux Standard.

- Netscape FastTrack Server™. This powerful Web server lets you manage information on the Internet and in your own intranet easily. FastTrack gives you industry-leading performance, flexibility, and security in an easy-to-use graphical environment. This Web server supports SSL encryption, access control, and NSAPI-compatible plug-in modules to protect your information and extend the server's functionality.
- Novell NetWare® client and administrative utilities. NetWare lets you seamlessly view and copy files on NetWare volumes and print to NetWare printers without any additional software on your NetWare servers. With

the administration utilities, you can provide complete NDS and bindery administration. For example, you can create and delete objects, view and set property values, and manage filesystem trustee assignments.

- Netscape Navigator™ 3.01 Gold. The Navigator lets you browse the World Wide Web, author Web pages, and view on-line help and other documentation.

- CRiSP-LiTE. This powerful program provides an intuitive interface for editing files from the desktop.

- X Servers. OpenLinux includes two X servers: Metro-X and XFree86. These X servers let you easily configure a graphical interface on a variety of popular high-performance video cards.

- OpenDOS™. This is a complete DOS operating system that you can use to run thousands of existing DOS programs. While running OpenLinux, you can access a DOS emulator and run DOS programs.

- Graphical desktop. A sophisticated desktop interface can be used to view and manage filesystems. For example, you can drag and drop files onto program icons to open the files. The desktop interface also lets you customize your workspace with icons and toolbars so you can quickly perform tasks with a click of the mouse.

B.3   Key Features of OpenLinux

Since OpenLinux is a distribution of Linux using the 2.0.29 kernel, the features inherent in Linux are also found in Caldera's OpenLinux. Here's a listing of some of the key features found in OpenLinux.

- TCP/IP. Uses TCP/IP, the Internet protocol, for high-speed networking.

- Menu-based Tools. Installs and configures OpenLinux easily with menu-based tools.

- POSIX-based Environment. Uses a POSIX-based multi-user operating environment with complete Internet connectivity tools, traditional UNIX® development environments, and a high-speed, preemptive multitasking architecture that takes full advantage of 32-bit microprocessors. (Caldera includes support for both ELF and a.out binary formats.)

- Unlimited Users. Sets up an unrestricted number of user accounts on each Caldera operating system for use on a single computer system.

- Internet/Intranet Connectivity. Integrates OpenLinux with the Internet, including the integration of these services: DNS/NIS (name services), HTTP (Web), SMTP (E-mail), FTP, SNMP (management), PPP/SLIP (dial-in), NNTP (Usenet News), and many others.

- Client Access to Windows and UNIX. Accesses all your existing systems as a client: UNIX, Windows NT®, Windows® 95, and Windows for Workgroups™ 3.11.

- Remote Management. Manage UNIX systems via remote login on networked or dial-in connections and access network resources from a remote site without requiring a separate machine as a dedicated gateway.

- Multitasking. Runs many DOS and SCO UNIX (ibcs2) applications at the same time your computer acts as an Internet gateway for your organization.

- Hardware Support. Obtains support for a variety of other networking protocols, filesystems, and networked operating systems. Obtains support for hundreds of hardware components, including CD-ROM, multimedia devices, laptop computers, high-speed networking cards, and high-performance video graphics cards. Product line

B.4   Getting Information

This guide represents a small part of the documentation for OpenLinux. The rest of the information is on-line. You can also contact Caldera for additional help.

This section explains how to get more information:

- Use on-line documentation.
- Contact Caldera.

Using On-line Documentation

To access on-line documentation, double-click the Caldera_Info icon on the Desktop. The on-line documentation includes links to this guide, plus other information you'll need. The information is displayed using the Netscape browser.

Some of the on-line manuals that are included with OpenLinux Standard are also available as paper books. Check with your local computer book reseller or Caldera for availability.

Contacting Caldera

In addition to the sources of information about Linux and UNIX available in bookstores and on the Internet, Caldera provides several electronic resources to assist you with installing and using Caldera OpenLinux. You can get information from Caldera in these ways:

- Email
- World Wide Web
- File Transfer Protocol (FTP)

Using E-mail to Contact Caldera

If you want information via E-mail, you can send messages to the following addresses:

Table B-1 *You can obtain information from Caldera by sending E-mail messages to these addresses.*

If you want this	Send e-mail here
Autoreply with general, non-technical information about Caldera. Caldera staff reviews all messages sent to this address. If your question requires a more detailed response than the autoreply gives, you'll also get an E-mail message from Caldera staff (usually within 24 hours).	info@caldera.com
Autoreply with frequently asked questions and answers	faq@caldera.com
Answers to technical questions regarding installing and using Caldera products. Your message is placed in a queue to be answered by a support engineer. In the meantime, you'll receive an autoreply with technical information about installing and using Caldera products.	support@caldera.com
Autoreply with information about Caldera-related E-mail lists	majordomo@caldera.com
Autoreply with information on ordering by fax, telephone, or E-mail.	order@caldera.com

Using the World Wide Web to Contact Caldera

If you want to contact Caldera through the Internet, access this site:

`http://www.caldera.com.`

This site gives you information about Caldera, Caldera products, Linux, and other related information.

Using File Transfer Protocol (FTP) to Contact Caldera

If you want to contact Caldera using FTP protocol, here's our site: ftp.caldera.com. This site includes this information:

- Lists of frequently asked questions and answers
- Release notes
- Updated programs
- Known bugs

A Word about Copyrights

Caldera OpenLinux products are unusual among commercial software because Caldera has added valuable components to freely distributable software. The components added by Caldera are copyrighted. The freely distributable software is available under the GNU General Public LicenseGNU General Public License (GPL) and the Berkeley license (explained in "License Statements").

This section explains these topics:

- Copyrighted components added to OpenLinux
- Freely distributed software

Copyrighted Components Added to OpenLinux

The following are some of the components added by Caldera:

- Netscape FastTrack Server™
- Netscape Navigator™
- Novell NetWare® client and administrative utilities
- Metro Link's Metro-X® server

- A commercial license for OpenDOS™
- A graphical desktop interface

These commercial components aren't freely distributable. You were licensed to use these components when you purchased this copy of Open-Linux Standard. However, you must have a separate license for each computer that runs any of these commercial components.

Freely Distributed Software

The following are the components that are freely distributable:

- Linux operating system kernel
- The utilities accompanying the Linux operating system

Though you can freely change and redistribute these programs, you should review the license agreements to find out about any exclusions. For example, some freely available software can't be redistributed without written permission from the copyright owner.

Appendix

Installing OpenLinux

This chapter explains how to install your new OpenLinux system. Before you install OpenLinux, you need to prepare your hard disk. That way, you won't lose any information that's currently on your hard disk and you can quickly install your system.

This section explains how to do these tasks:

- Prepare to install.
- Upgrade from existing Caldera or Linux systems.
- Share the hard disk.
- Install OpenLinux.
- Boot in emergency situations.

C.1 Preparing to Install

Before you install OpenLinux, you must obtain information about the hardware in your system. That way, you'll know if your computer is compatible with OpenLinux, and you'll be able to quickly the system.

This section explains these topics:

- System requirements
- Collecting hardware and network information

System Requirements

Your computer system must meet the following requirements in order to install OpenLinux .

- 32-bit Intel-based personal computer or compatibles, such as these processors: 386, 486, Pentium, Pentium Pro. Other processors are not supported in this release.
- Minimum 8-MB RAM (16-MB RAM to use graphical components).
- 266-MB free hard disk space for recommended installation. (You'll need more or less disk space, depending on the installation option you choose.)
- A supported mouse and video card (for use with the graphical components).

Collecting Hardware and Network Information

Before you install OpenLinux , you should collect information about your system's hardware and your network. You'll use this information as you install your new system. For example, if you have a CD-ROM drive, you'll be asked to specify your system's CD-ROM type and model.

This table lists the information you'll need to quickly install OpenLinux.

Collect the information in this table before you install OpenLinux . Items marked with an asterisk (*) are usually automatically detected when you install OpenLinux.

Collect this	Here's an example	Write your system's information here
2 3-1/2 inch floppy diskettes	IBM formatted	
CD-ROM Drive, make and model*	Sony, cdu31a	
Ethernet card, make and model*	3com, 3c509	
Mouse, manufacturer (and model)	Microsoft	
Mouse, port used (ps/2, or a serial port number)	ps/2 port	
Graphics card, manufacturer	Matrox	
Graphics card, model or number	Millennium	
Graphics card, memory size in MB	2MB	
Monitor, manufacturer and model or	NEC	
Monitor, maximum scan rate	76 MHz	
Modem, manufacturer and model	Hayes	
Modem, serial port used	COM 2	
Hostname for your computer	brighton	
Domain name of your network	caldera.com	
IP address assigned to your computer	192.168.12.44	
Network address of your organization or LAN	192.168.12.0	
Netmask of your organization or LAN	255.255.255.0	
Broadcast address of your network	192.168.12.255	
Gateway or router address (if you have one)	192.168.12.254	
DNS name server address (if you have one)	192.168.12.1	
Additional addresses for gateways or name servers (if you have more than one of either)		

C.2 Upgrading from Existing Caldera or Linux Systems

OpenLinux is an upgrade from Base and Caldera Network Desktop (CND). However, you may have personalized these systems with different settings (for example, the filesystems that automatically mount at startup). If you want, you can save these settings to a floppy diskette and add them to your new system. You may also have settings under another distribution of Linux that you want to save.

This section explains how to prepare your system if you already have a Caldera distribution of Linux or another distribution of Linux. This section explains how to do these tasks:

- Upgrade from existing Caldera systems.
- Add Caldera's commercial packages to other Linux distributions.

Upgrading from Existing Caldera Systems

Before upgrading from an existing Caldera system, you might want to copy certain files to a floppy diskette or your network because the Linux partition will be re-formatted, destroying all data on that partition.

Table C-1 lists some files you might want to copy:

Table C-1   *Files you may want to copy before installing your new system.*

If you want to preserve this	Copy this file or directory
X Windows configuration	/etc/Xaccel.ini or /etc/XF86config
Boot manager configuration parameters (such as boot parameters to recognize hardware) NOTE: Since OpenLinux uses the Linux 2.0.29 kernel, the boot parameters may be different than your existing Caldera system.	/etc/lilo.conf
IP networking information (such as, hosts, nameserver, and domain name)	/etc/hosts and /etc/resolv.conf
Filesystems mounted on your system	/etc/fstab
Names and passwords of all users on your system	/etc/passwd and /etc/group
Any home directories for users on your system	/home
Any of your user settings	/usr

Adding Caldera's Commercial Packages to Other Linux Distributions

You can upgrade to OpenLinux from another Linux distribution. Many users have successfully installed Caldera's commercial packages on other ELF-based Linux 2.x systems. However, before upgrading, you should know Caldera doesn't provide support for other Linux systems and the upgrade instructions provided here may not work on your system.

1. **Load a copy of the rpm** utility (for example, from the Internet).

   This file contains the RedHat Package Manager utility, which is used to install, query, and uninstall all software packages from the Caldera CD-ROM.

2. **Install this utility on your Linux system**.

3. **Enter** man rpm to review the man page for the rpm utility.

4. **Use the rpm** command to install, verify, or uninstall the packages located on the Caldera CD-ROM (for example, rpm -i OpenLinux-1.1-8.i386.rpm).

   NOTE: For a list of the available software packages, see "Choosing the Software Packages to Install."

C.3   Sharing the Hard Disk

If you're planning to run only OpenLinux on your system, you need only two partitions: a default partition of at least 266 MB and a swap partition of at least 16 MB. If you're planning to run additional operating systems with OpenLinux, you'll need more partitions on your hard drive. For example, you can run OpenLinux or Windows 95.

NOTE: If you're already using another operating system on your hard disk and you're planning to share it with OpenLinux, you might instead consider using a separate hard disk for OpenLinux. That way, you won't have to back up all the data and repartition your current hard disk.

This section explains how to do these tasks:

- Share hard disk with DOS or Windows.
- Share hard disk with other operating systems.

Sharing Hard Disk with OpenLinux and DOS/Windows

If you're already using DOS or Windows on your system, you can share the hard disk with a Caldera system without reinstalling them. To prepare the hard disk to use more than one operating system, you must defragment your current data and divide the partition. This section explains how to defragment your hard disk if you currently have DOS or Windows on your hard disk.

1. **Boot your computer to DOS or Windows**.

2. **To move all the data on your system to one area, defragment your filesystem.**

   NOTE: Most versions of DOS or Windows have a program to defragment your hard disk (for example, DEFRAG.EXE or OPTIMIZE.EXE).

3. **To shrink your filesystem, run this file from the Caldera CD-ROM: \COL\TOOLS\FIPS15\FIPS.EXE** (for example, from a command line in DOS, enter D:\COL\TOOLS\FIPS15\FIPS.EXE).

   The FIPS utility splits your current DOS/Windows partition in half without damaging the existing data on the hard disk.

4. **Carefully follow the on-screen instructions for the FIPS utility**.

   The recommended OpenLinux installation requires at least 266 MB of free disk space.

5. **Use FIPS to adjust the size of the DOS partition on your hard drive by using the arrow keys on your keyboard, then press** enter to set the size of the partitions.

6. **Confirm the reduced size of the new DOS partition**. FIPS writes the new partition information to your hard drive. You're now ready to install OpenLinux.

Sharing Hard Disk with OpenLinux and Other Operating Systems

You must create two partitions to install OpenLinux . If you're planning to run more than one operating system on your hard disk, you'll need to create additional partitions. This section explains how to prepare your hard disk for OpenLinux and partition your hard disk.

Note: If you're planning to install Windows 95 and OpenLinux, you should first install Windows 95. That way, you won't have to reconfigure LILO and the master boot record. (LILO lets you choose the operating system you want to start.)

1. **If you already have an operating system on your hard disk, you should back up the data before continuing**. Most operating systems come with utilities to back up your system.

2. **Using a hard disk utility on your current system, create enough space for these partitions**:

   • At least 266 MB for the root Linux filesystem (For more specific information on the software packages you can install, see "Selecting an Installation Option.")

   • At least 16 MB for a Swap partition

   • Enough space for your current operating system

3. **If necessary, reinstall your current operating system into the new, smaller partition that you created**. You're now ready to install OpenLinux.

C.4   Installing OpenLinux

Once you've prepared your hard disk by backing up any data and preparing space for OpenLinux , you're ready to install your new system. This section explains how to do these tasks:

   • Create boot and modules diskettes.

   • Start the installation and recognize the hardware.

   • Change partitions on hard disk.

   • Use the Kernel Module Manager.

   • Choose the partition for OpenLinux.

   • Select an installation option.

   • Do final configuration.

As you're installing OpenLinux, you can access other consoles. These consoles let you execute other programs as you're installing OpenLinux. Use the keystrokes in Table C-2 to access other consoles:

Table C-2   *Lists how to access consoles during the installation process*

To do this	Press and hold down these keys
Review installation messages (such as hardware detected)	left-Alt+F8
Return to installation process	left-Alt+F1
To get additional information (such as hardware parameters)	left-Alt+F2 or F3, then login as help or root.
To access help in certain fields	F1

Creating Install and Modules Diskettes

If you don't have a bootable CD-ROM, you will need diskettes to install OpenLinux. You can use the Caldera CD-ROM to create these diskettes.

1. **Insert the Caldera CD-ROM.**

2. **To create an Install diskette, use this table**:.

Table C-3   *Creating an Install diskette*

To copy the files from DOS/Windows	To copy the files from Linux
a. Insert a blank 3-1/2" floppy diskette.	a. Insert a blank 3-1/2" floppy diskette.
b. Access this file on your CD-ROM: `/COL/LAUNCH/FLOPPY/RAWRITE3.COM`	b. Mount your CD-ROM drive.
c. Enter drive letter and this file: `/COL/LAUNCH/FLOPPY/INSTALL.IMG` (for example, `D:/COL/LAUNCH/FLOPPY/INSTALL.img`)	c. Access the directory you mounted the CD-ROM to.
d. Enter the drive letter for the floppy diskette.	d. From a command line, enter dd `if=/col/launch/floppy/install.img of=/dev/fd0`.

Table C-3   *Creating an Install diskette*

To copy the files from DOS/Windows	To copy the files from Linux
e. Press ENTER `to continue`.	
f. Close RAWRITE3.	

Depending on your system's hardware, you may not need to create a Modules diskette.

3. **To create a Modules diskette, use this table**:.

Table C-4   *Creating a Modules diskette*

To copy the files from DOS/Windows	To copy the files from Linux
a. Insert a blank 3-1/2" floppy diskette.	a. Insert a blank 3-1/2" floppy diskette.
b. Access this file on your CD-ROM: `/COL/ LAUNCH/FLOPPY/RAWRITE3.COM`	b. Mount your CD-ROM drive.
c. Enter drive letter and this file: `/COL/LAUNCH/ FLOPPY/MODULES.IMG` (for example, `D:/COL/ LAUNCH/FLOPPY/INSTALL.img`)	c. If you're not already there, access the directory you mounted the CD-ROM to.
d. Enter the drive letter for the floppy diskette.	d. Enter dd `if=/col/ launch/floppy/mod- ules.img of=/dev/ fd0`.
e. Press ENTER `to continue`.	
f. Close RAWRITE3.	

Starting the Installation and Recognizing the Hardware

This section explains how to start the installation process and get your system to recognize your hardware.

1. **Do one of these, depending on how you're installing OpenLinux.**

Table C-5   *Steps for starting the installation process.*

To install from a bootable CD-ROM	To install using the Install diskette
a. Insert the CD-ROM.	a. Insert the CD-ROM and the install diskette.
b. Turn on your computer.	b. Turn on your computer. Note: If necessary, see the README file in the /col/launch directory.

After a few moments, a welcome message appears.

2. **If necessary, enter boot parameters; otherwise, press** enter to continue. If you've already tried to install OpenLinux and the system didn't recognize your hardware, you may want to enter boot parameters (explained in the "Using Hardware Parameters" chapter).

3. If your system has plug-n-play cards, enter pnp to disable this facility; otherwise, press enter. Plug-n-play cards may conflict with the installation.

A list of languages appears.

4. **Choose a language; then press** enter to continue. A list of keyboard maps appears.

5. **Choose a keyboard; then press** enter to continue. A list appears with the hardware detected by the system.

6. **After you've reviewed the hardware detected by your system, press** enter to continue.

7. **Depending on whether or not all your system's hardware was detected, use this table.**

Table C-6   *Recognizing your hardware*

System recognized all hardware	Autoprobe for more hardware	Manually choose hardware that wasn't recognized
a. Choose "Yes" and press enter.	a. Choose "No" and press enter.	a. Choose "No" and press enter.
b. Skip to "Choosing the Partition for OpenLinux "	b. Choose "Yes" to autoprobe, then press enter.	b. Choose "No" and press enter. You're prompted to use the Kernel manager.
	c. Press enter to continue. After autoprobing is done, a list of hardware appears.	c. See "Using the Kernel Module Manager"
	d. After you review the hardware, press enter to continue.	
	e. Depending on whether or not your system recognized your hardware, do one of these: –If the system recognized all your hardware, choose "Yes" and press enter. Then see "Choosing the Partition for OpenLinux." –If the system didn't recognize all your hardware, choose "No" and press enter. Then see "Using the Kernel Module Manager."	

Changing Partitions on Hard Disk

As you're installing OpenLinux, you're asked if you need to change the partitions on your hard disk. If you haven't already partitioned your hard disk, you should do it when you're prompted. The fdisk utility is used to make the partitions.

1. **Select the hard disk device to partition**. A message appears telling you that you should be familiar with the fdisk utility before continuing.

2. **Choose "Yes" and press enter.** The fdisk utility starts and a list of commands appears.

3. **Enter** p (print to screen) to see a list of existing partitions.

4. **If necessary, use this table to delete any unused partitions.**

Table C-7 *Deleting any existing partitions that aren't being used*

To delete any existing partitions
NOTE: When you delete a partition, you lose all the data on that partition.
a. Enter d (delete).
b. Enter the partition number you want to delete.

5. **Use this table to create and mark the partition for your swap area.**

Table C-8 *Creating and marking a swap partition*

To create and mark the swap partition
a. Enter n (new).
b. Enter p to mark the partition you're creating as a primary partition
c. Enter the partition number for the partition you're creating.
d. Enter the cylinder number where you want the partition to start (usually the first one displayed in parentheses).
e. Enter the last cylinder number or the size you want the partition to be. Make this partition between 16 and 64 MB in size. For example, to make the partition 32 MB, enter this: +32M
f. Enter t (type), then enter the number of the partition you're changing.
g. Enter 82 to mark the partition as type 82, Linux Swap.

6. **Use the table to create and mark the Linux root partition**.

Table C-9   *Creating and marking the main partition*

To create and mark the main partition
a. Enter n (new).
b. Enter p to mark the partition you're creating as a primary partition
c. Enter the partition number for the partition you're creating.
d. Enter the cylinder number where you want the partition to start (usually the first one displayed in parentheses).
e. Enter the last cylinder number or the size you want the partition to be. Depending on the software packages you're planning to install, make this partition at least 266 MB. For example, to make the partition 266 MB, enter this: +330M. The system automatically assigns this partition as the Linux native (type 83).

7. **Enter** w (write) to save these changes and exit the utility. To quit without saving these changes, enter q.

8. **Press** enter to continue. After a few moments, the system automatically reboots.

Using the Kernel Module Manager

If your system doesn't recognize your hardware, you can use kernel modules to help your system recognize the hardware. You can also analyze the hardware that was autoprobed by the installation.

1. **Choose "Load kernel module."** A list of modules appears.

2. **Choose the type of hardware support you want to load, then press** enter. A list of modules appears.

3. **Choose the module you want to load, then press** enter.

4. **If necessary, enter any parameters that are needed to correctly recognize your hardware**. (For a list of parameters, press and hold down alt+F2, then log in as help; or see "Using Hardware Parameters.")

5. **Press** enter to continue. A list of your system's hardware appears.

6. **After reviewing the new list of hardware detected, press** enter to continue.

7. **To load other modules, repeat steps 2–6; otherwise, choose "Return to previous menu" and press** enter.

8. **Choose "Finish kernel module management" and press** enter. You're prompted to set up partitions on your hard disk.

   To review the modules you have loaded and how they're affecting your installation, choose "Analyze kernel modules."

9. **Depending on what you want to do, use this table**.

To change any partitions on your hard disk	To continue without making changes to any partitions
a. Choose "Yes" and press enter. A list of hard disks appears.	b. See "Changing Partitions on Hard Disk."
a. Choose "No" and press enter.	b. See "Choosing the Partition for OpenLinux ."

Choosing the Partition for OpenLinux

After your system's hardware is detected and your hard disk is partitioned, you're ready to choose the partition for OpenLinux. In this section, you format the partition for OpenLinux and the system checks for defective sectors on your hard disk.

1. **Select the swap partition to initialize the area**. Depending on the size of your system's swap partition, this may take several minutes to initialize.

2. **Select a source to install from**.

Table C-10   *Selecting a source to install from*

If you're installing from this source	Do this
CD-ROM	a. Choose "CD-ROM" and press enter. A list of CD-ROM types appears.
	b. Press enter to choose the default device path; otherwise, choose one from the list.
	c. Press enter to continue.
Network (NFS)	a. Choose "Network (NFS)" and press enter.
	b. Enter your hostname (for example, `drift.caldera.com`).
	c. Enter the device name of the network interface.
	d. Enter your IP address.
	e. Enter the network mask.
	f. Enter the broadcast address.
	g. If you have a default router/gateway, choose "Yes" and press enter; otherwise, choose "No" and press enter.
	h. If necessary, enter the default router/gateway.
	i. Enter the NFS server's IP address.
	j. Enter the exported directory on the NFS server where the installation data are.

3. **Choose the Linux native partition (type 83) to install the Caldera system, then press** enter.

4. **Choose "Yes" and press** enter to format the partition you chose.

5. **Do one of these:**
   - To check for defective sectors, choose "Yes" and press enter. The system checks for bad sectors, then it writes these changes to your hard disk. Depending on your system's disk size, this process may take several minutes to complete.

- To continue without checking for defective sectors, choose "No" and press enter.

After the system formats the partitions you selected, you're prompted to select a package to install. See the next task, "Selecting an Installation Option," to install the package you want.

Selecting an Installation Option

After you format the partition for OpenLinux, you choose what software packages you want to install. You can choose from one of the defaults or choose specific software packages. Here are the options.

1. **Choose one of these installation options, then press** enter:
   - **Minimal system (without X11).** This installs the OpenLinux system, but it doesn't install the graphical system. It requires 45 MB of free disk space.
   - **Minimal system (with X11).** This installs the OpenLinux system, development tools, other utilities, and the graphical X Window System. It requires 71 MB of free disk space.
   - **Small standard system (commonly required packages).** This installs commonly used utilities, the graphical X Window System, and the desktop interface. However, it doesn't include some development tools, additional utilities, and Internet services. It requires 104MB of free disk space.
   - **Standard system**. This is the default installation for OpenLinux . This installation includes the graphical desktop and other development tools, and so forth. It requires 266 MB of free disk space.
   - **Install all packages**. This installs all the contents of the CD-ROM. It requires 732 MB of free disk space.
   - **Quick and compact selection**. This lets you choose certain groups of items to install. This installation option is similar to selecting individual packages, but it's faster because groups of related packages (such as games or text processing) can be selected together.
   - **Individual series selection**. This lets you choose the packages you want to install. Unlike the "quick and compact" installation, you can choose from individual packages. Packages marked with a "#" are required for the operating system. Packages marked with "X" are preselected according to categories, but you can deselect them.

NOTE: Only use this option if you're an experienced Linux user.

A list of X servers appears.

2. **Choose an X server, then press** enter.

   NOTE: The system automatically chooses the minimum XFree86 servers and you can't deselect them.

3. **Press** enter to begin the installation. A box appears showing you the installation progress.

   During the installation, you can review a list of help topics. To get a list of help topics, press left-alt+f2 and enter help. Choose a help topic, then choose "Call" and press enter. To move around the help screens, use the commands listed at the bottom of the screen. To return to the installation process, press alt+f1. (Make sure you log off before returning to the installation process.)

   When the installation completes, you're prompted to enter your system's hostname. (See "Doing Final Configuration.")

Doing Final Configuration

After you install the packages, you configure your OpenLinux system. You can later review and change these configuration options using the LISA utility.

1. **Enter the hostname of this computer (for example,** `drift.caldera.com`).

2. **If you have a network card, choose "Yes" and press** enter; otherwise, choose "No" and press enter.

3. **Press** enter to use the default network card, or enter the device name of the network card.

4. **Enter your system's IP address**.

5. **Enter the network mask**.

6. **Enter the broadcast address**. You're asked if you have a default router/gateway.

7. **If you have a default router and gateway, choose "Yes" and press** enter; otherwise, choose "No" and press enter. Then skip to step 9.

8. **Enter the IP address of the default router/gateway.** You're asked if your network uses a DNS nameserver.

9. **If your network uses a DNS nameserver, choose "Yes" and press** enter; otherwise, choose "No" and press enter, then skip to step 11.

10. **Enter the IP address of the DNS nameserver**.

11. **To configure the NIS system, use this table; otherwise, choose "Do not use NIS" and press** enter.

Table C-11   *Configuring NIS services*

To configure host as NIS client	To configure host as NIS client and server
a. Choose "Configure host as NIS client," then press enter.	a. Choose "Configure host as NIS client and server," then press enter.
b. Enter your NIS domain.	b. Enter your NIS domain.
c. Enter the IP address of your NIS server. NOTE: You can enter up to three different NIS servers.	

12. **Choose Local Time or GMT Time for your system clock, then press** enter.

   If you're planning to use another operating system with OpenLinux, you should choose "Local Time" to avoid possible system problems.

13. **Choose your time zone, then press** enter.

14. **Choose your mouse type, then press** enter. This information determines which device to link to.

15. **Use this table to set up your printer**.

Table C-12   *Setting up the printer*

To set up printer
a. Choose the appropriate printer driver.
b. Enter the printer port.
c. Choose a default printer resolution.
d. Choose a default paper size.

You're ready to set up a password for the root user.

16.**Press** enter to continue. You're prompted to enter a password.

17.**Enter a password, then reenter the password to confirm it**. This is your root password that you use when you want to administer your system.

You're ready to set up a password for the default col user. The col user is the initial, non-root user of the system you're installing.

18.**Press** enter to continue.

19.**Enter a password, then re-enter the password to confirm it.** This is your default password. (To set up other users later, see "Adding a User.") A list of your current setup appears.

20.**Press** enter to continue.

21.**Choose the partition where the LILO Boot Manager should be installed, then press** enter. Normally, you should choose the Linux root partition for LILO.

22.**Choose the boot image (operating system) you want to start when you boot your system**. This is the image that will boot, unless you choose image at boot time.

You're asked to choose a boot name for the Linux operating system. If you're sharing your hard disk with multiple operating systems, you'll type a name of the operating system you want to be able to start.

23.**To use the default boot name, press** enter; otherwise, enter a new name (without spaces) for the boot name.

24.**If necessary, enter boot parameters**. (For more information on boot parameters, see "Using Hardware Parameters.")

25.**If necessary, repeat steps 22–24 to choose other images to boot; otherwise, choose "No further entries to add to LILO" and press** enter. The LILO configuration file appears.

26.**After reviewing** the LILO file, press enter to continue.

27.**If the LILO file is ready to configure, choose "Yes" and press** enter. LILO is installed.

28.**Press** enter to continue.

29.**Choose all services that should automatically boot each time you start your system, then press** enter. (To select an item, highlight it, then press the spacebar.)

30.**Choose the X server to configure**, then press enter.

31.**Depending on whether or not you want to configure your graphical system now or later, do one of these**:

Table C-13   *Configuring the graphical system*

To configure the graphical system now	To configure the graphical system later
a. Choose "Yes" and press enter.	a. Choose "No" and press enter. You're prompted to re-boot your system.
b. Press enter to continue. You'll configure the graphical system in a few moments.	b. Press enter to continue. After a few moments, your system reboots.
c. Press enter to continue, then see "Configuring the X Window System."	

Booting in Emergency Situations

If you have trouble rebooting the system and getting back into Caldera,

1. **Insert the Install diskette**.

2. **Restart your system**. The welcome message appears.

3. **At the boot prompt, enter boot ro root=,** then enter where the root Linux partition is (for example, `boot ro root=/dev/hda2`).

Appendix D

D.1 DOS Installation README (\col\launch\dos)

This directory contains the files necessary to launch the OpenLinux(TM) installation from DOS. This is useful in instances where an install floppy cannot be used, for example, on a laptop where either a CD-ROM or floppy drive is available but not both.

The contents of this directory are

- install.bat—a DOS batch file program that utilizes the remaining files to launch the OpenLinux installation from DOS.

- loadlin.exe—a DOS program that loads the installation program. Documentation for this can be found in "..\.\tools\loadlin."

- vmlinuz—an OpenLinux kernel to be used during installation.

- initrd.gz—a file used by the OpenLinux kernel during installation.

The easiest way to use these files is to boot the machine into DOS, change directory to this directory, and run "install.bat."

In some instances, you will not be able to run "install.bat" directly from the CD-ROM due to conflicts between the loading install program and the loaded drivers. If you observe this problem, do the following:

1. Make a directory on your DOS hard drive.

2. Copy all files in this directory to the newly created directory on your DOS hard drive.

3. Reboot into DOS and hold down the <LEFT SHIFT> key as DOS is loading. This will cause DOS to not load any additional drivers.

4. Change directory to the directory you created in (1) on your DOS hard drive.

5. Run "install.bat."

D.2   README for Floppy installation (\col\launch\floppy)

Some OpenLinux(TM) products include manufactured installation diskettes. In such instances there is no need to create the diskettes as below.

The process outlined below is the same used to produce master copies of manufactured installation diskettes.

Updated installation diskette images may be available on Caldera's Web site. If the installation on your system encounters problems, please refer to http://www.caldera.com/ for any related updated images.

To create OpenLinux(TM) installation diskettes and launch an install:

• Create and label an installation diskette:

Write the installation diskette image to a 1.44-MB floppy.

From Linux, use a command such as

```
dd if=install.img of=/dev/fd0H1440
```

or

```
cat install.img >/dev/fd0
```

From DOS, use the RAWRITE3 command and follow the prompts to transfer INSTALL.IMG to a floppy.

- Create and label a modules diskette:

  Write the modules diskette image to a 1.44-MB floppy.

  In Linux, use a command such as

  ```
  dd if=modules.img of=/dev/fd0H1440
  ```

  or

  ```
  cat modules.img >/dev/fd0
  ```

From DOS, use the RAWRITE3 command and follow the prompts to transfer MODULES.IMG to a floppy.

- Put the installation diskette in your floppy drive and restart your computer.

D.3   Problems Using Very Large Hard Disks

Using very large hard disks in PCs can lead to problems because of the limitations of the BIOS and IDE standards on which most PCs are based. Problems arise because the BIOS can manage only hard disks with a maximum of 256 heads, 63 sectors, and 1024 cylinders because the IDE standard is based on a model that specifies the Cylinders, Heads, and Sectors of the hard disks (CHS model), but only allows a maximum of 16 heads, 255 sectors, and 65536 cylinders. The lowest limits of both of these standards combine to give a maximum size for standard hard disks of 504 MB (16 heads, 63 sectors, and 1024 cylinders).

The newer Enhanced-IDE (EIDE) standard avoids this limitation by not using the CHS model. Instead, a Logical Block Addressing model is used (LBA). This model numbers all sectors on the disk sequentially.

Newer BIOS versions overcome the 504-MB limitation by using an Extended CHS model that extends the maximum number of heads to 256. The new upper size limit, from the Enhanced IDE and Extended CHS models, is almost 7.9 GB.

Linux does not use the BIOS to access your hard disk, so IDE and EIDE hard disks should not cause problems on Linux systems. If problems occur, however, Linux might be obtaining incorrect hard disk size parameters from the BIOS. To correct this problem, use boot parameters to pass the correct information to Linux. The parameter topassis "hdx=cyl,heads,sect," where hdx is the hard disk device (hda, hdb, hdc, or hdd). More information is provided below on using these parameters to create cylinder counts of less than 1024.

SCSI Hard Disks

In general, all SCSI hard disks use the LBA mode mentioned above. SCSI hard disks do have a separate problem that EIDE hard disks do not have, however. SCSI hard disks larger than 1 GB must have special treatment with the "fdisk" utility and while configuring the LILO boot manager. If your SCSI hard disk is affected by this problem, "fdisk" will display messages regarding the problem when you prepare your hard disk. The expert mode of "fdisk" can be used to correct the SCSI problems. The LILO problems are fixed by adjusting the "/etc/disktab" file. Both of these fixes are described below with an example.

Why the Problem Arises

The problem with these larger hard disks is that the partition table must be read before any operating system becomes active. The partition table is accessed via the BIOS, which is limited to 256 heads, 63 sectors, and 1023 cylinders. Because of this, the hard disk controller attempts to convert (or translate) the true parameters of hard disks with more than 1023 cylinders into values that can be accepted by the BIOS.

The partition table itself can always be found at the first cylinder, first sector, and first header (which is the same in any translation); but because of this translation from the controller, if all data for the boot process (such as the boot loader and operating system kernel) are not found in the first 1024 cylinders, the BIOS cannot successfully boot the system.

Partitions can be created above 1024 cylinders, but you cannot boot these partitions because boot data in those high partitions cannot be accessed until after the system is booted. This only causes trouble when a system has multiple operating systems, and the user attempts to choose which to boot.

A work-around solution is to create a small Linux partition below 1023 cylinders that can be used to boot the Linux system. This partition can be as little as 15 MB, because it only needs to contain the kernel and the root filesystem. The "/usr" directory and other information can be stored in a second Linux partition located above 1024 cylinders. Use the "fdisk" utility of another operating system such as OS/2 to create these partitions. Then use the Linux "fdisk" during installation to mark the partitions as Type 0x83, Linux.

A better solution is to enter the correct combination of cylinders, sectors, and heads that the hard disk controller is passing to the BIOS. Use the "fdisk" expert mode, as described below. The following diagram shows an example of the translation of the physical values of the hard disk to LBA direct block addressing, which is finally used by the operating system to access the hard disk.

On the left, you can see that the physical layout of the hard disk is very different from the logical (LBA) values reported. Most hard disks have significantly fewer heads than are externally reported. The logical values reported by the hard disk should conform to the limitations of IDE or BIOS. In the case of an EIDE or SCSI controller, the controller itself will do another translation.

SCSI hard disks are usually reported as 64 heads and 32 sectors, giving a size of 64*32*512 Bytes = 1 MB per cylinder. EIDE usually reports 255 heads. The last translation is done by the operating system itself. Here Linux uses Logical Block Addressing (LBA) to refer to the blocks sequentially from the first block to the last block on the hard disk.

Many controllers use two different models in order to provide cylinder numbers under 1024. In most cases, the controller first tries to double the number of heads. If this does not result in a cylinder count less than 1024, the controller increases the actual values for heads and sectors to the maximum possible number in order to minimize the number of cylinders. This process is used, for example, by the Extended Translation of the Adaptec controllers AH 274x/284x/294x. The NCR controller uses a variant by which the number of heads and sectors is chosen to provide the correct size while being within the 1024 cylinder limit. Overlap between partitions is thereby minimized because each partition begins and ends on a cylinder boundary.

The translation by an Adaptec controller of a 4-GB disk gives a count of 255 heads, 63 sectors, and 522 cylinders.

Your task is to find out the translation that the controller is doing and enter the values that it passes for the hard disk into the expert mode of "fdisk." As you do this, remember that the total size of the hard disk must remain constant.

For example, assume that we have a computer with a 4-GB SCSI hard disk. This is more than 1024 cylinders, so "fdisk" gives a warning during installation:

```
The number of cylinders for this disk is set to 4095.
This is larger than 1024, and may cause problems with:

1. software that runs at boot time (e.g., LILO)
2. booting and partitioning software form other OSs
   (e.g., DOS FDISK, OS/2 FDISK)
```

When you use the "p" command to display the partition table, you see a sequence of error messages:

```
Device Boot    Begin   Start   End    Blocks    Id   System
/dev/sda1        1      1      754    771088+   6    DOS 16-bit>32M
Partition 1 does not end on cylinder boundary:
   phys=(95, 254, 63) should be (95, 63, 32)
/dev/sda2   *    97     754    1954   1228972+  82   Linux swap
Partition 2 does not end on cylinder boundary:
   phys=(248, 254, 63) should be (248, 63, 32)
/dev/sda3       1274    1954   2456   514080    a5   BSD/386
Partition 3 does not end on cylinder boundary:
   phys=(312, 254, 63) should be (312, 63, 32)
/dev/sda4       2362    2456   4095   1678792+  5    Extended
Partition 4 does not end on cylinder boundary:
   phys=(521, 254, 63) should be (521, 63, 32)
/dev/sda5       2362    2456   2707   257008+   83   Linux
/dev/sda6       2394    2707   2770   64228+    83   Linux native
/dev/sda7       2402    2770   3436   682731    6    DOS 16-bit>32M
/dev/sda8       2487    3436   4095   674698+   6    DOS 16-bit>32M
```

To correct these errors, new values must be provided for "fdisk" so that the partition boundaries match the values reported by the hard disk and controller. In this example, the 4-GB hard disk shown above has 64 heads, 32 sectors, and 4095 cylinders, for a total capacity of 64*32*4095 bytes = 4095 MB.

If you set the number of heads to 255, and the number of sectors to 63 (a hint that this value is correct appears in the error messages shown above), the partition still must have 4095 MB. So if 255*63*cylinders = 4095 MB, then the number of cylinders would be 522.

These new values must be entered in "fdisk." First, you must change to the expert mode with the "x" command; and then enter the new parameters for the heads, sectors, and cylinders. In expert mode the commands "c" (cylinders), "h" (heads), and "s" (sectors) can be used. According to the calculation above, these values should be 255 heads and 63 sectors.

NOTE: If you are using DOS on your system, never enter a head count of 256. This value will cause DOS to crash without comment.

Below is how the screen might look as you enter these new values in "fdisk."

```
Expert command (m for help): h Number of heads (1-256): 255
Expert command (m for help): s Number of sectors (1-63): 63
   Warning: Setting sector offset for DOS compatibility
Expert command (m for help): c Number of cylinders (1-65535): 522
```

After these values are entered in the "fdisk" expert mode, return to the normal main menu of "fdisk" with "r." Now using the "p" command should show all partitions without the warnings shown in the first listing above.

```
Command (m for help): p Disk /dev/sda: 255 heads, 63 sectors, 522
cylinders Units = cylinders of 16065 * 512 bytes
```

Device Boot	Begin	Start	End	Blocks	Id	System
/dev/sda1	1	1	96	771088+	6	DOS 16-bit>32M
/dev/sda2 *	97	97	249	1228972+	82	Linux swap
/dev/sda3	250	250	313	514080	a5	BSD/386
/dev/sda4	314	314	522	1678792+	5	Extended
/dev/sda5	314	314	345	257008+	83	Linux native
/dev/sda6	346	346	353	64228+	83	Linux native
/dev/sda7	354	354	438	682731	6	DOS 16-bit>32M
/dev/sda8	439	439	522	674698+	6	DOS 16-bit>32M

If the error messages have not disappeared, you have not yet found the right values. Try again with new values until the error messages do not appear.

When you find the correct values, make a note of them in your system documentation. You must enter these values each time you need to run "fdisk." They are not saved.

After the correct values are entered in expert mode, you can continue working normally with "fdisk" to create the partitions that you need to install Linux on.

If you want to use LILO to boot Linux directly from the hard disk, you must list the correct partitions in the file "/etc/fstab/." These partitions are shown from the main menu of "fdisk" once you have corrected the information in expert mode. Change the partition display of "fdisk" from units to sectors with the "u" command. The sector values shown correspond to the block values of the LBA mode.

```
Command (m for help): u Changing display/entry units to sectors

Display the revised partition table:

Command (m for help): p

Disk /dev/sda: 255 heads, 63 sectors, 522 cylinders
Units = sectors of 1 * 512 bytes
```

Device Boot	Begin	Start	End	Blocks	Id	System
/dev/sda1	63	63	1542239	771088+	6	DOS 16-bit>32M
/dev/sda2 *	1542240	1542240	4000184	1228972+	82	Linux swap
/dev/sda3	4000185	4000185	5028344	514080	a5	BSD/386
/dev/sda4	5028345	5028345	8385929	1678792+	5	Extended

```
/dev/sda5      5028408    5028408 5542424   257008+  83    Linux native
/dev/sda6      5542488    5542488 5670944    64228+  83    Linux native
/dev/sda7      5671008    5671008 7036469   682731    6    DOS 16-bit>32M
/dev/sda8      7036533    7036533 8385929   674698+   6    DOS 16-bit>32M
```

Now the start, size, and end of the partition are no-longer displayed in cylinders, but in sectors (which Linux uses to access the hard disk). Enter these sector values in the file "/etc/disktab." The entries in this file would look like this for our example:

```
# Dev.   BIOS   Secs/   Heads/   Cylin   Part.
# num.   code   track   cylin.   ders    offset

0x801    0x80   63      255      522     63        # /dev/sda1
0x802    0x80   63      255      522     1542240   # /dev/sda2
0x803    0x80   63      255      522     4000185   # /dev/sda3
0x805    0x80   63      255      522     5028408   # /dev/sda5
0x806    0x80   63      255      522     5542488   # /dev/sda6
0x807    0x80   63      255      522     5671008   # /dev/sda7
0x808    0x80   63      255      522     7036533   # /dev/sda8
```

The process described here is a difficult one, and we cannot guarantee your success for any particular hardware configuration. We hope that the principal steps and concepts are clear, however. If you have trouble, please contact Caldera for additional information or suggestions.

D.4   Linux Allocated Devices

Maintained by H. Peter Anvin <Peter.Anvin@linux.org>
Last revised: May 29, 1995

This list is the successor to Rick Miller's Linux Device List, which he stopped maintaining when he lost network access in 1993. It is a registry of allocated major device numbers, as well as the recommended /dev directory nodes for these devices.

This list is available via FTP from ftp.yggdrasil.com in the directory /pub/device-list; filename is devices.<format> where <format> is txt (ASCII), tex (LaTeX), dvi (DVI) or ps (PostScript). In cases of discrepancy, the LaTeX version has priority.

This document is included by reference into the Linux Filesystem Standard (FSSTND). The FSSTND is available via FTP from tsx-11.mit.edu in the directory /pub/linux/docs/linux-standards/fsstnd.

To have a major number allocated, or a minor number in situations where that applies (e.g. busmice), please contact me. Also, if you have additional information regarding any of the devices listed below, I would like to know.

Allocations marked (68k) apply to Linux/68k only.

```
0       Unnamed devices (NFS mounts, loopback devices)
        0 = reserved as null device number

1 char Memory devices
        1 = /dev/mem    Physical memory access
        2 = /dev/kmem   Kernel virtual memory access
        3 = /dev/null   Null device
        4 = /dev/port   I/O port access
        5 = /dev/zero   Null byte source
        6 = /dev/core   OBSOLETE - replaced by /proc/kcore
        7 = /dev/full   Returns ENOSPC on write
  block RAM disk
        1 = /dev/ramdiskRAM disk

2 char Reserved for PTY's <tytso@athena.mit.edu>

  block Floppy disks
        0 = /dev/fd0 First floppy disk autodetect
        1 = /dev/fd1 Second floppy disk autodetect
        2 = /dev/fd2 Third floppy disk autodetect
        3 = /dev/fd3 Fourth floppy disk autodetect

To specify format, add to the autodetect device number:
        0 = /dev/fd?         Autodetect format
        4 = /dev/fd?d360     5.25"  360K in a 360K  drive
       20 = /dev/fd?h360     5.25"  360K in a 1200K drive
       48 = /dev/fd?h410     5.25"  410K in a 1200K drive
       64 = /dev/fd?h420     5.25"  420K in a 1200K drive
       24 = /dev/fd?h720     5.25"  720K in a 1200K drive
       80 = /dev/fd?h880     5.25"  880K in a 1200K drive
        8 = /dev/fd?h1200    5.25" 1200K in a 1200K drive
       40 = /dev/fd?h1440    5.25" 1440K in a 1200K drive
       56 = /dev/fd?h1476    5.25" 1476K in a 1200K drive
       72 = /dev/fd?h1494    5.25" 1494K in a 1200K drive
       92 = /dev/fd?h1600    5.25" 1600K in a 1200K drive

       12 = /dev/fd?u360     3.5"    360K Double Density
      120 = /dev/fd?u800     3.5"    800K Double Density
       52 = /dev/fd?u820     3.5"    820K Double Density
       68 = /dev/fd?u830     3.5"    830K Double Density
       84 = /dev/fd?u1040    3.5"   1040K Double Density
       88 = /dev/fd?u1120    3.5"   1120K Double Density
       28 = /dev/fd?u1440    3.5"   1440K High Density
      124 = /dev/fd?u1600    3.5"   1600K High Density
```

```
 44 = /dev/fd?u1680   3.5"  1680K High Density
 60 = /dev/fd?u1722   3.5"  1722K High Density
 76 = /dev/fd?u1743   3.5"  1743K High Density
 96 = /dev/fd?u1760   3.5"  1760K High Density
116 = /dev/fd?u1840   3.5"  1840K High Density
100 = /dev/fd?u1920   3.5"  1920K High Density
 32 = /dev/fd?u2880   3.5"  2880K Extra Density
104 = /dev/fd?u3200   3.5"  3200K Extra Density
108 = /dev/fd?u3520   3.5"  3520K Extra Density
112 = /dev/fd?u3840   3.5"  3840K Extra Density

 36 = /dev/fd?CompaQ  Compaq 2880K drive; obsolete?
```

NOTE: The letter in the device name (d, q, h or u) signifies the type of
drive: 5.25" Double Density (d), 5.25" Quad Density (q), 5.25" High
Density (h) or 3.5" (any model, u). The use of the capital letters D,
H and E for the 3.5" models have been deprecated, since the drive
type is insignificant for these devices.

```
3 char Reserved for pty's <tytso@athena.mit.edu>
      block First MFM, RLL and IDE hard disk/CD-ROM interface
          0 = /dev/hda       Master: whole disk (or CD-ROM)
         64 = /dev/hdb       Slave: whole disk (or CD-ROM)
```

For partitions, add to the whole disk device number:
```
          0 = /dev/hd?       Whole disk
          1 = /dev/hd?1      First primary partition
          2 = /dev/hd?2      Second primary partition
          3 = /dev/hd?3      Third primary partition
          4 = /dev/hd?4      Fourth primary partition
          5 = /dev/hd?5      First logical partition
          6 = /dev/hd?6      Second logical partition
          7 = /dev/hd?7      Third logical partition
          ...
         63 = /dev/hd?63     59th logical partition
```

```
4 char TTY devices
          0 = /dev/console   Console device

          1 = /dev/tty1      First virtual console
          ...
         63 = /dev/tty63     63rd virtual console
         64 = /dev/ttyS0     First serial port
          ...
        127 = /dev/ttyS63    64th serial port
        128 = /dev/ptyp0     First pseudo-tty master
          ...
        191 = /dev/ptysf     64th pseudo-tty master
        192 = /dev/ttyp0     First pseudo-tty slave
          ...
```

```
            255 = /dev/ttysf        64th pseudo-tty slave

         Pseudo-tty's are named as follows:
         * Masters are "pty", slaves are "tty";
         * the fourth letter is one of p, q, r, s indicating
           the 1st, 2nd, 3rd, 4th series of 16 pseudo-ttys each, and
         * the fifth letter is one of 0123456789abcdef indicating
           the position within the series.

 5 char Alternate TTY devices
           0 = /dev/tty           Current TTY device
          64 = /dev/cua0          Callout device corresponding to ttyS0
           ...
         127 = /dev/cua63         Callout device corresponding to ttyS63

 6 char Parallel printer devices
           0 = /dev/lp0           First parallel printer (0x3bc)
           1 = /dev/lp1           Second parallel printer (0x378)
           2 = /dev/lp2           Third parallel printer (0x278)

         Not all computers have the 0x3bc parallel port; hence
         the "first" printer may be either /dev/lp0 or
         /dev/lp1.

 7 char Virtual console capture devices
           0 = /dev/vcs           Current vc text contents
           1 = /dev/vcs1          tty1 text contents
          ...
          63 = /dev/vcs63         tty63 text contents
         128 = /dev/vcsa          Current vc text/attribute contents
         129 = /dev/vcsa1         tty1 text/attribute contents
          ...
         191 = /dev/vcsa63        tty63 text/attribute contents

NOTE: These devices permit both read and write access.

 8 block SCSI disk devices
           0 = /dev/sda           First SCSI disk whole disk
          16 = /dev/sdb           Second SCSI disk whole disk
          32 = /dev/sdc           Third SCSI disk whole disk
          ...
         240 = /dev/sdp           Sixteenth SCSI disk whole disk

Partitions are handled in the same way as for IDE
disks (see major number 3) except that the limit on
logical partitions is 11.

 9 char SCSI tape devices
           0 = /dev/st0           First SCSI tape
           1 = /dev/st1           Second SCSI tape
```

```
           ...
       128 = /dev/nst0         First SCSI tape, no rewind-on-close
       129 = /dev/nst1         Second SCSI tape, no rewind-on-close
           ...
   block Multiple disk devices
         0 = /dev/md0          First device group
         1 = /dev/md1          Second device group
       ...
```

The multiple devices driver is used to span a filesystem across multiple physical disks.

```
10 char Non-serial mice, misc features
         0 = /dev/logibm       Logitech bus mouse
         1 = /dev/psaux        PS/2-style mouse port
         2 = /dev/inportbm     Microsoft Inport bus mouse
         3 = /dev/atibm        ATI XL bus mouse
         4 = /dev/jbm          J-mouse
         4 = /dev/amigamouse   Amiga Mouse (68k)
         5 = /dev/atarimouse   Atari Mouse (68k)
       128 = /dev/beep         Fancy beep device
       129 = /dev/modreq       Kernel module load request
```

The use of the suffix -mouse instead of -bm or -aux has also been used.

```
11 block SCSI CD-ROM devices
         0 = /dev/sr0          First SCSI CD-ROM
         1 = /dev/sr1          Second SCSI CD-ROM
          ...
```

The prefix /dev/scd instead of /dev/sr has been used as well, and might make more sense.

```
12 char QIC-02 tape
         2 = /dev/ntpqic11     QIC-11, no rewind-on-close
         3 = /dev/tpqic11      QIC-11, rewind-on-close
         4 = /dev/ntpqic24     QIC-24, no rewind-on-close
         5 = /dev/tpqic24      QIC-24, rewind-on-close
         6 = /dev/ntpqic120    QIC-120, no rewind-on-close
         7 = /dev/tpqic120     QIC-120, rewind-on-close
         8 = /dev/ntpqic150    QIC-150, no rewind-on-close
         9 = /dev/tpqic150     QIC-150, rewind-on-close
```

The device names specified are proposed -- if there are "standard" names for these devices, please let me know.

```
   block MSCDEX CD-ROM callback support
         0 = /dev/dos_cd0      First MSCDEX CD-ROM
         1 = /dev/dos_cd1      Second MSCDEX CD-ROM
```

```
            ...

13 char PC speaker
        0 = /dev/pcmixer     Emulates /dev/mixer
        1 = /dev/pcsp        Emulates /dev/dsp (8-bit)
        4 = /dev/pcaudio     Emulates /dev/audio
        5 = /dev/pcsp16      Emulates /dev/dsp (16-bit)
    block 8-bit MFM/RLL/IDE controller
        0 = /dev/xda         First XT disk whole disk
       64 = /dev/xdb         Second XT disk whole disk

        Partitions are handled in the same way as IDE disks
        (see major number 3).

14 char Sound card
        0 = /dev/mixer       Mixer control
        1 = /dev/sequencer   Audio sequencer
        2 = /dev/midi00      First MIDI port
        3 = /dev/dsp         Digital audio
        4 = /dev/audio       Sun-compatible digital audio
        6 = /dev/sndstat     Sound card status information
        8 = /dev/sequencer2  Sequencer -- alternate device
       16 = /dev/mixer1      Second soundcard mixer control
       17 = /dev/patmgr0     Sequencer patch manager
       18 = /dev/midi01      Second MIDI port
       19 = /dev/dsp1        Second soundcard digital audio
       20 = /dev/audio1      Second soundcard Sun digital audio
       33 = /dev/patmgr1     Sequencer patch manager
       34 = /dev/midi02      Third MIDI port
       50 = /dev/midi03      Fourth MIDI port
    block BIOS harddrive callback support
        0 = /dev/dos_hda     First BIOS harddrive whole disk
       64 = /dev/dos_hdb     Second BIOS harddrive whole disk
      128 = /dev/dos_hdc     Third BIOS harddrive whole disk
      192 = /dev/dos_hdd     Fourth BIOS harddrive whole disk

        Partitions are handled in the same way as IDE disks
        (see major number 3).

15 char Joystick
        0 = /dev/js0         First joystick
        1 = /dev/js1         Second joystick
    block Sony CDU-31A/CDU-33A CD-ROM
        0 = /dev/sonycd      Sony CDU-31a CD-ROM

16 char Reserved for scanners
    block GoldStar CD-ROM
        0 = /dev/gscd        GoldStar CD-ROM

17 char Chase serial card
```

```
          0 = /dev/ttyH0        First Chase port
          1 = /dev/ttyH1        Second Chase port
          ...
   block Optics Storage CD-ROM (under development)
          0 = /dev/optcd        Optics Storage CD-ROM

18 char Chase serial card - alternate devices
          0 = /dev/cuh0         Callout device corresponding to ttyH0
          1 = /dev/cuh1         Callout device corresponding to ttyH1
          ...
   block Sanyo CD-ROM (under development)
          0 = ?                 Sanyo CD-ROM

19 char Cyclades serial card
         32 = /dev/ttyC0        First Cyclades port
          ...
         63 = /dev/ttyC31       32nd Cyclades port

       It would make more sense for these to start at 0...

   block Double" compressed disk
          0 = /dev/double0      First compressed disk
          ...
          7 = /dev/double7      Eighth compressed disk
        128 = /dev/cdouble0     Mirror of first compressed disk
          ...
        135 = /dev/cdouble7     Mirror of eighth compressed disk

       See the Double documentation for the meaning of the
       mirror devices.

20 char Cyclades serial card - alternate devices
         32 = /dev/cub0         Callout device corresponding to ttyC0
          ...
         63 = /dev/cub31        Callout device corresponding to ttyC31
   block Hitachi CD-ROM (under development)
          0 = /dev/hitcd        Hitachi CD-ROM

21 char Generic SCSI access
          0 = /dev/sg0          First generic SCSI device
          1 = /dev/sg1          Second generic SCSI device
          ...

22 char Digiboard serial card
          0 = /dev/ttyD0        First Digiboard port
          1 = /dev/ttyD1        Second Digiboard port
          ...
   block Second MFM, RLL and IDE hard disk/CD-ROM interface
          0 = /dev/hdc          Master: whole disk (or CD-ROM)
         64 = /dev/hdd          Slave: whole disk (or CD-ROM)
```

```
              Partitions are handled the same way as for the first
              interface (see major number 3).

23 char Digiboard serial card - alternate devices
           0 = /dev/cud0       Callout device corresponding to ttyD0
           1 = /dev/cud1       Callout device corresponding to ttyD1
           ...
   block Mitsumi proprietary CD-ROM
           0 = /dev/mcd        Mitsumi CD-ROM

24 char Stallion serial card
           0 = /dev/ttyE0      Stallion port 0 card 0
           1 = /dev/ttyE1      Stallion port 1 card 0
           ...
          64 = /dev/ttyE64     Stallion port 0 card 1
          65 = /dev/ttyE65     Stallion port 1 card 1
           ...
         128 = /dev/ttyE128    Stallion port 0 card 2
         129 = /dev/ttyE129    Stallion port 1 card 2
           ...
         192 = /dev/ttyE192    Stallion port 0 card 3
         193 = /dev/ttyE193    Stallion port 1 card 3
           ...
   block Sony CDU-535 CD-ROM
           0 = /dev/cdu535     Sony CDU-535 CD-ROM

25 char Stallion serial card - alternate devices
           0 = /dev/cue0       Callout device corresponding to ttyE0
           1 = /dev/cue1       Callout device corresponding to ttyE1
           ...
          64 = /dev/cue64      Callout device corresponding to ttyE64
          65 = /dev/cue65      Callout device corresponding to ttyE65
           ...
         128 = /dev/cue128     Callout device corresponding to ttyE128
         129 = /dev/cue129     Callout device corresponding to ttyE129
           ...
         192 = /dev/cue192     Callout device corresponding to ttyE192
         193 = /dev/cue193     Callout device corresponding to ttyE193
           ...
   block First Matsushita (Panasonic/SoundBlaster) CD-ROM
           0 = /dev/sbpcd0     Panasonic CD-ROM controller 0 unit 0
           1 = /dev/sbpcd1     Panasonic CD-ROM controller 0 unit 1
           2 = /dev/sbpcd2     Panasonic CD-ROM controller 0 unit 2
           3 = /dev/sbpcd3     Panasonic CD-ROM controller 0 unit 3

26 char Frame grabbers
           0 = /dev/wvisfgrab  Quanta WinVision frame grabber
   block Second Matsushita (Panasonic/SoundBlaster) CD-ROM
           0 = /dev/sbpcd4     Panasonic CD-ROM controller 1 unit 0
```

```
        1 = /dev/sbpcd5      Panasonic CD-ROM controller 1 unit 1
        2 = /dev/sbpcd6      Panasonic CD-ROM controller 1 unit 2
        3 = /dev/sbpcd7      Panasonic CD-ROM controller 1 unit 3

27 char  QIC-117 tape
        0 = /dev/ftape       QIC-117 tape
    block Third Matsushita (Panasonic/SoundBlaster) CD-ROM
        0 = /dev/sbpcd8      Panasonic CD-ROM controller 2 unit 0
        1 = /dev/sbpcd9      Panasonic CD-ROM controller 2 unit 1
        2 = /dev/sbpcd10     Panasonic CD-ROM controller 2 unit 2
        3 = /dev/sbpcd11     Panasonic CD-ROM controller 2 unit 3

28 char  Stallion serial card - card programming
        0 = /dev/staliomem0  First Stallion card I/O memory
        1 = /dev/staliomem1  Second Stallion card I/O memory
        2 = /dev/staliomem2  Third Stallion card I/O memory
        3 = /dev/staliomem3  Fourth Stallion card I/O memory
    block Fourth Matsushita (Panasonic/SoundBlaster) CD-ROM
        0 = /dev/sbpcd12     Panasonic CD-ROM controller 3 unit 0
        1 = /dev/sbpcd13     Panasonic CD-ROM controller 3 unit 1
        2 = /dev/sbpcd14     Panasonic CD-ROM controller 3 unit 2
        3 = /dev/sbpcd15     Panasonic CD-ROM controller 3 unit 3
    block ACSI disk (68k)
        0 = /dev/ada         First ACSI disk whole disk
       16 = /dev/adb         Second ACSI disk whole disk
       32 = /dev/adc         Third ACSI disk whole disk
        ...
      240 = /dev/adp         16th ACSI disk whole disk

      Partitions are handled in the same way as for IDE
      disks (see major number 3) except that the limit on
      logical partitions is 11.

29 char  Universal frame buffer
        0 = /dev/fb0current  First frame buffer
        1 = /dev/fb0autodetect
        ...
       16 = /dev/fb1current  Second frame buffer
       17 = /dev/fb1autodetect
        ...
    block Aztech/Orchid/Okano/Wearnes CD-ROM
        0 = /dev/aztcd       Aztech CD-ROM

      The universal frame buffer device is currently only
      supported on Linux/68k.  The "current" device accesses
      the fame buffer at current resolution; the
      "autodetect" one at bootup (default) resolution.
      Minor numbers 2-15 within each frame buffer assignment
      are used for specific device-dependent resolutions.
      There appears to be no standard naming for these devices.
```

```
30 char    iBCS-2 compatibility devices
            0 = /dev/socksys     Socket access
            1 = /dev/spx         SVR3 local X interface
            2 = /dev/inet/arp    Network access
            2 = /dev/inet/icmp   Network access
            2 = /dev/inet/ip     Network access
            2 = /dev/inet/udp    Network access
            2 = /dev/inet/tcp    Network access

            iBCS-2 requires /dev/nfsd to be a link to
            /dev/socksys, and /dev/X0R to be a link to /dev/null.

      block Philips LMS CM-205 CD-ROM
            0 = /dev/cm205cd     Philips LMS CM-205 CD-ROM

            /dev/lmscd is an older name for this device.  This
            driver does not work with the CM-205MS CD-ROM.

31 char    MPU-401 MIDI
            0 = /dev/mpu401data MPU-401 data port
            1 = /dev/mpu401stat MPU-401 status port
      block ROM/flash memory card
            0 = /dev/rom0        First ROM card (rw)
              ...
            7 = /dev/rom7        Eighth ROM card (rw)
            8 = /dev/rrom0       First ROM card (ro)
              ...
           15 = /dev/rrom7       Eighth ROM card (ro)
           16 = /dev/flash0      First flash memory card (rw)
              ...
           23 = /dev/flash7      Eighth flash memory card (rw)
           24 = /dev/rflash0     First flash memory card (ro)
              ...
           31 = /dev/rflash7     Eighth flash memory card (ro)

            The read-write (rw) devices support back-caching
            written data in RAM, as well as writing to flash RAM
            devices.  The read-only devices (ro) support reading
      only.

32 block   Philips LMS CM-206 CD-ROM
            0 = /dev/cm206cd     Philips LMS CM-206 CD-ROM

33 block   Modular RAM disk device
            0 = /dev/ram0        First modular RAM disk
            1 = /dev/ram1        Second modular RAM disk
              ...
          255 = /dev/ram255      256th modular RAM disk
```

```
34-223 UNALLOCATED

224-254 LOCAL USE
       Allocated for local/experimental use

       Please note that MAX_CHRDEV and MAX_BLKDEV in
       linux/include/linux/major.h must be set to a value
       greater than the highest used major number.  For a
       kernel using local/experimental devices, it is
       probably easiest to set both of these equal to 256.  The
       memory cost above using the default value of 64 is 3K.

255 RESERVED
```

D.5   Additional /dev Directory Entries

This section details additional entries that should or may exist in the /dev directory. It is preferred that symbolic links use the same form (absolute or relative) as is indicated here. Links are classified as "hard" or "symbolic" depending on the preferred type of link; if possible, the indicated type of link should be used.

Compulsory links

These links should exist on all systems:

```
/dev/fd       /proc/self/fd    symbolic    File descriptors
/dev/stdin    fd/0 symbolic    stdin file descriptor
/dev/stdout   fd/1 symbolic    stdout file descriptor
/dev/stderr   fd/2 symbolic    stderr file descriptor
```

Recommended links

It is recommended that these links exist on all systems:

```
/dev/X0R     null        symbolic  Used by iBCS-2
/dev/nfsd    socksys     symbolic  Used by iBCS-2
/dev/core    /proc/kcore symbolic  Backward compatibility
/dev/scd?    /dev/cd? hard Alternate SCSI CD-ROM name
```

Locally defined links

The following links may be established locally to conform to the configuration of the system. This is merely a tabulation of existing practice, and does not constitute a recommendation. However, if they exist, they should have the following uses.

```
/dev/mouse   mouse port      symbolic  Current mouse device
/dev/tape    tape device     symbolic  Current tape device
/dev/cdrom   CD-ROM device   symbolic  Current CD-ROM device
/dev/modem   modem port      symbolic  Current dialout device
/dev/root    root device     symbolic  Current root filesystem
/dev/swap    swap device     symbolic  Current swap device
```

   /dev/modem should not be used for a modem which supports dialin as well as dialout, as it tends to cause lock file problems. If it exists, /dev/modem should point to the appropriate dialout (alternate) device.

Sockets and pipes

Non-transient sockets and named pipes may exist in /dev. Common entries are:

```
/dev/printer   socket  lpd local socket
/dev/log       socket  syslog local socket
```

Index

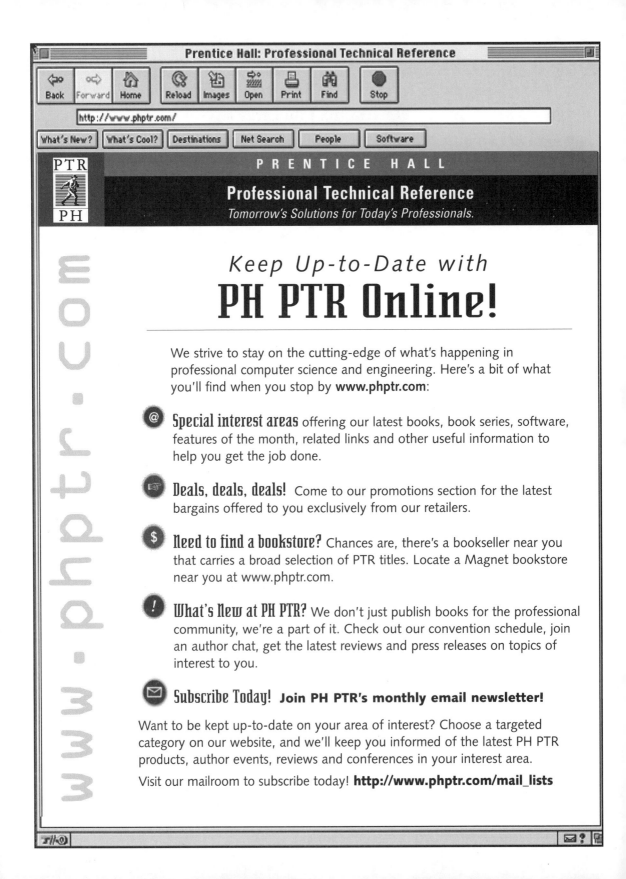

OpenLinux Lite License

Nearly all of the components that make up the OpenLinux Lite product are distributed under the terms of the GNU General Public License or similar licenses which permit free and unrestricted redistribution.

However, several components of OpenLinux Lite are not governed by these licenses. The following components are distributed as part of the OpenLinux Lite product with the permission of the noted copyright holder, and with the noted licenses granted:

1. Looking Glass desktop metaphor—Copyright Visix Software, Inc., 90 day license for personal or commercial evaluation

2. LISA installation and administration utility—Copyright Caldera and Linux Support Team, license for personal and commercial use, without time restriction

3. CRiSP-LiTE™ text editor—Copyright Vital, Inc., license for personal and commercial use, without time restriction.

OpenLinux Lite is provided without technical support of any kind, though we invite you to browse the technical resources at our Web site: http://www.caldera.com. Caldera welcomes feedback on OpenLinux Lite. Please send comments by E-mail to info@caldera.com.

About the CD-ROM

The accompanying CD-ROM is a copy of Caldera OpenLinux Base. Caldera distributes a commercial version of Linux which has some nice features and custom programs. The CD-ROM has a 90-day license to Looking Glass fro, VISIX and a few other programs. Looking Glass is a powerful variation of MS Windows Program Manager. It combines drag-and-drop, sounds, and easy customization of the desktop.

Quick-start note:

To launch an OpenLinux™ install, change directory to ./col/launch ("cd col" then "cd launch" and proceed per the instructions in that directory's README.

System Requirements

Your computer system must meet the following requirements in order to install OpenLinux .

- 32-bit Intel-based personal computer or compatibles, such as these processors: 386, 486, Pentium, Pentium Pro. Other processors are not supported in this release.
- Minimum 8MB RAM (16MB RAM to use graphical components)
- 266MB free hard disk space for recommended installation (You'll need more or less disk space, depending on the installation option you choose.)
- A supported mouse and video card (for use with the graphical components).

Technical Support

Prentice Hall does not offer technical support for this software. However, if there is a problem with the media, you may obtain a replacement copy by E-mailing us with your problem at:

discexchange@phptr.com